GARRISONS AND GARRISON WARFARE IN THE BRITISH CIVIL WARS, 1638-1653

Andrew Abram

Helion & Company

Helion & Company Limited
Unit 8 Amherst Business Centre
Budbrooke Road
Warwick
CV34 5WE
England
Tel. 01926 499 619
Email: info@helion.co.uk
Website: www.helion.co.uk
Twitter: @helionbooks
Visit our blog https://helionbooks.wordpress.com/

Published by Helion & Company 2025
Designed and typeset by Mach 3 Solutions (www.mach3solutions.co.uk)
Cover designed by Paul Hewitt, Battlefield Design (www.battlefield-design.co.uk)

Text © Andrew Abram 2025
Photographs and illustrations as individually credited
Front cover artwork by Seán Ó Brógain © Helion & Company 2025

Maps by Mark Thompson © Helion & Company 2025

Every reasonable effort has been made to trace copyright holders and to obtain their permission for the use of copyright material. The author and publisher apologize for any errors or omissions in this work and would be grateful if notified of any corrections that should be incorporated in future reprints or editions of this book.

ISBN 978-1-804518-37-3

British Library Cataloguing-in-Publication Data.
A catalogue record for this book is available from the British Library.

All rights reserved. No part of this publication may be reproduced, stored in a retrieval system, or transmitted, in any form, or by any means, electronic, mechanical, photocopying, recording or otherwise, without the express written consent of Helion & Company Limited.

For details of other military history titles published by Helion & Company Limited contact the above address or visit our website: http://www.helion.co.uk.

We always welcome receiving book proposals from prospective authors.

Contents

List of Illustrations   iv
List of Maps   v
List of Tables   vi
List of Abbreviations   vii
Acknowledgements   viii
Explanatory Notes and Conventions   ix
Introduction   x

1. 'A place of greatest strength in this part of the Kingdom': Windsor Castle   13
2. 'A place strongly fortified': The Royalist Garrison of Reading   48
3. 'A frontline fortress': The Parliamentarian Garrison of Aylesbury   90
4. The Parliamentarian Garrisons of Nantwich and Halton   112
5. The Parliamentarian Garrisons of Norton, Northwich, Tarvin, Hooton, and Puddington   139
6. The Parliamentarian Garrison of Warwick   165
7. The Parliamentarian Garrisons of Coventry and Kenilworth   193

Bibliography   215

List of Illustrations

A most famous victory obtained by that vallant religious gentleman, Collonell Venne. TT, E126[42]	19
Captain, later Colonel John Barkstead.	23
Windsor Castle in 1658 as seen from the south-east, by Wenceslas Hollar.	28
Monies sent to Colonel John Venn's Regiment, 29 October 1642-3 June 1644. (TNA, SP28/126/1, f. 14r.)	33
Victuals sent to the garrison of Windsor, 29 October 1642. (TNA, SP28/263, f. 70r.)	38
Map of Reading by John Speed (1611).	58
Sir Jacob Astley, governor of Reading, 1643-1644.	68
Ruins of Reading Abbey, which were incorporated into the town's fortifications. (Photo by Paul Wright)	77
Good and Joyfull Newes Out of Buckinghamshire. TT, E126[99]	95
Robert Devereux, Earl of Essex, Captain-General and Chief Commander of the Parliamentarian army (1591-1646)	99
Welsh Row, Nantwich. (Photo by Paul Wright)	117
List of work done at the mud walls of Nantwich, 19 July 1645. (TNA, SP28/224, f. 13r.)	121
Halton Castle. (Photo by Paul Wright)	131
Warrant signed by Sir William Brereton to the constables of Aston to bring teams and carts to Halton Castle for the transportation of ammunition, 7 July 1644 (Unlisted warrant, Aston Collection)	135
Norton Abbey, showing the Tudor manor house on the remains of the medieval undercroft, by Samuel and Nathaniel Buck (1727).	141
Warrant signed by Captain John Brooke to the constables of Aston to send men to Norton with complete arms, 2 March 1644. (Unlisted warrant, Aston Collection)	151
Muster roll of Sergeant Major William Daniell's Company, part of the Tarvin garrison. (TNA, SP28/123/1, unf.)	155
Richard Grenville, 2nd Baron Brooke (1607-43).	171
Basil Fielding, Earl of Denbigh (c. 1608-75).	179
List of Parliamentarian forces in Warwickshire. (TNA, SP28/34/1, f. 64r.)	186
Map of Coventry by John Speed (1611).	199
Cook Street Gate in Coventry's town walls. (Photo by author)	203
Prospect of Kenilworth Castle, from William Dugdale, *Antiquities of Warwickshire* (1653).	212

List of Maps

1	The King's campaign towards London, autumn 1642.	14
2	The Royalist advance towards London, autumn 1642.	49
3	Reading in the 1640s.	51

List of Tables

1	Monies Received for the Garrison of Windsor Castle since Their Marching Out of the City of London to Windsor, 13–29 October 1642	21
2	Sent to Windsor for the Victualling of the Castle, 29 October 1642	39
3	'Upon report from the Committee of Both Kingdoms, it is ordered that this Establishment of Windsor Castle following, shall stand *pro tempore*'	45
4	A Selection of Receipts of Arms, Munitions, and Other Stores into 'his Majesty's Magazine at Reading'	71
5	Foot Regiments in the Garrison of Reading, April 1644	78
6	Payments for the Maintenance and Quartering of the Garrison of Aylesbury, 1646	101
7	Payments Due for Work on the Fortifications of the Garrison of Aylesbury, April–July 1646	106
8	Contributions from the Parish of Haddenham, Buckinghamshire, to the Garrison of Aylesbury	107
9	Composite of Abstracted Military Accounts of Captain Richard Grenville, 1642–1645	108
10		136
11	Charges for the Right Honourable the Lord Brooke at Stratford at the Settling the Militia at Stratford-upon-Avon, 30 June 1642	166
12	'Colonel Purefoy, his regiment of horse'	180
13	'Disbursements to Colonel Godfrey Bosvile's regiment of foot the regiment 12 October 1643 the space of 5 weeks, ending 17 November 1643'	191
14	Disbursements for the Construction of the Fortifications at Coventry from August to November 1642	197
15	Purchases Made by Colonel John Barker for the Equipping of His Troop, March–May 1643	200
16	List of Colonel Barker's Foot Regiment, Taken 24 January 1644	201
17	Colonel Willoughby's Company, Mustered 30 October 1645	204
18	Lieutenant Colonel Robert Phipps' Company, Mustered 30 October 1645	205
19	Sergeant Major Gamaliel Purefoy's Company, 15 September 1645	207
20	Accounts of John Mascall, Treasurer of Kenilworth Castle, 12 September–28 November 1644	209
21	Colonel John Needham's 'Account of what arms I received from the State since I received my commissions'	210
22	'An account of what horses have been in the castle of Kenilworth and how disposed of them from 12 May 1643 to 5 April 1644'	211

List of Abbreviations

BA – Buckinghamshire Archives
BL – British Library
Bodl. Lib. – Bodleian Library
BRO – Berkshire Record Office
CA – Coventry Archives
CJ – Journals of the House of Commons
CRO – Cheshire Record Office/Cheshire Archives
CSPD – Calendar of State Papers Domestic
DRO – Devon Record Office
ESRO – East Sussex Record Office
HMC – Historical Manuscripts Commission
HR – Historical Research
JSAHR – Journal of the Society for Army Historical Research
LJ – Journals of the House of Lords
ML – London Museum
MP – member of Parliament
Ms – Manuscript
Mss – Manuscripts
NLW – National Library of Wales
THSLC – Transactions of the Historical Society of Lancashire and Cheshire
TNA – The National Archives
TT – Thomason Tracts
WA – Warwickshire Archives
WorcsA – Worcestershire Archives
WSHC – Wiltshire and Swindon History Centre/Wiltshire and Swindon Archives
WSL – William Salt Library

Acknowledgements

I would like to thank Charles Singleton of Helion & Co. for his continued advice and encouragement throughout this and other projects. This book is dedicated, with love, to my wife, Professor Kathryn Hurlock.

Explanatory Notes and Conventions

Although dates prior to 1752 are recorded with the year beginning 25 March, modern dating is used throughout, with the New Year being taken to start on 1 January. Spellings in contemporary manuscripts and printed sources (which varied considerably during the seventeenth century) have been modernised, while, where appropriate, current forms of punctuation have been added to period accounts.

According to the imperial system, contemporary monetary values have been quoted throughout. Hence, 12 pennies (12d.) = one shilling (1s.); 20 shillings = one pound sterling (£1); £1 = 240d. Moreover, lengths and distances are given in inches, feet, yards, ells, and miles; weights in pounds (lb), 112lb = one hundredweight (cwt), 20cwt = one ton.

Introduction

Military histories of the British Civil Wars (1638–1653) have tended to concentrate on battles, military campaigns, and field armies to the exclusion of the role, organisation, and composition of garrisons, as well as sieges and garrison warfare. Historians such as Malcolm Wanklyn, for instance, have interpreted events enacted on the battlefield as being more significant than anything else in determining the outcome of the conflict.[1] This is at odds with the main aspects of the conflict, as the most typical forms of combat and military activity – rather than set-piece engagements and skirmishes – involved sieges of and assaults on fortified positions. Moreover, except perhaps with the formation of Parliament's New Model Army in 1645, significant numbers of troops and military resources went into the garrisoning of cities, towns, and ports (such as Reading and Warwick), while the provisioning and supply of these garrisons often stretched local civilian populations on whom taxes and other resources (such as horses and foodstuffs) were levied.

Troops from garrisons also marched out to join or augment other forces and returned to them for their safety. Urban centres with their various garrisons also controlled trade and movements by dominating the hinterland between transportation routes and other areas of military operations. It was in this light that the Earl of Clarendon reported that, when Royalist ammunition convoys were forced to pass through regions sympathetic to Parliament in 1642–1643, 'the enemy was much superior in all the counties between Yorkshire and Oxford and had planted garrisons so near all the roads that the most private messengers travelled with great hazard, three being intercepted for one that escaped'.[2] Moreover, as centres of intelligence networks, the importance of garrisons increased as the civil wars progressed.

One reason for the general neglect by historians of sustained studies of garrisons and garrison warfare – as pointed out by authors such as Andrew Hopper in his work on the papers of the Hotham governors of Hull during the civil wars and Ian Atherton in his study of the Royalist garrison of Lichfield – is that relatively insufficient garrison accounts have survived in

---

1 Malcolm Wanklyn, *Decisive Battles of the English Civil War* (Barnsley: Pen & Sword, 2006).
2 W. D. Macray (ed.), Edward Hyde, Earl of Clarendon, *The History of the Rebellion and Civil Wars in England* (Oxford: Clarendon Press, 1888), III, p. 23.

manuscript form.³ With some notable exceptions, fewer still have found their way into print. Nevertheless, comprehensive and detailed accounts for some major Parliamentarian garrisons survive (mainly in The National Archives). One exception to this is Malcolm Gratton's work on the town and port of Liverpool, which greatly contributes to our understanding of its Parliamentarian garrison.⁴ Albeit from a slightly later period is the present author's focused assessment of the raising, equipping, composition, and experience of the English military garrison at Tangier on the Mediterranean Coast of Morocco, between 1661 and 1684.⁵ The English occupation of Tangier is well-served by a large quantity of manuscript and published material, including journals, letters collections, and narrative accounts, mostly generated by English participants and government officials but also Moroccan and Iberian sources, which provide a much wider perspective on events.

Hence, where surviving, primary source material provides a valuable insight into the existence, composition, strength, funding, and logistics of garrison life during the civil wars. These include the Parliamentarian garrisons of Warwickshire – including Warwick, Coventry, and Kenilworth; Yorkshire – Hull and Beverley; in addition to the Thames Valley in the form of Reading and Windsor. To a lesser extent, Nantwich and other garrisons in Cheshire provide some insight into garrison life. Owing partly to a more general lack of surviving records, Royalist garrisons such as Reading, Lichfield, and Chester paint a similar picture. Atherton contends that garrison archives rarely survive because of their fleeting nature and because most were discarded after the war. Therefore, those belonging to Lichfield, Windsor, and Warwickshire, for instance, can be regarded as exceptional and possess a rich seam of research material.

Based on detailed primary archival research (particularly among the manuscript collections deposited in The National Archives, British Library, and various regional archives), as well as published sources, the following book aims to assess the role of garrison warfare, composition, logistics, financing, arming, and clothing of a selection of civil war garrisons. As such, muster lists and pay warrants provide much information about the make-up and payment of military units, albeit they mainly survive from 1645 to 1646. In terms of historiography, such a work also emphasises the importance of the early modern sense of 'locality' or 'regionalism', thus enhancing important studies by authors such as R. N. Dore (Cheshire), Clive Holmes (Eastern

---

3   Andrew Hopper (ed.), *The Papers of the Hothams, Governors of Hull during the Civil War*, Camden 5th Series, 39 (Cambridge: Cambridge University Press, 2011); Ian Atherton, 'Royalist Finances in the English Civil War: The Case of the Lichfield Garrison, 1643-5', *Midland History*, 33 (2008), pp. 43–67.

4   Malcolm Gratton, 'Liverpool under Parliament: The Anatomy of a Civil War Garrison, May 1643 to June 1644', *THSLC*, 156 (2007), pp. 51–74. See also Andrew Hopper, '"Tinker" Fox and the Politics of Garrison Warfare in the West Midlands, 1643-50', *Midland History*, 24 (1999), pp. 98–113.

5   Andrew Abram, *The English Garrison of Tangier: Charles II's Colonial Venture in the Mediterranean, 1661-1684* (Solihull: Helion & Co., 2022).

Association), Tony Brighton (Derbyshire), and Martin Bennett (Royalist Midlands).

Richard Israel's recent study of sieges in the Severn Valley between 1642 and 1646 illustrates not only that 'Siege warfare is often the forgotten aspect of the English Civil War' but also that locating common aspects of the conflict in particular geographical regions can be fruitful.[6] This is echoed, to an extent, by Stuart B. Jennings' work on Newark, which details the various accounts of the sieges of the town whilst considering wider context during the British Civil Wars.[7] The primary focus of the present study is the Thames Valley, Cheshire, and Warwickshire area of the Midlands. Moreover, it will further address the imbalance presented by various writers by focusing on the impact of garrisons in both a regional and national context, to provide a deeper understanding of the conflict.

---

6   Richard Israel, *Cannon Played from the Great Fort: Sieges in the Severn Valley during the English Civil War 1642-1646* (Solihull: Helion & Co., 2021).
7   Stuart B. Jennings, *Royalist Newark, 1642-1646: Sieges and Siege Works* (Solihull: Helion & Co., 2024).

Chapter 1

'A place of greatest strength in this part of the Kingdom': Windsor Castle

On 28 October 1642, Colonel John Venn, a radical Presbyterian and London MP, was ordered, upon recommendation by the Commons, to take possession of Windsor Castle as governor and commanding officer of a regiment of foot, consisting of 800 common soldiers besides officers in 10 companies.[1] Pay warrants for the regiment from 28 October to 29 December 1642, and 30 December 1642 to 10 February 1643, indicate that, following the establishment of the garrison, there was money to pay the regiment's officers and soldiers during the early months of its existence.[2] In terms of recruitment, commissioned officers may have been lured by the promise of receiving some of their pay in advance, whilst the sum of £30 (seemingly in the form of a bounty) was laid out on the initial recruitment of common soldiers. Similarly, several new recruits were conscripted into Venn's own company, commanded by Captain Lieutenant Robert Holland, and £25 was put up 'for the impressment money and receiving recruits'.[3] Even so, recruits for the garrison were occasionally enlisted from 'the well-affected in Windsor'.[4]

Among the disbursements made by the Committee of the Militia of the City of London in preparation for the seizing of Windsor Castle were those for the raising of Venn's regiment, its transportation to Windsor, and the carriage of ammunition and provisions from the City of London upriver via Brentford in October 1642. Thus, between 17 and 28 October, Colonel Venn received payment 'for the raising of his regiment, and the entertainment of himself and the officers and soldiers of the same, due 11 November 1642'; £169 7s. 6d. went to John Taylor 'for transporting the said Colonel's men with their provisions to Windsor with the hire of porters and barges', whereas

---
1   *CJ*, II, p. 811.
2   TNA, SP28/263, ff. 234r., 297r.–v.
3   TNA, SP28/298/1, ff. 239r.–240v.; SP28/126/1, ff. 14v.–15v.
4   *CSPD 1645–1647*, p. 217.

GARRISONS AND GARRISON WARFARE IN THE BRITISH CIVIL WARS, 1638-1653

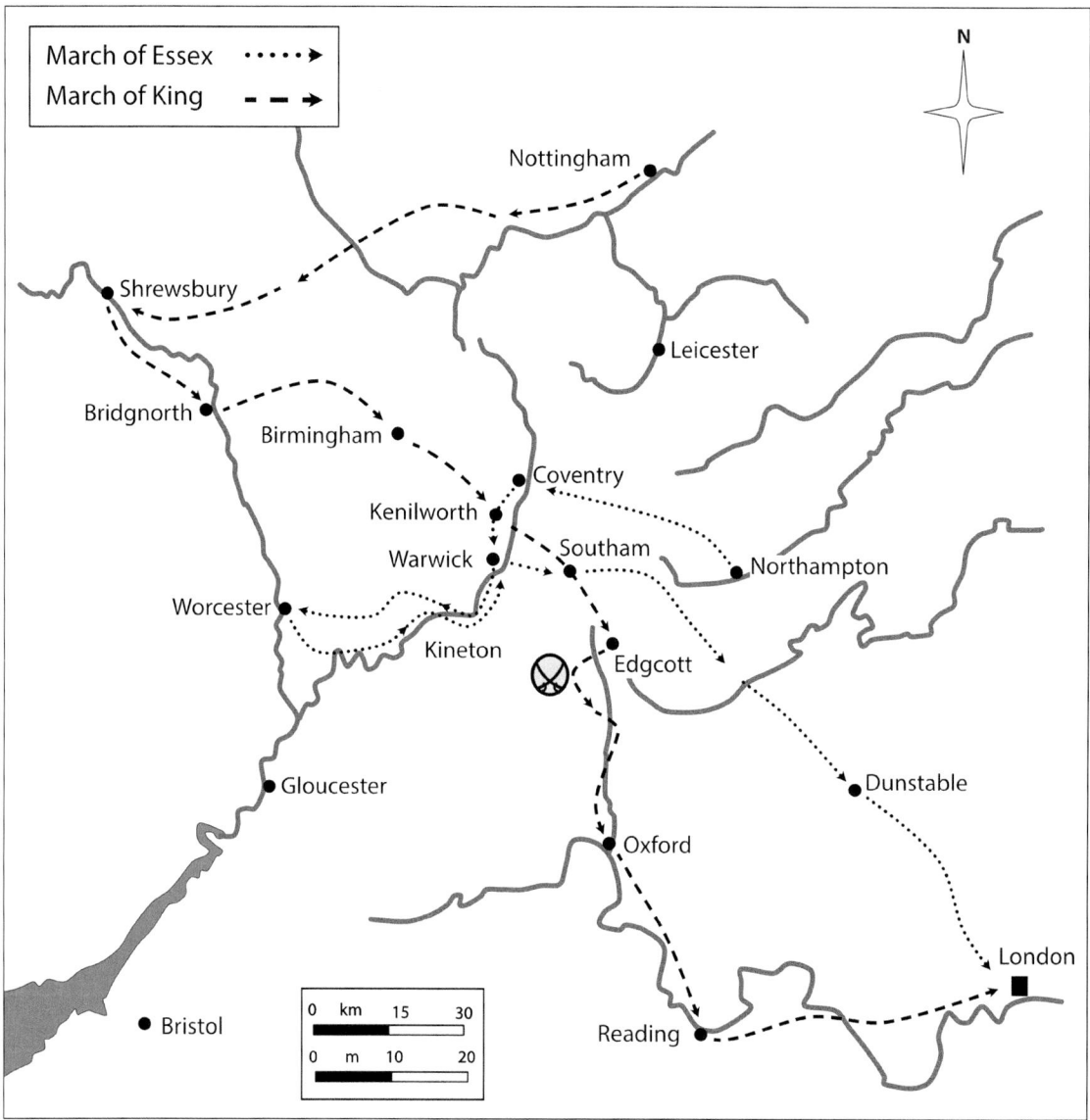

Map 1 The King's campaign towards London, autumn 1642.

payment was made to Benjamin Blunden, 'commissary for Windsor, for impressed men for service the sum of £100, and 4 November £100 for which is to account for that regiment at Windsor'.[5] In appointing Colonel Venn to command a garrison at Windsor, Parliament's first intention was to protect the castle, which acted as the western bulwark in defence of Parliamentarian London, from the advancing Royalist army. According to one report on 20 October 1642, the King 'intended to draw to Windsor and to take possession of the castle, that being a place of greatest strength in this part of the Kingdom, by reason of the height and strength, the country lying under it so that the castle can command it round about'.

---

5   TNA, SP28/34/2, ff. 171r.–v.

Hence, the King's objective in advancing along the Thames Valley towards London would be thwarted:

> for by the appointment of the Parliament, several-well affected gentlemen and valiant religious commanders are gone into Essex, Middlesex, Buckinghamshire, Berkshire, Surrey, Hampshire, and other adjoining counties, to raise several troops of dragoons and volunteers, some of which are arrived already at Windsor, and have taken possession of the castle, for the use of his Majesty and Parliament, others are in their march towards Windsor, where being arrived, they intend to fortify themselves, and to make outworks, so that the Cavaliers have lost their labour.[6]

Moreover, another contemporary source declared:

> The King's Majesty having altered his intention of staying at Shrewsbury (as is conceived by the persuasion of that *Cavalero* rout, which have destined all to ruin and destruction) hath lately bent his course toward London, being persuaded that here he shall have more aid and assistance, (as is pretended) then he hath yet obtained, this pretense of theirs hath drawn his Majesty into this course, although it is apparently manifest that they march up to London with an intent to plunder it, and bring all to ruin and destruction, that stand well affected to the King and Parliament. For the perfecting of which practice, they intended to draw to Windsor, and to take possession of the castle, that being a place of greatest strength in this part of the Kingdom, by reason of the height and strength, the country lying under it, so that the castle can command it round about. Could they have obtained this castle, they would there have fortified themselves, till such times as they could have gathered strength, which having obtained, they then intended (as is generally thought) to have marched against London that being their only aim, but God which sees the secrets of all hearts has brought their practices to light and made them apparent to the eye of the world, their intentions were discovered to the high court of Parliament, who by God's assistance and direction have taken the most speedy and effectual course to prevent so great a mischief.[7]

Colonel Venn took possession of the royal castle of Windsor in the name of the King and Parliament unopposed. He acted as governor from October 1642 to June 1645. Venn's newly raised regiment began arriving at Windsor on 26 October, when the sum of 17s. 8d. was paid 'for 6 wherries [light rowing boats, chiefly for carrying passengers] from Brentford to Windsor

---

6 *Exceeding true and happy newes from the Castle of Windsor. Declaring how severall troopes of dragooners have taken possession of the said castle, to keepe it for the use of the King ann Parliament* (London: T. Franklin, 1642). TT, E123[20].

7 *A most famous victory obtained by that vallant religious gentleman, Collonell Venne, against Prince Robert, who came against Windsor on Munday the 7th of November, promising Collonell Vann great preferment if that he would deliver up the said castle to his Majesites use, also Collonell Vens answer to Prince Roberts propositions likewise declaring how the said towne is beat downe, and men, women, and children, forced to fly into the woods to save themselves from the cruelty of the cavaliers* (London: J. Rich, 1642). TT, E126[42].

with soldiers', whilst, on 29 October, 17s. 6d. was laid out 'for towing the last barges with soldiers to Windsor', and a further 2s. 6d. 'for unloading provisions and ammunition'.[8] Not only did Windsor possess enormous strategic value as the western bulwark for London, but it was also a major magazine and distribution point for supplying goods to the garrisons of the Thames Valley, in addition to the southwest of England and the Midlands. Likewise, from November 1642, Windsor Castle acted as the headquarters for the Parliamentarian army under the Earl of Essex and, in 1645, the New Model Army commanded by Sir Thomas Fairfax, although a separate garrison remained there for most of this time.

The son of a Somerset yeoman, John Venn (1586–1650) was apprenticed to the Merchant Taylors' Company in 1602 and became a full member from 1621. In 1614, he was admitted to the Company of the Artillery Garden, became a captain in the London Trained Bands, and, in 1642, was lieutenant colonel of the Yellow Regiment. Venn subsequently commanded a regiment of foot in the Earl of Essex's army, before being appointed governor of Windsor Castle by Parliament on 28 October 1642. Largely recruited out of London volunteers, Colonel Venn's newly raised regiment, which garrisoned Windsor Castle, was initially transported from London in October 1642 with all its personnel, arms, horses, ammunition, and supplies in 'boats and barges', while various sums were paid to bargemen for carriage. Thus, some troops, with their provisions, were transported from Brentford in 28 barges, with some craft making to up to three journeys. More soldiers arrived at Windsor during the following weeks in 12 barges and a wherry.[9]

When Colonel Venn's soldiers arrived at Windsor, they broke into the treasury and pillaged the Chapel's collection of plate. On 27 May 1643, the House of Lords decreed that 'the plate, sent from Windsor to the treasurers at Guildhall, be forthwith melted down and coined; and the proceeds thereof paid to Mr White, agent to the Lord Fairfax, for supply of the army in the north under the command of the said Lord Fairfax, and that it be employed to no other use'. In attempting to preserve the College of St George from harm, they ordered the Speaker to instruct Venn 'to take care that there be no disorders and disturbances made in the Chapel at Windsor; and that the evidences, registers, monuments there and all things that belong to the Order of the Garter, may be preserved without any defacings, and that he permit the Prebends to live in their own houses'.[10] This was of little use, though, because the soldiers destroyed the fifteenth-century chapter house, and, among various things, lead was stripped off the chapel roofs, parts of Henry VIII's unfinished funeral monument were removed, and the Dean and canons ejected. Taking a somewhat softer line, in December 1643, the Commons ordered Venn to 'put the ordinance for removal of scandalous monuments and pictures in execution in the several churches and chapels of Windsor and Eton'.[11] Royalist propaganda was rife, however, with one source reporting for 7 September 1643:

---

8 TNA, SP28/34/2, f. 170r.
9 TNA, SP28/16/2, ff. 171r.–v.; SP28/34/2, f. 171r.; SP28/126/1, ff. 8r.–22v.; SP28/263, ff. 76r.–79r.
10 *LJ*, VI, p. 30.
11 *CJ*, III, pp. 106, 341, 348.

Though they dare not fight with men, they dare with images, for Captain [*recte* Colonel] Venn (as were this day advertised) who had hitherto so indulgent to his castle of Windsor, as not to ruin and deface the chief beauties of it, had at last broke down the curious organs in the castle church, demolished all the painted glass, and committed many other outrages of that barbarous nature, not sparing the carved work on the very walls, perhaps to make it fitter for his winter stable, which use his soldiers put it when they first came thither.[12]

Once the Parliamentarian garrison at Windsor was established, the construction of substantial fortifications began in earnest. The Royalist Sir Philip Warwick described the castle as 'no than a house of magnificence, being no little strength, though it was called a castle'.[13] Even so, Wenceslaus Hollar's perspective drawings, rendered in 1658, show that the main structures, including the keep on the motte, remained in very good condition. Because Windsor Castle and its location on the Thames was of such strategic importance to the Parliamentarian cause, funding came principally from central London sources. Thus, the initial costs included £131 12s. 'expended for fortifications of the first coming to Windsor allowed by the House of Commons'; £197 10s. 9d. was provided for 'repairing the castle and other incidental charges', whilst £257 6s. 1d. was spent 'about the new fortifications by my Lord General's order'. The accounts of Sir Edward Peyto, lieutenant general of the Earl of Essex's Train of Artillery from November 1642 to his death in September 1643, provide an often tantalising picture of their development. The first phase of construction, involving a series of riverside fortifications that occurred in late November and early December 1642, comprised of a series of breastworks and connecting trenches, protected by a redoubt on the western side of the town. Peyto's accounts refer to batteries and fortifications, such as monies disbursed 'for the batteries behind his Excellency's lodgings in Windsor', for employment at 'the redoubt and line at the west end of the town', for 'the sconce at Eaton College', and 'for fortifications from the Castle way to the rivers side'.

The second period of construction was begun on 25 April 1643 and continued for the next three months. This was concentrated around the castle and the town of Windsor. Garrison accounts include not only various payments to a considerable number of men involved in the construction but also the remarkable scale of the completed fortifications.[14] The sum of £1 12s. was paid to 'Mr Evans, surveyor of the work and the engineer'; £7 to Henry Clark, 'surveyor of the works for 7 months' pay at 5s. per week'. Pioneers were paid 1s. a day for a fortnight to excavate ditches. Turf was laid on top of the ditches and banks to prevent erosion, while more could have been positioned against the sides of the castle walls and at weak points within the fabric of the castle. Palisades were constructed along the top of the fortifications. Moreover, in November, supplementary work saw the construction of timber platforms, batteries, palisades, and draw bridges.

---

12 *Mercurius Aulicus*, 9 September 1643. TT, E245[36].
13 Sir Philip Warwick, *Memoirs of the Reign of King Charles I* (London: Ri. Chifwell, 1702), p. 254.
14 TNA, SP28/126/1, ff. 19r.–36r.

The latter were positioned across the moat at the Henry VIII Gate and on Windsor Bridge. Among various disbursements, £52 15s. 8d. was given 'to the carpenters for work done by them in making platforms for batteries and palisades about the fortifications, and other works about the castle', and £31 1s. 'for cutting down timber in the forest to make palisades, platforms and 2 drawbridges'. The latter was rendered by the Dutch artist Dirk van der Aa in 1705, although the drawbridge workings and castle gateway were removed in the late eighteenth century.[15]

Several stonemasons and labourers were employed in the 'stopping of vaults under the castle and other work'. Unsurprisingly, quantities of tools were procured for the workmen. In December 1642, Captain Jonathan Gawthorne – a company commander in Venn's regiment – was reimbursed the sum of £4 4s. 6d. for pickaxes, spades, and shovels that had been transported to Windsor from London. While the quantities of such tools cannot be inferred from this example, a month earlier, 92 spades were purchased for the fortifications at the Parliamentarian garrison at Coventry at a cost of £5 11s., while £2 18s. 2d. was disbursed for 49 shovels for the pioneers.[16] Likewise, the Ordnance Office supplied the Train of Artillery, which provided the ordnance and logistical support to the New Model, both during field operations and siege conditions. According to the Establishment of Sir Thomas Fairfax's army, there were two companies of pioneers among the Train, each with a captain (paid 5s. per day), a lieutenant (3s.), two overseers (2s.), and 60 pioneers (receiving 12d. a day).[17] Large quantities of tools and technical equipment were received from specialist suppliers. On 15 April 1645, John Gace of Eastcheap in London, a turner and former Master of the Turners' Company, delivered 800 shovels and spades at 1s. 3d. apiece 'according to the contract made with the said Committee, amounting to £50' to the Ordnance Office, with a further 100 spades at 3s. (probably metal-shod at that price) on 17 June.[18]

In early November 1642, the Earl of Essex hastened his army to the defence of London, while the King followed at a rather sluggish pace. On 7 November, Essex's forces arrived, and, the same day, a large cavalry force under Prince Rupert, the King's nephew and leading Royalist commander, attacked the town and castle at Windsor, barely weeks after the garrison's arrival. Colonel Venn may have felt exposed there, especially as his inexperienced regiment was so far untested; however, it would acquit itself well. The Parliamentarian newsbook *A Perfect diurnall of the passages in Parliament* reported for 7 November:

> Information was given to Parliament that Prince Robert [*recte* Rupert] with a part of the King's forces has besieged Windsor, but they are driven back by Colonel Venn and the forces in the castle, and that with some loss, and some of them taken prisoners; but Prince Robert, finding it too great a difficulty to gain Windsor, as

---

15 Dirk van der Aa, *View of Windsor Castle* (1705), Royal Collection, RCIN 404917.
16 TNA, SP28/136/19, f. 8v.
17 TNA, SP28/145, ff. 60r.–63v.
18 TNA, WO47/1, f. 211r.; SP28/29/1, f. 123r.; SP28/30/5, ff. 636r.–v.

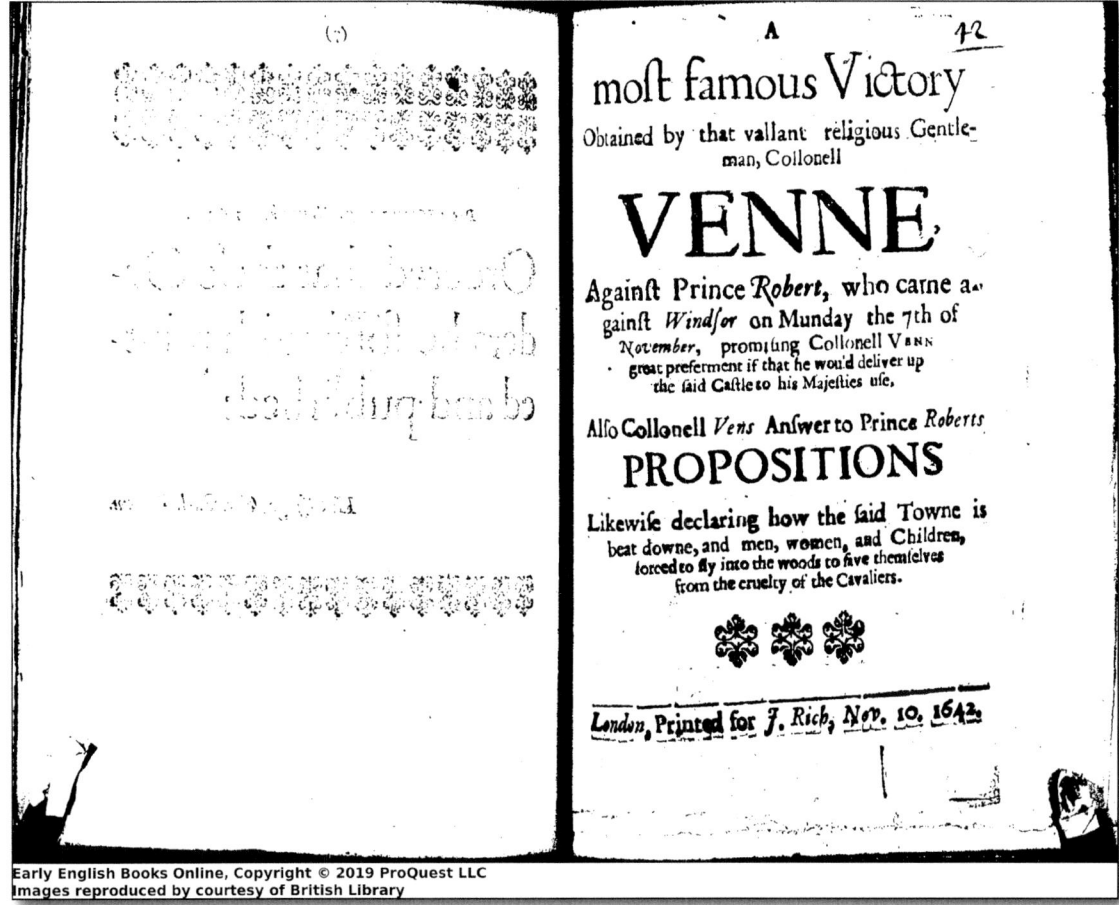

A most famous victory obtained by that vallant religious gentleman, Collonell Venne. TT, E126[42]

better fitting with his valour and wonted practice went and plundered Staines, and divers other places within 10 miles of London, and has made great spoil there.[19]

Nevertheless, in covering Colonel Venn's refusal to deliver up the castle, a more fulsome account narrated:

> Prince Robert, having received this answer, was struck into a fearful and terrible outrage, and commanded all his horse and foot to discharge against the inhabitants of the said town, commanding his cannoneers to plant those 5 pieces of ordnance that they had with them against the castle. Yet all this could not prevail, for Colonel Venn planted 7 pieces of ordnance right opposite against the Cavaliers; this fight began about 10 of the clock in the forenoon Monday last, and continued until 6 at night. But the Prince Robert's troops, being many in number, prevailed against the inhabitants of the said town, so that they were forced to retreat into the castle for their safeguard, which being done, Prince Robert drew his forces into the said town, and with his ordnance from Eton College, which he had raised to be planted there, he began to let fly at the castle, thus they continued shooting for

---

19   *A Perfect diurnall of the passages in Parliament*, 7–14 November 1642. TT, E240[14].

the space of 7 hours, doing great execution on both sides, for there was slain near 1,000 of the Prince's forces, and many of our men, only not 1 of note, but Captain Sanders, a noble honest gentleman and a good soldier, who went down thither with Colonel Venn for the true Protestant religion. Also Colonel Venn behaved himself very bravely, to the wonder and amazement of the beholders, so that in spite of Prince Robert's policy, he and his Cavaliers were forced to retreat, and leave to assault the castle. As for the town that is mightily battered and ruined, and the inhabitants very much damnified. All which stood well-affected to the Parliament, went into the castle and are safe, as to the rest they are left to the wide world, as well they deserve it, for had they been true, they had not come to this misery that they are now like to endure.[20]

Rupert left a detachment to keep the Windsor garrison from venturing forth to threaten his line of communications, whilst, on 10 November, three Royalist infantry regiments under Colonel Henry Wentworth and a tertia commanded by Lord Fielding quartered temporarily at nearby Old Windsor. Keeping ahead of Charles I's main body, Rupert had advanced with his horse to Maidenhead, and, from there, he pillaged Staines and Egham on the outskirts of London.

The composition and quality of Colonel John Venn's regiment is reflected in the origins of some of its company commanders. Lieutenant Colonel John Bradley was a gentleman of the City of London, who in July 1642 had been entrusted by Parliament with the shipment of arms from the magazine of Hull to London and its subsequent storage.[21] Probably a sergeant major of the Yellow Regiment, London Trained Bands – commanded by Colonel Sir John Wollaston and in which Venn served as lieutenant colonel – he was a captain in Essex's forces by 16 August 1642, when a warrant was issued to compensate him for sums paid out for carbines, pistols, and arms for the troops of cuirassiers.[22] Sergeant Major Thomas Buxton had been a captain in the Orange Regiment, London Trained Bands, in April 1642 and was promoted later in the year before service in Venn's regiment of foot, forming the garrison of Windsor. Captain Jonathan Gawthorne had been captain lieutenant in the Red Regiment, London Trained Bands, in mid-1642, before transferring into Colonel Venn's infantry regiment at Windsor Castle.[23]

Likewise, Captain William Stackhouse was a lieutenant in the Green Regiment, London Trained Bands, commanded by Colonel John Warner, in summer 1642. Stackhouse also served as captain in Sir John Seton's regiment of dragoons and was one of the officers specified in Parliament's commission of 29 September 1642 as a recruiter for the regiment in London.[24] Captain John Barkstead was a London goldsmith before service in Venn's regiment. In August 1645, he became governor of Reading, whilst, two years later,

---

20   *Most famous victory*. TT, E126[42].
21   *CJ*, V, p. 215.
22   TNA, SP28/1A, f. 119v.
23   TNA, SP28/262/19, f. 219r.
24   TNA, SP28/4, f. 359r.; SP28/5, ff. 204v.–6r., 340r.; *A True Relation of the late proceedings of the London Dragoneers, sent down to Oxford, consisting of foure Companies under the command of Sir John Seaton* (London: Henry Overton, 1642). TT, E118[39].

he replaced Colonel Richard Fortescue – he having been made governor of Pendennis Castle – as commanding officer of his foot regiment.[25] The background and service record of Captains Henry Sanders, Joseph Symonds, Richard Lane, and Phillip Purchon before joining Venn's regiment remain uncertain, but, as with their comrades above, membership of the London Trained Bands is a possibility.

Table 1 Monies Received for the Garrison of Windsor Castle since Their Marching Out of the City of London to Windsor, 13–29 October 1642 (TNA, SP28/126/1, ff. 19r.–36r.)

	£	s.	d.
October 1642. Borrowed from the Militia of London at the time of the regiment's advancing	815	0	0
Received and borrowed from the Militia of London at several times in victuals for the supply of the garrison by the hands of the commissary	649	18	2
Borrowed from the Colonel, being his own money, lent to pay the commissary for provision of victuals for the garrison	343	6	5
Borrowed from Commissary Blundell, being so much by him disbursed for victuals for the garrison	170	0	0
29 October 1642. Monies laid out and disbursed for same:			
Paid to the Colonel's captain-lieutenant to pay the officers and soldiers belonging to the Colonel's company	2134	3	9
Paid to the Colonel himself towards his own pay	199	10	0
Paid to Lieutenant Colonel John Bradley for himself, his officers and soldiers	1843	1	1
Paid to Sergeant Major Thomas Buxton for same	1752	7	8
Paid to Captain Henry Saunders for same	1546	8	11
Paid to Captain Jonathan Gawthorne for same	1440	2	3
Paid to Captain Joseph Symons for same	1592	7	4
Paid to Captain Richard Lane for same	1476	10	1
Paid to Captain John Barkstead for same	1617	10	1
Paid to Captain William Stackhouse for same	1581	1	0
Paid to Captain Phillip Pinchon for same	1515	4	4
Paid to the gunners and matrosses	919	16	11
Paid to Mr Christopher Love, minister of the regiment	128	0	0
Paid to the quartermaster of the regiment	70	0	0
Paid to Robert Leonard, marshal of the regiment	84	6	1
Paid to the doctor, apothecary and his man	110	16	0
Paid more to him to provide drugs	35	0	0
Paid to Meredith Jones, surgeon towards his own and 2 mates' pay	112	3	0
Paid to the gunsmith and armourer	66	17	0
Paid to the commissary of victuals towards his and his 2 men's pay	22	0	0
Paid to the engineer	47	1	8
Paid to the commissary towards the expense of the dragoons' horses	5	15	0
Expended on the regiment at its first coming and before we were settled in provisions of bread, beer, and cheese when the enemy lay about us	189	2	6
Paid for bread, beer, and cheese for the poor common prisoners	347	16	3
Paid for provisions delivered to the Lord General	116	3	4
Paid to the conductors and woodcutters for the several guards in the castle for fuel for 1 whole year, ending 3 June 1644	39	2	3
Paid for intelligence at the first coming to Windsor allowed by the House of Commons	10	0	0

---

25   Bodl. Lib., Ms Tanner 60/1, f. 512r.; *CJ*, IV, p. 239.

	£	s.	d.
Paid for incidental charges allowed by the House of Commons	167	7	0
Expended by the commissary for candles for the use of the castle guard	28	16	10
Paid for money bags		1	0
Paid for the hire of a horse to bring up money and given to the clerks by Quartermaster Lee	1	2	0
Paid for what came short in 1 bag	2	10	0
Paid for what came short in another bag	2	10	0
Paid for 40 fathoms of rope for the well		19	0

Although no actual muster lists appear to have survived for Venn's regiment, the 'accounts of Robert Holland, Captain-Lieutenant of the company of Colonel Venn in the garrison of Windsor' record various disbursements to troops. Hence, between 13 and 28 October 1642, payments were made to one captain lieutenant, one ensign, three sergeants, four corporals, three drummers, one drum major, and 58 private soldiers of Venn's own company; from 28 October 1642 to 6 December 1643, the same number of commissioned officers, non-commissioned officers, and 144 soldiers were present, whilst, between 6 December 1643 and 3 June 1644, these were paid along with 119 men. As might be expected, given levels of recruitment, wounds, and sickness, the number of common soldiers in Venn's regiment fluctuated. Hence, 71 were mustered among his company on 29 December 1642, 65 men on 2 March 1643, 60 on 13 April 1642, 47 on 5 May 1644, 72 on 28 February, and 48 on 29 May 1645. Between 4 June and 1 November 1644, Ensign Hutton, Sergeant Lilly, and Corporal Cooke are listed as present, whilst, during the period from 21 November 1644 to 23 May 1645, the company consisted of a captain lieutenant, one ensign, two sergeants, three corporals, two drummers, and 66–68 soldiers.[26] Moreover, a document entitled 'Monies due unto the Colonel, commanders, and officers of the regiment of Colonel Venn in the garrison of Windsor from 28 October 1642 to 3 June 1644, being the whole charge of the said regiment during said time' includes the following:

> To the colonel himself for 83 weeks £15 15s. per week comes to £1,307 15s.
> To the officers and soldiers of his company £2,905 5s. 6d.
> For recruiting of his said company £30
>
> Company commanders:
> Colonel Venn (Captain-Lieutenant Robert Holland)
> Lieutenant Colonel Bradley
> Sergeant Major Buxton
> Captain Sanders
> Captain Gawthorne
> Captain Symonds
> Captain Lane
> Captain Barkstead

---

26   TNA, SP28/16/2, ff. 62v.–63v.; SP28/126/1, ff. 14r.–15v., 45v.–48v.

Captain Stackhouse
Captain Purchon.

Also included in the garrison were one provost marshal, one surgeon, two mates, one quartermaster, one engineer, one commissary and his two assistants, unspecified gunners and matrosses, one apothecary and his assistant, one gunsmith, and one armourer. The sum of £29 6s. was paid to six gunners from 20 October to 16 December 1642, being seven weeks at 14s. per week.

Several other disbursements of pay to Venn's regiment during its occupation of Windsor Castle offer clues to its composition and strength. On 3 November 1642, Lieutenant Colonel Bradley's company mustered Lieutenant Showell, two sergeants, three corporals, two drummers, and 120 soldiers; there were 126 soldiers on 10 November, 132 on 17 November, 138 on 24 November, 144 on 1 December, 148 on 8 December, whereas, between January and April 1644, between 101 and 107 private sentinels were mustered, and, between 2 November 1644 and 3 June 1645, Bradley's company contained 108–130 of them. There are fewer references to Sergeant Major Buxton's company in the pay accounts, yet, upon discharge on 22 November 165, it contained one lieutenant, one ensign, two sergeants, three corporals, one drummer, and 41 soldiers. From 1 December 1642 to 6 December 1643, Captain Henry Sanders' company mustered one lieutenant, one ensign, two sergeants, three corporals, one drummer, with between 66 to 92 soldiers; similarly, between 3 November and 7 December 1644, 60 private soldiers were mustered, although, between 8 and 15 December 1644, 90 were present. However, in mid-1645, the strength of the unit had been reduced to one lieutenant, one ensign, one sergeant, two corporals, one drummer, and 32–46 soldiers. The total pay apportioned to Sanders' company was £1551 19s. 4d., but only £893 was received, with the sum of £658 14s. 4d. remaining owed.

Furthermore, in mid-1645, Captain Symonds' company possessed one lieutenant, one ensign, one sergeant, two corporals, one drummer, and 19–26 soldiers. During the same period, Captain Gawthorne's command mustered one lieutenant, one ensign, one sergeant, two corporals, one drummer, and between 20 and 36 common soldiers; Captain Lane's had one lieutenant, one ensign, two sergeants, two corporals, one drummer, and between 26 and 49 men; Captain Barkstead's company comprised one lieutenant, one ensign (Howell Morris), one sergeant (Robert Styche), one corporal, one drummer, and 17–24 soldiers. Captain William Stackhouse's company is better documented – from 8 December 1642 to 13 December 1643, it mustered one lieutenant, one ensign, two sergeants, three corporals, one drummer, and

Captain, later Colonel John Barkstead.

between 66 to 90 soldiers; in mid-1645, there was one lieutenant, one ensign, one corporal, one drummer, and 26–48 soldiers. The total pay assigned to the unit was £1307 16s. 8d., although £379 12s. 8d. was received and £928 4s. left in arrears. Likewise, in mid-1645, Captain Purchon's company consisted of one lieutenant, one ensign (Thornell), one sergeant, one corporal, one drummer, and between 15 and 33 soldiers.[27]

Soon after the garrison was established in October 1642, Parliament disbursed money for 'the raising of dragoon horses employed under the command of the Lord General at Windsor and elsewhere', with money for meat and pad-saddles for the horses.[28] The garrison accounts mention the purchase of items in November 1643 of horse tack, such as bridles, girths, and halters, and state that a number of saddles had been sent for mending. There appears to have been roughly 50 dragoons in the garrison, who were primarily employed in patrolling the hinterland about Windsor and the Thames Valley area. The 'account of what horses for dragoons have been sent into the castle of Windsor' between 28 October 1642 and 3 June 1644 provides evidence of the origin, description, and price of various animals procured from the locality as well as others in the Thames Valley area. These include the following: 'from Mr Child of Wraysbury, a sad bay mare £3; from Humphrey Hedges of Egham, 1 roan gelding £3; from Andrew Durdant of Staines, 1 black mare £2 10s.; from Mr Harrison of High Harefield, 1 gray gelding £3; [and] from Mr Symerson of Binfield, 1 sorrel nag £2 10s.'[29]

Such prices are somewhat lower than the £4 paid by the Ordnance Office to Smithfield dealers for dragoon mounts for the New Model Army in 1645–1646, but the Windsor horses seem to have been purchased directly locally, and their price might reflect a slightly inferior quality and lower overheads on the part of the vendors.[30] Another list of mounts maintained by the Windsor garrison between August 1643 and June 1644 records that, from 29 August to 13 September 1643, there were 20; between 13 September and 30 October 1643, there were 36; between 30 October and 17 December 1643, there were 54; from 17 December 1643 to 12 January 1644, 54 were mustered; from 12 January to 30 March 1644, there were 48; between 30 March and 14 April 1644, 34 were present; whilst, from 14 April to 2 June 1644, the garrison accounted for 20 horses. According to a note by Commissary Benjamin Blundell, however, 'all sent out with the party to Greenland House and not yet returned'.[31]

This refers to the military operations following the fruitless attempts by the Earl of Essex and Sir William Waller in June 1644 to capture Oxford and the King. Consequently, Sergeant Major General John Browne was given command of the Parliamentarian forces in the area, with instructions to reduce Oxford, Banbury, Wallingford, and the Fort of Greenland House. The following month, Lieutenant Colonel John Bradley led 300 foot from the

---

27 TNA, SP28/126/1, ff. 47v.–59r.; SP28/126/2, ff. 185r.–191v.
28 *CSPD 1642*, p. 451.
29 TNA, SP28/126/1, ff. 28r.–v.
30 TNA, SP28/29/1, ff. 166r.–v., 204r.; SP28/29/2, f. 258v.; SP28/31/5, f. 542r.; SP28/140/7, f. 276v.
31 TNA, SP28/43/1, f. 20r.

Windsor garrison at the siege of Greenland. Under the heading 'Dragoon horses dead' was reported that, on 6 October 1643, one grey nag had died; on 14 January 1644, one horse; on 20 January, one horse; on 30 January, one horse; on 13 February, two horses; on 17 February, one white nag; on 26 February, one flea-bitten mare; on 1 March, a bay nag; on 15 March, a roan nag; on 20 April, a bay gelding, one white mare, and a sorrel nag were deceased. Moreover, '17 several' additional horses were stated 'lost and stolen'; one white mare had been pilfered by Sergeant Sawyer; another brown nag was lost, sent by Lieutenant Cole to Farnham (possibly the Captain Cole in Colonel Richard Norton's regiment of dragoons, whose company attempted to seize Basing House in July 1643); one gray nag was 'taken away by Sir William Waller's coming from Basing', whereas a brown gelding was sent and never returned. In total, 13 mounts were reported dead, 18 lost or stolen, and a further three horses were provided to support other Parliamentarian operations and did not come back.

The financial accounts of the Parliamentarian garrison of Windsor give an idea of the welfare of its horses and the supplies purchased to keep them healthy. William Wright and other farriers were employed to shoe mounts, whilst, between August 1643 and July 1644, the garrison had up to five grooms who were paid 2s. 4d. a week. The accounts also contain payments for items such as curry combs, cantles, girths, bridles, and halters, in addition to supplies 'for medicines at several times for horse baths', 'medicines for horse backs', 'bleeding and drenching', among other treatments.[32] When the Parliamentarian garrison arrived at Windsor in October 1642, there was only a fraction of the amount of fodder required to feed its horses. As Gavin Robinson observed, by the end of the following year, the whole of Berkshire was drained of hay and oats and was unable to support the Parliamentarian forces, which also included the armies of the Earl of Essex and Sir William Waller.[33] The accounts of the garrison's treasurer confirm that, because of the shortage in the Windsor area in particular, fodder had to be procured from surrounding counties. During the harvest period of September–October 1643, 60 cartloads of hay (including 10 from Eaton College Meadow), 13 quarts of oats, 1,210 bushels of grain, two quarts of beans, one of barley, and 'malt for the mash' from unnamed localities are recorded as having been purchased by the Windsor Castle garrison and supplied to the dragoons for their mounts.[34]

Colonel John Venn's newly established garrison at Windsor Castle was transported from London in October 1642 with all its personnel, arms, horses, ammunition, and supplies in 'boats and barges', while various sums were paid to bargemen for carriage.[35] Such vessels were flat-bottomed barges or lighters that carried goods on the River Thames. After 1642, the Earl of Essex's infantry benefitted from two major clothing deliveries – one at

---

32　TNA, SP28/126/1, ff. 28v.–29r., 34r., 40r.
33　Gavin Robinson, 'Horse Supply in the English Civil War 1642–1646', PhD thesis (University of Reading, 2001), p. 228.
34　TNA, SP28/126/1, ff. 20v., 28v.
35　TNA, SP28/16/2, ff. 171r.–v.; SP28/34/2, ff. 171r.; SP28/126/1, ff. 8r.–22v.; SP28/263, ff. 76r.–79r.

Bierton, near Aylesbury, in October 1643 and the other at Portsmouth in September 1644. Regarding the first, a single consignment of 6,000 pairs of shoes and 2,000 shirts, snapsacks, and stockings were sent to Windsor for distribution to the army, probably on 26 October.[36] In 1644, various loads of clothing, arms, ordnance, and ammunition were transported to both Reading and Windsor for the Parliamentarian forces from Thames wharfs in London.[37] During the autumn, the Earl of Essex established a supply centre and headquarters to sustain his army during military operations that led to the Second Battle of Newbury.

On 24 October, the Committee of Both Kingdoms informed the Earl of Essex:

> we learn of your want of provisions and your desire to have them sent to Reading. Upon our first notice of your departure from Basingstoke, we appointed them to go to Windsor, as a place nearer and fitter for a further transportation. The provisions are now upon the water and may easily come to Reading if you send order to that purpose.[38]

Hence, these supplies were sent by boats from Windsor to Reading, where they were distributed to Essex's troops. On 18 November 1644, the sum of £7 was laid out by Thomas Richardson, commissary and waggonmaster to Essex's army, to Henry Russell and Thomas Waters 'for the hire of their boats with 6 oars apiece, carrying 2 tons of match and 4 tons of bullet to Reading (but left by them at Windsor by order) according to their contract with Sir Walter Earle and the rest of the Officers of the Ordnance'. Moreover, John Arnold received payment, 'which he disbursed for hire of timber to take up the 3 great brass pieces out of Morgan's barge into Windsor Castle with the round-shot, etc. And also to [the] gunners, carpenters, and labourers for their assistance as by his bill of particulars to the sum of £1 9s. 6s.'[39] During the harsh winter of 1642–1643, when the main armies in the south of England went into winter quarters, the Earl of Essex located his troops in the western suburbs of London and established his headquarters at Windsor Castle, billeting in the Round Tower. This caused considerable discord with the governor, Colonel Venn.

Nevertheless, the logistical deficiencies in supplying Essex's army in 1644 were revealed by the following letter sent by Commissaries Martin Pindar and Thomas Herbert to Speaker William Lenthall on 24 October from Reading. After detailing the army's movements 'about Reading and Newbury', they wrote:

> Touching the necessities of our own army, give us leave to represent some things to your consideration. The army most part of this march from Portsmouth has suffered in want of provision, partly through the indigency of the country through

---

36 TNA, SP28/140/4, ff. 27r., 35v.–36v., 85v.
37 TNA, SP28/140/4, f. 40v.; SP28/262/2, ff. 217r., 219r.
38 *CSPD 1644–1645*, p. 69.
39 TNA, SP28/140/4, ff. 46v., 47v.

which we passed and partly due to want of commissioners whose continued absence is of extraordinary prejudice, it being an employment both of care and pains; and though a deputy may endeavour yet wanting the reputation the work fails much in the practice. Wherefore we beseech you to take some course, both to expedite the commissaries of provisions – both which are and have long been absent – to attend their charge, and if the House seem pleased to hasten some biscuit and cheese hither, the passage being safe, the way not bad, and the soldier thereby would be exceedingly cheered.[40]

Weapons and ammunition sent to the Windsor garrison were in part supplied by the London Militia, although various items came from the Ordnance Office stores in the Tower. By warrant of the Committee of Safety, dated 20 October 1642, 628 matchlock muskets at 20s. apiece, a pair of pistols at £3, and one firelock carbine at £1 10s. were delivered to Colonel Venn. The total cost of these arms (including carriers' fees) came to £632 16s. The following day, the sum of 15s. was disbursed 'for carriage of 50 barrels of powder, 200 muskets and 300 swords from the Magazine in London [that is, Ordnance Office stores]'.[41] Additionally, 7s. 6d. went on 'bringing up the 5 chests of muskets from the waterside to Bulls Wharf, London, and then on to Windsor'.[42] Upon arrival, these were brought up to the castle. Other references to arms supplied to the garrison are discernible, although, on 9 August 1643, it was ordered that 'Lieutenant Colonel Rowe do forthwith deliver unto Colonel John Venn, Governor of Windsor Castle, 50 barrels of powder out of the store remaining in his hand that came in the Danish ship 300 swords, 200 muskets, with rests and belts'.[43] Rowe, being one of the principal agents for the Committee of Safety, distributed various quantities of weapons and ammunition from the Ordnance Office to a number of garrisons, such as Aylesbury, Pembroke, Evesham, and Worcester, in early 1645. He had previously supplied munitions to Essex's army, in addition to other forces.[44] The supply of over 1,000 matchlock muskets to Venn's regiment between October 1642 and August 1643, in addition to no references to pikes, corslets, and helmets, indicates that the Windsor garrison consisted of musketeers.

Significant quantities of pikes, swords, bandoliers, and firearms were imported into Britain from the Low Countries, especially via the ports of Dunkirk and Ostend in Flanders as well as Amsterdam in the United Provinces. In autumn 1642, the Committee of Safety authorised the purchase of 12,000 muskets with rests, 1,500 pairs of pistols, 1,200 carbines, 6,000 pikes, 600 sets of cavalry armour, and 6,000 corslets through Thomas Andrews and Stephen Estwick, who in turn 'asked their factors in Holland and France to obtain the weapons and by 4 October 2,690 muskets and 3,956

---

40 HMC, *Thirteenth Report, App. I* (London: HMSO, 1894), pp. 188–89.
41 TNA, SP28/34/2, f. 171v.
42 TNA, SP28/126/1, ff. 33v.–34v.
43 *CJ*, III, p. 199.
44 TNA, WO49/82, ff. 114r.–116v., 291r., 321r., 329r.; WSL, Ms Salt 463, unf.; *CSPD 1644–1645*, pp. 365, 367, 605, 609, 622, 625.

Windsor Castle in 1658 as seen from the south-east, by Wenceslas Hollar.

rests, 246 carbines, 66 dragoons, 980 pairs of pistols with cases, 401 suits of harquebusier armour and 2,331 corslets had been received'.[45] A further warrant was to the Ordnance Office on 10 June 1645 for two tons of match and 50 snaphaunce muskets to be delivered out of the stores for the use of the Windsor garrison.[46] In comparison, 200 muskets, 'full-bore with rests, at the rate of 17s. 6d. the musket and rest', were ordered for the Earl of Essex's army in September 1642.[47] Likewise, in 1645, the New Model was supplied with matchlock muskets, 'full bore and proof', costing between 10s. and 11s. 6d. each; snaphaunce muskets, 'English, full bore and proof, and 4 feet long', at 14s. 4d. and 15s. 6d. apiece; pistols with holsters costing £1 8s. a pair; and snaphaunce cavalry carbines.[48] Carbines were supplied to troops of the London City horse in 1643–1644 priced 22s. apiece, along with pistols, armours, and saddles.[49]

In addition to arms, several quantities of powder and ammunition were supplied to the garrison, although various consignments were also received at Windsor for distribution to the Earl of Essex's army. On 22 October 1642, 21 barrels of powder, 9cwt of bullet, and 60 bundles and eight shanks of match valued at £141 7s. 6d. were received by Commissary Blundell. Five days later, 20 barrels of powder at £4 4s. 10d. per barrel were ordered to be dispatched for the use of Venn's regiment, whilst, on 3 November 1642, 30 barrels of powder, 3cwt of bullet, and 60 bundles of match valued at £202 10s. were received. Such consignments were sent from the London Guildhall via Bull Wharf at the Tower of London. Similarly, on 21 December, the sum of 8s. was paid to a bargeman for carriage of four tons of powder, match, and swords and for 'bringing them up'. A further 30 barrels of powder, 30cwt of musket bullet, and 60 bundles of match were supplied to Blundell, who was responsible for supplying Venn's troops. A warrant dated 30 March 1643 was issued to pay £17 1s. to John Davies for the charge of eight barges that carried soldiers to Windsor to guard ammunition, arms, and provisions sent to it on 2 March. On 24 April, there was a shipment of 12 barrels of powder, 12cwt of bullet, and 12 bundles of match, valued at £82 4s., received by Sergeant Major Buxton from the Guildhall for the garrison.[50] Equally, following appeals by Colonel Venn to the Committee of Both Kingdoms 'concerning the wants of

---

45 TNA, SP28/161/3, f. 284r.
46 *CSPD 1645–1647*, p. 583.
47 TNA, SP28/227/1, ff. 6r.–7v.
48 TNA, WO47/1, ff. 208v., 210r.; SP28/30/1, f. 18r.; SP28/352/1, unf.; Bodl. Lib., Ms Eng. hist. C14, ff. 5r.–6v., 9v.
49 TNA, SP28/14, ff. 47r., 55v.; SP28/131/1, f. 2r.
50 TNA, SP28/34/2, ff. 171r.–180v.; SP28/16/2, f. 171v.

the garrison', on 19 August 1644, it was agreed that 10 barrels of gunpowder and half a ton of match should be delivered to Windsor Castle.[51]

Match cord, or slow match, used by musketeers, some dragoons, and gunners to ignite their charges, was made by steeping hemp cord or tow in saltpetre and limewater (vinegar being a substitute) then immersing it in sulphur. The principal suppliers of match for land service to the Ordnance Office and the Committee of Safety were John Freeman and Thomas Steventon.[52] Between 7 October and 8 November 1644, Freeman delivered over 11 tons of 'good and serviceable English match to be supplied to Essex's train of artillery'. In April and July 1645, he delivered a further 11 tons for the New Model Army, including the two-and-a-half tons of English match at £34 per ton that he was paid for on 10 July.[53] Likewise, Steventon was contracted with for seven tons of match on 6 September 1644, and, thereafter, he was a regular supplier of that commodity. Between April and August 1645, he furnished 11 tons for the New Model Army. Amongst the debentures made out to him is that for '68cwt of English match in fatts' and 12cwt of Spanish match. On 1 June, Steventon received a payment of £34 for one ton of match 'made up in fatts, by him provided and by him brought into his Majesty's stores for the service at Farnham Castle'. By 11 July, he had delivered two-and-a-half tons of English match and the like of Spanish, and, on 2 August, he provided 39cwt 4lbs of English match at £1 13s. per cwt and three tons 19lbs of Flemish at £3 per ton for the New Model, for which he received £155 19s. 6d.[54]

During the 1670s, the British professional soldier the Earl of Orrery recounted that, formerly, corporals were issued with an unspecified quantity of skeins (120 yards in length) and distributed to individual soldiers several links (being slightly under eight inches). He also suggested that 'it might also do well, if the soldiers tied their links of match about their middle, and under their coats, and doublets, instead of tying them to their bandolier belt, or collar; for by that means, the match would be kept dryer, and fitter for service, in time of action'.[55] Moreover, in distributing powder and match each day, the corporals of divisions or squadrons of shot were required to issue rations and ammunition to sentinels. According to Richard Elton, a one-time officer in the New Model Army:

> He must advise his sentinels how to demean themselves upon the discovery of an enemy, either to give an alarm, or else to give notice without making a noise. And if upon his guard he shall either observe or be advertised by his sentinels of the approach of the enemy, then he is to have his men in readiness with bullets in their muskets, and their matches lighted; himself secretly coming in, giving intelligence unto his captain, or other superior officer, whereby they may all be in

---

51 *CSPD 1644*, p. 437.
52 TNA, WO47/1, ff. 206v., 267r.; WO55/1660, f. 7r.
53 TNA, SP28/31/5, f. 516r.; Bodl. Lib., Ms Eng. hist. C14, ff. 10v, 35r.
54 TNA, WO47/1, f. 99v.; SP28/31/3, ff. 327r., 331r.; SP28/31/5, f. 517r.
55 Roger Boyle, Earl of Orrery, *A Treatise of the Art of War Dedicated to the King's Most Excellent Majesty* (Savoy: T. N., 1677), p. 32.

a readiness before the alarm be given. He is likewise to distribute victual, powder, bullet and match, unto his squadron, and to take notice of the best experienced men, and accordingly to employ them upon action upon the watches.[56]

Beginning in October 1642, various quantities of ordnance were sent to Windsor Castle, seemingly for the Parliamentarian garrison but also as pieces of artillery intended for Essex's army in 1643–1644. Substantial consignments were also conveyed from the Ordnance Office stores to Windsor to be distributed to the New Model Army. On 6 October 1642, the bargemen Henry Sheils and Richard Hewerton delivered '4 pieces of ordnance and other ammunition'.[57] Moreover, the accounts of Commissary Blundell mention his payment on 25 November 1642 of 7s. to '7 labourers about the ordnance mount' and 4s. 6d. 'to the gunners which they disbursed in getting in the ordnance'.[58] The garrison accounts also mention the conveyance of other guns to Windsor between October 1642 and June 1644; for instance, an undated receipt is for '3 pieces of ordnance and charge in London, being brought to Windsor'.[59] Even so, it is difficult to ascertain from them exactly when they arrived and who they were intended for, given that the magazine there was also used for supplying other military forces and garrisons. In March 1643, 12 cannons, and six carriages, with ammunition and fireworks were removed from the castle's magazine by the Earl of Essex's troops for their advance toward Oxford.[60] Also, a note from the officers of the Ordnance – undated but probably 1644 – states that '2 brass sakers, 1 weighing 740lbs, the other 555lbs with their several carriages and wheels, which were sent forth in the brigade of Sir James Harrington from London were left by the Yellow Regiment of the Hamlet Auxiliaries at Windsor and are there remaining'.[61]

In spring 1645, the headquarters of the New Model Army was established at Windsor. On 3 April, Sir Thomas Fairfax departed London for Windsor, and, the following day, £7,000 was delivered to the town, while another £3,000 went to Reading 'towards the payment of 14 days' pay to such officers and soldiers as shall appear in the muster rolls, under the hands of such person or persons as shall be appointed to take the muster and listed under my command there'.[62] There was also an additional £10,000 at Windsor on 27 May for the soldiers, along with provisions for the siege of Oxford, including 20 close waggons for provisions. This was ordered to be conveyed via St Albans and Newport Pagnell on 13 June. On 9 April 1645, one-third of the Earl of Essex's train of artillery was reduced, although several officers, artificers, and carters were brought into the new formation.[63] On 22 April 1645, Parliament ordered that '2 brass demi-culverins, and 8 brass sakers,

---

56   Richard Elton, *The Compleat Body of the Art Military* (London: Robert Leybourn, 1650), p. 179.
57   TNA, SP28/262/2, ff. 217r., 219r.
58   TNA, SP28/147/2, ff. 358v.–361r.
59   TNA, SP28/126/1, f. 33v.
60   *The Kingdomes Weekly Intelligencer*, 7–14 March 1643. TT, E93[6].
61   TNA, SP28/16/2, f. 171v.
62   TNA, SP28/29/1, ff. 4r., 23r., 168r.
63   TNA, SP28/29/1, f. 30r.; SP28/29/3, ff. 325r.–326v., 334r.–344v., 379r.

formerly made use of in the Navy, and now lying upon the Tower Wharf, shall be taken thence, and employed towards the Train of Artillery in the army under the command of Sir Thomas Fairfax'.[64] These were transported by barge to Fairfax's headquarters at Windsor. Moreover, when the 10 pieces of ordnance were dispatched from the Tower of London to Windsor on 29 April, they were accompanied by '12 waggons and carriages, comprising 5 loads of match, 2 loads of bullets, and 6 carriages for the ordnance'.[65]

On 23 May 1645, the Commons gave the Committee for the Army orders to 'make provision for such money and necessaries for the siege of Oxford, as they have or shall receive directions for from the Committee of Both Kingdoms, not exceeding the sum of £6,000'. Moreover, it had previously been agreed that £10,000 was to await Fairfax at Windsor, along with the following provision for a siege: two demi cannons and three whole culverins (ready at Windsor and Northampton); 1,200 spades and shovels; 500 pickaxes; 300 steel spades; 200 scaling ladders; 500 barrels of gunpowder; 40 tons of match; 30 tons of bullet; 300 great grenadoe shells; 300 small grenadoe shells; 1,000 hand grenades; 20 carriages for provisions; and 200 horse harnesses.[66] Likewise, following the rapid equipping of the army's Train, a warrant was issued for the disbursement of £32 to John Petty on 18 June for 'a demi-cannon new field carriage complete at Windsor'.[67] In September, among the substantial quantities of small arms, ammunition, clothing, and artillery for the supply of the New Model Army sent by sea to commissaries at Lyme during Fairfax's advance westwards was 'a new carriage belonging to the demi-cannon that came from Windsor and a draught rope in the stores as serviceable to the demi-cannon'.[68]

On 24 October 1644, five tons of match, musket bullet, and a quantity of cannon shot was received into the magazine at Windsor. Some of this ammunition was forwarded to the garrison at Reading, the Earl of Essex being notified, 'Upon Wednesday next there will be 20 cartloads of ammunition and provisions for your own train at Windsor to be from thence conveyed to the armies, for the safe transport of which you are desired to send a party of horse'. Correspondingly, on 6 November, the Commons ordered £290 to be paid to Sir Walter Erle, lieutenant of the Ordnance, 'upon account, out of Haberdashers' Hall, for providing 5 tons of match and 5 of bullets, with cask, and carriages complete for culverin to be sent to the armies; likewise £28 for 1 ton of match with cask for the garrison at Windsor Castle'. A week later, the Committee of Both Kingdoms commanded that 'the ordnance now at Windsor with the bullet thereto belonging be put into Windsor Castle, and that the match and bullet to be sent to the army be put into the barge ready to be conveyed to Reading, and the 2 lighters (which brought these) to be discharged'.[69]

---

64   *CJ*, IV pp. 74, 117; *LJ*, VII, p. 330.
65   *The Moderate Intelligencer*, 23–29 April 1645. TT, E337[20].
66   *CJ*, IV, pp. 151–52.
67   TNA, SP28/30/5, f. 639r.
68   TNA, WO55/460, unf.; WO55/1647, unf.
69   *CSPD 1644–1645*, pp. 78, 99, 118.

The accounts of the Windsor garrison record that, on 21 December 1642, £10 10s. was paid for bullet moulds for musket shot, whereas further sums were disbursed for 'melting and casting 1,000lb of bullets' and for casting 32cwt of the same items.[70] Instructions issued in 1636 for arming the English and Welsh militia declared that muskets were meant to be of one standard bore (12 bullets to the pound 'rolled in', resulting in a barrel bore roughly matching the diameter of a 10-bore bullet) and that each musketeer 'shall be furnished with a sufficient whole musket, the barrel thereof shall be four feet in length and no more', the total length of the weapon being five feet two inches. Furthermore:

> every such person appointed to serve with a full musket shall be further furnished and armed with a good bandolier, and with fifteen good and serviceable charges of turned wood, covered with leather and fastened there unto. Also with a good primer, worm and scourer, and a bullet bag annexed unto it, with a mould to cast such bullets as aforesaid.[71]

Sir Thomas Fairfax's army possessed its own means of manufacturing musket ammunition, thus when required, making it self-sufficient in the field, especially during siege operations and when regular supplies were slow in arriving. On 5 March 1645, it was determined that distributed between three close waggons and six open carts of the Train of Artillery – under the auspices of the Commissary of Ammunition – were to be '2,000 moulds to make bullets 1 dozen of 1lb, 6 dozen of bastard musket shot [weighing 14 to the pound] with nippers, pots and ladles', for the express use of the army's ladle maker. Other equipment required specifically for the casting of musket shot, including 12 melting ladles at 3s. apiece, 24 dipping ladles at 6d. each, and 2cwt of sheet lead, is itemised in the accounts of Sir Walter Erle, the lieutenant of the Ordnance, between April and June 1645.[72]

In 1643, when stocks of artillery shot in the Windsor magazine were low, money was paid to 'Mr Browne the founder for shot for the castle'.[73] This must have been John Browne, who was the principal supplier of round shot and other ordnance to both Essex's forces and the New Model Army. He operated furnaces at Cowden, Barden, Brenchley, and Horsmonden in Kent. On 11 April 1645, he was paid for delivering into the Ordnance Office 250 round shot for demi-culverin and 1,000 saker shot, amounting to £40 3s. 7d., in addition to an unspecified quantity of 'hand grenades for sakers', costing £125. Similarly, on 25 May, Sir Walter Erle advised his officers, 'You are to take notice that Richard Pearson, agent unto Mr John Browne, gun founder, is contracted with for 300 grenadoe shells for the greater mortar piece in Sir Thomas Fairfax his Train of Artillery, at the rate of £2 2s. per cwt,

---

70 TNA, SP28/126/1, ff. 34r.–35v.
71 Walter Rye (ed.), *State Papers Relating to Musters, Beacons, Ship-money, &c. in Norfolk from 1626 Chiefly to the Beginning of the Civil War* (Norwich: Goose and Son, 1907), p. 89; David R. Lawrence, *The Complete Soldier: Military Books and Military Culture in Early Stuart England, 1603–1645* (Brill: Leiden, 2008), p. 189.
72 TNA, SP28/140/1, ff. 3r.–6v.; SP28/145, f. 60r.; WO47/1, f. 210r.
73 TNA, SP28/147/2, f. 359v.

Monies sent to Colonel John Venn's Regiment, 29 October 1642-3 June 1644. (TNA, SP28/126/1, f. 14r.)

which accordingly are to be received into the stores'. A further indenture with Pearson, notified on 30 June, was for the supply of 300 demi-culverin shot, 300 saker shot, and 210 grenadoe shells of 12-inch diameter. These were duly delivered on 1 August 1645.[74]

Colonel Venn's regiment was initially furnished with a full set of clothing. It is probable that the auxiliaries to the Trained Band regiments of the City and Tower Hamlet suburb of London did not receive soldiers' coats, shoes, and snapsacks.[75] Nonetheless, a Royalist account of the First Battle of Newbury, fought on 20 September 1643, records that 'much of the slaughter fell upon the London Trained bands and their Auxiliaries, many of whose buff coats our soldiers now have'. There is no record of such garments being issued, and it is likely that the citizen-soldiers bought these expensive items themselves.[76] During late 1642, the infantry of the Windsor garrison seems to have been equipped in common with other regiments of the Earl of Essex's forces and the projected army of the Earl of Warwick. Thus, a warrant was issued by the Committee of Safety to Stephen Estwick on 18 November 1642, ordering him 'out of the store remaining in your hands to deliver to Alderman Fouke 900 hundred coats, shirts, and other usual and allowed necessaries for the

---

74 TNA, SP28/29/1, f. 137r.; WO49/82, f. 317r.; ML, 46-78/708, ff. 65r., 95v.
75 Lawson C. Nagel, 'The Militia of London 1641-1649', PhD thesis (University of London, 1982), pp. 88, 218; Simon Marsh, 'The Arming of the London Auxiliary Regiments to the Trained Bands during the Civil War', *Arquebusier*, 34:6 (2016), pp. 1–19.
76 *Mercurius Aulicus*, 20 September 1643. TT, E264[16].

clothing of so many soldiers in a special service to be directed by the Lord General and for the delivery thereof'.[77] This was followed by another warrant, issued on 30 October 1642, to supply Colonel Venn's regiment with 1,200 coats, caps, shirts, and 'other necessaries'. His acquittance, dated 21 December 1642, records the receipt of 300 coats, 300 pairs of shoes, 300 shirts, and 630 snapsacks, while the coats were coloured grey lined with yellow.[78] The delivery of the latter is confirmed in the garrison accounts, which list '5s. paid for bringing up the soldiers' coats'.[79]

In the Early Modern period, the hue grey was the product of mixing black and white sheep fleeces, or of using dark fleeces unmixed. Grey is often referred to in relation to countrymen, and, as it was undyed, it may have been cheaper than coloured fabric. The Yorkshire sheep farmer Henry Best reported that 'three or four black sheep do well in a flock, to furnish one with wool for grey stockings and other uses; but many black sheep in a keeping are neither seemly nor profitable, for their wool is usually hairy, scarce vendible'.[80] Shades of grey would differ considerably depending on the hues of black, brown, or white of the original fleeces and the quantities mixed. In similar fashion to Venn's soldiers, on 12 November 1642 following its capture and stripping of its clothes at Brentford, Colonel Denzil Holles' London-raised regiment was re-equipped from the Ordnance Office stores with red magazine coats, breeches, doublets, caps, and stockings.[81] Around the same time, Sergeant Major Skippon's regiment, then part of the Earl of Warwick's forces, was supplied with red coats faced with yellow.[82]

The shoes obtained for Venn's soldiers may have been from London sources, although, in May 1642, the cordwainers of Northampton had provided 7,000 pairs at 2s. 4d. a pair for the troops in Ireland while, on 24 June, a further 8,000 pairs were shipped there from Chester.[83] Moreover, when the Earl of Essex's army was recruiting in the summer of 1644, ready to begin its drive on Oxford, the Northampton Commissioners supplied 2,000 pairs of shoes to be distributed to his regiments of foot.[84] From 1645 onwards, however, the New Model Army was supplied with shoes almost entirely procured from members of the Livery of the Cordwainers Company in London. Manufactured in sizes equating to modern UK sizes seven to 10, they cost 2s. 3d. a pair. Moreover, these were made of 'good neates leather with good soles' and, unlike earlier footwear sent to Ireland, were curried or lacquered – the working in of a mixture of tallow (animal fat) and beeswax

---

77 TNA, SP28/262/3, f. 306v.
78 TNA, SP28/261/2, ff. 294r.–v.; SP28/262/2, f. 219r.
79 TNA, SP28/126/1, f. 35v.
80 George Andrews (ed.), *Rural Economy in Yorkshire in 1641: Being the Farming and Account Books of Henry Best, of Elmswell, in the East Riding of the County of York* (Edinburgh: William Blackwood and Sons, 1857), p. 84.
81 TNA, SP28/262/2, f. 374r.; *CJ*, II, p. 866.
82 TNA, SP28/3B, f. 412r.; *Most Happy Newes from the Earle of Essex. Wherein is declared the relation of two famous Victories obtained by the Parliament Forces* (London: T. Rider, 1643). TT, E85[30].
83 TNA, SP28/1B, ff. 532r., 657r.; SP28/170/1, ff. 26v., 29r., 44v.
84 *CSPD 1644*, p. 285.

– and possibly hobnailed. Hence, 32,000 pairs of shoes were provided to Fairfax's army during 1645–1646 via the Ordnance Office.[85]

In September 1642, Parliament ordered clothing for 7,000 infantrymen in Ulster, at a total cost of £15,937 10s. or 42s. 6d. per set of clothes. This provided each soldier with a cap, canvas doublet, cassock, breeches, two pairs of stockings, two pairs of shoes, and two shirts. Moreover, a tender to supply the British forces in Ireland, dated 27 March 1648, included '16,000 shirts, at 2s. 10d. per shirt. The shirts to be made of Lockram, good Osnaburg or Lübeck cloth'.[86] Three thousand pairs of 'grey knitted' stockings were issued to soldiers going to Ireland in early 1642, which cost between 15d. and 17d. per pair.[87] Nonetheless, most of those supplied for Irish service in 1642–1643 and the New Model Army were described in Ordnance Office contracts as 'Irish stockings', 'stockings', or 'stockings of good Welsh cotton'. One order placed for 2,500 pairs of stockings with Francis Butcher on 9 October 1645 states that they were 'to be of the largest sizes [and] equal goodness of cloth'.[88] The most numerous purchases for the New Model – particularly in 1645 – were for Irish stockings, which cost 12d. a pair. Given that this price remained consistent, it must be presumed that batches referred to as 'stockings' were also of this type. Such 'cotton' stockings were probably constructed of frieze, generally a coarse woollen fabric best suited to winter gowns and rough overcoating, in addition to doublets and jerkins.

Snapsacks were sausage-shaped bags worn over the shoulder, with a drawstring either at one or both ends to close them. Essentially made of leather, they were important pieces of equipment supplied to soldiers during the British Civil Wars and other seventeenth-century conflicts. They were used for carrying victuals, spare clothing, and any personal items the soldier may have possessed. The soldiers of the Earl of Essex's army marching to the relief of Gloucester in 1643 were described as carrying three days' rations in their snapsacks, and, when the Red Regiment of the London Trained Bands entered the Wiltshire village of Chiseldon in September 1643, its soldiers reportedly 'could get no accommodation either for meat or drink but what we brought with us in our snapsacks'.[89] Described as 'large and of good leather', large quantities of these were procured for the New Model in 1645 at 8s. per dozen (8d. each).[90] Also, a tender submitted to Parliament for supplying English forces in Ireland, dated 27 March 1648, included '10,000 snapsacks at 15d. per piece'.[91]

In terms of clothing the London Trained Bands, on 15 October 1644, Major General Richard Browne, the Parliamentarian governor of Abingdon – which had been a Royalist stronghold in the Thames Valley, falling to

---

85 TNA, WO55/1662, ff. 21v., 67v.; WO47/1, f. 209v.; SP28/29/1, f. 195r.; Bod. Lib., Ms Eng. hist. C14, f.48r.; ML, 46-78/708, ff. 86r., 114v.
86 *LJ*, X, pp. 158–59.
87 TNA, SP28/139/4, ff. 62r.–v.
88 Bodl. Lib., Ms Eng. hist. C14, f. 53r.; ML, 46-78/708, f. 4r.
89 *Speciall Passages and Certaine Informations*, 11–18 September 1643. TT, E117[41].
90 TNA, WO49/55, f. 174r.; WO47/1, f. 209v.; SP28/29/1, *passim*; ML, 46-78/708, *passim*.
91 TNA, SP28/140/3, unf.; WO55/1646, unf.

Essex's army on 26 May 1644 – and former captain in the Orange Regiment of the London Trained Bands, informed the Committee of Both Kingdoms:

> our strength instead of being augmented is of late much weakened, because those who are come back are not able to do duty for want of clothes and shoes. We have 500 fallen sick of late, and one or two being perished for want of clothes have died in the streets. I beg you to pity our sad condition and to think of ammunition so much wanted for this garrison … The officers of my own regiments and of the Windsor party being left almost without men, humbly desire there may be present course taken for recruiting their companies and clothing the soldiers they have left, or else that these may be disbanded.

The Red, White, and Blue Auxiliaries were garrisoned in Abingdon during this period. Browne appealed to the committee again on 30 October, 'The condition of our poor foot is still very sad. I hear there is £2000 coming to us, but that will do little good, only supplying the soldiers shoes to run away, besides the officers are 6 times that proportion already out of purse to their soldiers'. Consequently, on 20 December, the committee informed him:

> We have taken care to send provisions to Abingdon for the relief and clothing of the forces in your garrison there. You are to take care that those only be clothed of whom you can have assurance that they intend to tarry there during the winter and to do service, and not to depart when they are refurnished. We desire you to keep an account of clothes delivered to Manchester's forces [there], because he has undertaken here to make payment for them. The quantity [sent] is 1,500 suits, 2,000 pairs of shoes, and 2,000 pairs of stockings.[92]

On 21 March 1645, the Commons declared, 'each common soldier, that shall be pressed [for service in the New Model Army], shall be furnished with a coat, breeches, a shirt, a pair of stockings and shoes, and snapsack, by the several committees of the several countries [*recte* counties]; so as the charge do not exceed 24s. for each, besides the conduct money'.[93] Furthermore, the Parliamentarian-leaning *The Kingdomes Weekly Intelligencer* reported for 4 April 1645:

> This day also the House of Commons brought up an additional ordinance to that of 27 February last, for the raising and impressing of soldiers for Sir Thomas Fairfax his Army, concerning the manner of securing, and disposing those that were pressed, and for the providing of money, clothes, stockings and snapsacks, and other necessaries for them, that so they might have all fit encouragement to go on in the service; also, that care might be taken to have their names and habitations, that so in case they shall desert the service they might be proceeded against.[94]

---

92 *CSPD 1644–1645*, pp. 45, 84, 193.
93 *CJ*, IV, p. 85.
94 *Kingdomes Weekly*, 1–7 April 1645. TT, E276[22].

The importance of providing soldiers in field conditions, but also occasionally in garrisons, with complete suits is outlined in a letter from Lords Justices and Council to the Lord Lieutenant of Ireland, dated 7 June 1642, which states:

> we find that 1,000 coats, caps, stockings and shoes are to be brought in there weekly and sent hither, but therein we find no mention of breeches for the soldier, and therefore we must mind your Lordship to provide that their suits of clothes be entire, and such as may preserve them from cold as well in winter, when they must be put to hard duty in night watches, as now in their marches and services in the field.[95]

In May 1642, Parliament acknowledged that a group of suppliers had provided clothing that included 10,000 coats at 8s. 6d. each and 8,000 coats at 11s. apiece to Commissary George Wood for dispatch to Ireland. That the number of doublets and breeches provided in the same consignments is identical at 15,000 suggests that the suits referred to as being sent there are doublet and breeches combinations.[96]

The clothing issued to Venn's regiment in 1642 was produced by London manufacturers and distributed by the Committee of Safety directly to military units. However, large quantities were provided to Parliamentarian troops sent to and already serving in Ireland in 1642–1643 and 1645. These were procured and dispatched by the officers of the Ordnance Office from their stores in the Tower of London. Stores ordered to be sent to the troops in Ulster in April 1645 included 7,000 coats and breeches, 7,000 pair of shoes, 7,000 pair of stockings, 7,000 caps, and £4,000 worth of cloth.[97] The coats for Irish service provided by the Ordnance Office between 1642 and 1646 were unlined and almost entirely grey in colour. Such 'magazine suits' or clothing were issued to the infantry of the New Model and Commonwealth Armies from 1645 onwards. Estwick was an important merchant who played a prominent part in the supply of clothing and footwear to the Parliamentarian forces, through the auspices of both the Committee of Safety and the Ordnance Office. Between August and October 1642, he received the sum of £3,000 from the army treasurer for the provision of coats, shirts, shoes, and snapsacks for the Earl of Essex's army.[98] In 1645–1646, Estwick also led a consortium of London tailors and merchants who provided the Ordnance Office, and, in turn, the New Model, with major quantities of coats, breeches, shorts, and stockings.[99]

The procurement, organisation, accounting, and transportation of provisions (victuals and other foodstuffs) for seventeenth-century armies was essential to military operations, as well as the maintenance of good health,

---

95 HMC, *Calendar of the Manuscripts of the Marquess of Ormonde, K. P., Preserved at Kilkenny Castle* (London: HMSO, 1902–1920), VIII, p. 148.
96 TNA, SP28/139/4, f. 62r.; SP28/139/9, ff. 103r.–104v.
97 *CJ*, IV, p. 120.
98 TNA, SP28/1A, *passim*; SP28/2A, *passim*; SP28/261, unf.
99 TNA, SP28/140/3, unf.; Bodl. Lib., Ms Eng. hist. C14, f. 78v.; Ms Eng. hist. C244, f. 14v.

Victuals sent to the garrison of Windsor, 29 October 1642. (TNA, SP28/263, f. 70r.)

effective performance, and high morale among troops. Soldiers needed to be fed and provided with beverage, whereas horses and draught animals required considerable amounts of fodder. Though troops in garrisons might fare better than those in marching armies, benefitting from a more varied and plentiful diet, much depended upon the resources of the locality, in addition to the attitude of the inhabitants who proffered them. There was a difference between the types of food that were suitable for storage in garrisons and transportation with an army in the field. The professional soldier Francis Markham, who had been in the Dutch service, observed, 'if it be in marching or journeying, then he [the commissary] shall give them the victuals which is most easy for carriage, and the longest lasting, as biscuit, beef ready boiled, cheese and the like'.[100]

Among the Protestant forces in Ireland during 1642–1643, soldiers' rations consisted of salt beef, herrings, cheese, butter, and wheat and other cereals (such as rye) baked into biscuits. Such a diet was, however, blamed for the poor health of the men. The Earl of Cork commented that salted beef, biscuit, and butter without drinking water was only good for 'a rich churchyard and weak garrison'. Biscuits made this way seem to have been

---

100 Francis Markham, *Five Decades of Epistles of Warre* (London: Augustine Matthewes, 1622), p. 103.

standard practice and one that retained its calorific properties and made it easier for soldiers to carry on the march. An estimate for provisioning 2,000 troops with a daily ration of one pound of bread and half a pound of cheese records that, instead of the latter, '1lb more of biscuit is needful for each man per day'. Nonetheless, it was also stated that 'when this country did afford (in the time the soldiers were on the march) some provision, then 1lb of biscuits per man per day (and a pint of salt per man for a ten-day march) did well serve'.[101] On 7 February 1642, Parliament ordered the Commissary of Victuals to:

> with as much speed as conveniently you can, provide victual for 10,000 men for 3 months, after the rate of 4d. the day for every man, in bread, beef, butter, and cheese. Wherein you shall be careful of the goodness and wholesomeness of the provision; and likewise of the prices, that they be as cheap as the markets will afford. You shall, as near the prices will bear, provide for every man after the proportion of 1lb of bread, 1lb of beef, or, in lieu thereof, ½lb of cheese, or fish, as near the value thereof as you can; and ¼lb of butter, for every day.[102]

This corresponds with instructions given for the victualling of the Royalist garrison at Worcester in January 1645, which state, 'every common soldier's allowance per day is 1lb of biscuit and ½lb of cheese'.[103]

Table 2 Sent to Windsor for the Victualling of the Castle, 29 October 1642 (TNA, SP28/262/2, f. 219r.; SP28/263, f. 76r.)

	£	s.	d.
Biscuit (brown) 412 bags containing each 100lbs of biscuit at 12s. per cwt	220	14	3
For carriage from the lighter at Bull Wharf £1 19s. 6d.; biscuit (white) 3 bags at 18s. per cwt	2	8	2
Carriage from Tower Hill to Bull Wharf 1s.; bags 415 at 12d. per bag	20	15	0
Cheeses 1,122 containing 81cwt 15lbs at 52s. per cwt £211 8s.; butter 60 firkins at 22s. per firkin	66	0	0
For cordage of 12 loads of butter and cheese from Botolph Lane to Bull Wharf at 20d. per load	1	0	0
For portage of it into the barges		2	6
For wharfage for the whole		10	0
To Mr Taylor 10cwt of cheese, which he put aboard the boats with the soldiers when they went to Windsor	–	–	–
Total expenditure	535	18	5

A list of foodstuffs provided by the Militia in the City of London by the Lords and Commons includes the entry, 'Together with the goods there was advice sent to issue the biscuits at 1½d. the pound; the cheese at 3d.; the butter at 5d., which was as cheap a rate as they could at that time buy anywhere. The

---

101 James Hogan (ed.), *Letters and Papers Relating to the Irish Rebellion between 1642–46* (Dublin: Stationery Office, 1936), pp. 119, 135.
102 *CJ*, II, p. 417.
103 WorcsA, BA1714/899/192, ff. 519r.–523v.

butter and cheese being of the very best sort of Suffolk'.[104] Included amongst the warrants issued by the Committee of Safety in 1643 for the supply of the Windsor garrison is that dated 26 April for '80cwt of cheese, 70 firkins of butter and 140 bags of biscuit sent to Windsor for the use of Colonel Venn's regiment valued at £357 15s., and [paid] to the bargemen for carriage £5 13s. 4d.'; another, sent on 30 October, ordered that 'cheese, butter and biscuit with charges amounting to £180 be sent to Colonel Venn at Windsor'.[105] Likewise, the accounts of the garrison commissary at Windsor include various sums disbursed for the garrison in October–December 1642. These included £3 16s. for 19 tons of biscuit and cheese from London; an unspecified sum for '114 bags of brown biscuit, 3 bags of white biscuit, 1,522cwt of cheese, and 60 firkins of butter'; £1 9s. 8d. to Mr Lee for disbursements in sending a barge load of provisions; 10s. for sealing and salting meat; 3s. to butchers for dressing flesh and innards, 1s. for dressing hogs' heads; 5s. for a firkin (a small barrel containing nine imperial gallons or roughly 41 litres) of beer for the soldiers then upon duty; 4s. to Mr Price for drawing beer; £1 8s. to Mr Coggs for drawing beer for four weeks; and £1 for the carriage of 29 tuns (large casks containing 210 gallons) of beer from the waterside.[106]

Such victuals were supplied by London sources, although the large quantities of beer consumed by the Windsor garrison meant that several local brewers were called upon to provide regular batches. Consequently, in 1645, Eleanor and Thomas Hobbes claimed the sum of £5 9s. 10s. for beer, among other food commodities they had supplied to the garrison.[107] Being an essential element of a soldier's diet, beer (usually lower-strength small beer) purchases by commissaries or local officials were common, probably since brewing was often a localised activity and the product would be consumed quickly. Nevertheless, beer was sent to Ireland in large quantities. For instance, in July 1649, one commissary was paid £400 on account for 450 tuns of beer for Ireland, whereas, on 13 August, he received £800 for double the amount.[108] No inventories of stores held in the magazine at Windsor exist, but among the substantial amounts of warlike stores captured at Winchester by the New Model Army on 5 October 1645 were the following victuals: 38 hogsheads of beef and pork; 16,800lbs of cheese; 800lbs of butter; 140 quarters of wheat and meal; three hogsheads of French wine; 10 quarters of salt; 20 bushels of oatmeal; 14 sheep; four quarters of fresh beef; 7,840lbs of biscuit; and 112 hogsheads of strong beer.[109]

The Parliamentarian garrison of Newport Pagnell was described in October 1644 by a London-based newsbook as 'a warm nest for the soldier in winter'.[110] Troops located in a town or garrison set among agricultural areas might anticipate a better quality or at least more varied diet. Similarly, garrison soldiers would commonly fare better than their colleagues in marching armies,

---

104 TNA, SP28/263, f. 70v.
105 TNA, SP28/16/2, ff. 171r.–v.
106 TNA, SP28/147/2, ff. 358v.–361r.
107 TNA, SP28/43/1, ff. 125r.–126r.
108 *CSPD Interregnum, 1649–1650*, pp. 585–87.
109 Joshua Sprigge, *Anglia Rediviva or England's Recovery* (London: R. W., 1647), pp. 124–25.
110 *Mercurius Britannicus*, 21–28 October 1644. TT, E68[5].

for they would often be quartered in castles or other buildings within a garrison town. Commonly, 'free quarter' – not free in the sense that no payment would be made but was so called because no immediate payment was required – was taken, whereby tickets or vouchers were left with individual householders, noting the number of men and animals they had quartered and the total charge incurred by them. Once endorsed by a commissioned officer, tickets were to be given to the relevant army's treasury (if possible), where the sum would be reimbursed. Theoretically, regulations governed the requirements that troops could make of a householder, yet, although bills for free quarter were sometimes honoured by the soldiers and officers themselves, they were sometimes left unpaid, the objective being that the petitioner would claim them later. The exception to the norm was the New Model Army, amongst which neither provision nor quarter was to be taken without payment of ready cash. Nonetheless, in the event of lack of pay, these were to be itemised by the captain or quartermaster of individual troops and companies.

On 16 May 1645, Parliament issued its 'Instructions to the Parliamentary Commissioners sent to reside with the [New Model] Army', which included the observation of the following rules:

> For the ease of the country, the said Commissioners are to endeavour that no officer or soldier be quartered in any place but by the quartermaster, first showing his commission, if it be required, and by what authority he takes up such quarters; and giving a ticket of the names of every person which he shall quarter, expressing of what regiment, troop, or company the same person so quartered is; and the number of horses there quartered, and at whose house; together with the day of the month, and to subscribe his name thereunto. Saving whereby reason of the great numbers of them cannot be inserted, and then their numbers to be expressed in place of their names. That no quarter or provisions for man or horse in any quarters be taken without payment of ready money; but in case of necessity for want of pay; which the Parliament will use all means possible to prevent. And in case any quarter or provision shall be taken without payment, the captain or quartermaster shall by writing under their or one of their hands, certify what provisions have been so had, within what time, by whom, and of what regiment, troop, and company, from whom and the value thereof. Provided, that where the Army shall be upon their march, not staying above 24 hours in a place, the rates shall be 4d. a night for hay, 3d. a night for grass, 4d. a peck for oats, 6d. a peck for peas and beans, and 7d. for a peck for barley and malt (which provision of barley and malt is not to be taken but where no other grain for horse-meat is to be had), 8d. a day is to be paid for the diet of every trooper or horseman, 7d. a day for every dragoon, and 6d. a day for every foot soldier, pioneer, waggoner, or carter, that shall not be officers by commission, or of the Life Guard troop. Provided also that no inhabitant whatsoever shall be compelled to furnish any provision but what he has in his house of his own. And that no officer or soldier shall compel him to do otherwise, upon pain of cashiering, or such other punishment as the commander-in-chief shall think fit.[111]

---

111 John Rushworth, *Historical Collections of Private Passages of State* (London: D. Browne, 1721), VI, pp. 32–33; *Kingdomes Weekly*, 13–20 May 1645. TT, E284[23].

Armies and garrisons of the civil wars depended greatly upon the existing civilian infrastructure, so, in supplementing the biscuit and cheese provided from the Ordnance Office stores in London, the procurement of foodstuffs from the local population was particularly important. A small number of loss accounts prepared by local parish constables in Berkshire contain references to sums owed for the feeding and quartering of the officers and soldiers of Windsor garrison. Such documents include taxation, voluntary contributions from civilians, and costs borne via free quarter and plunder, although, by their nature, the entries need to be treated with caution and accurate dating (if any dates are included) can be unreliable. In July 1643, the parishioners of Harlington protested:

> All last winter we were charged with billeting of soldiers, both horse and foot, to our exceeding great hinderance and loss; and now upon the Lord General [Essex] coming to Windsor, the horse troop belonging to the Earl of Bedford is returned upon us again, to be billeted as formerly; so that we are no way able to do what we would in this case, for we shall be hardly able to subsist, especially if they should continue any time with us.[112]

Victuals or 'diet' was generally provided by local inhabitants in their homes, such as Mistress Ellis, who claimed £2 'for diet for Robert Hemmington, soldier to Captain Gawthorne under the command of Colonel Venn'. In March 1645, food and beer were provided at the inn of John Baldwyn, while he later claimed the sum of £4 4s. for the 'dieting of soldiers under the command of Colonel Venn'. Another innkeeper accommodated members of Captain Lane's company, including £7 9s. 3d. for their diet.[113] Like other civil war garrisons, the one at Windsor also procured quantities of commodities such as bread, beer, and meat from its neighbourhood of local parishes.

Financial accounts pertaining to Windsor offer a good idea of the composition, strength, and pay of at least some of the Parliamentarian garrison (including gunners and officials) for most of the period of its occupation. In terms of pay, in late 1642, the weekly bill for the garrison was around £144, and, between 1642 and 1644, the non-commissioned officers and soldiers of each company were provided with roughly 70 percent of their wages, with the remainder being in arrears. From this period onwards, monthly payments to commissioned officers became irregular and often did not correspond with that disbursed to their men. The accounts indicate also that, by June 1644, the total pay arrears owing to Colonel Venn's regiment was £11,220 16s. 6d.[114] The pay of the Windsor garrison was then a constant source of anxiety and struggle. On 20 December 1642, the pay and entertainment of Colonel Venn's regiment, besides dragoons, artillery, and other garrison members, was £3,047 16s. a month, against which only £1,000 had been forthcoming. But, within months, the arrears in pay had become acute. In attempting to alleviate this, on 13 May 1643, the Commons ordered:

---

112 *CSPD 1641–1643*, p. 474.
113 TNA, SP28/43/1, ff. 65r.–v., 102v.
114 TNA, SP28/126/1, ff. 20r.–45v.

that the whole regiment of foot forces together with a troop of horse [*recte* dragoons] under the command of Colonel John Venn in the town and castle of Windsor, with their several and respective officers, gunners and others employed in service there, be from time to time paid by Sir Gilbert Gerrard, Treasurer of the Army, out of the monies that shall be levied and received within the County of Berks, upon the ordinance for the weekly assessments, and for seizing and sequestering the estates of papists and delinquents: And for the better accommodation of the county for return of their monies, the treasurers appointed for the said assessments and sequestrations in the said county, are hereby required to make payment unto the said Colonel Venn from time to time [of] all such sums of money as shall be ordered and appointed [to] be paid unto him by Sir Gilbert Gerrard, and shall be due unto the said Colonel Venn by account passed under the hands of the auditors appointed for that purpose, and ordered to be paid unto the said Colonel Venn by the House of Commons or Committee for the safety of either of them.[115]

In November 1643, the Commons authorised the disbursement of £2,000 to the soldiers, while reportedly Colonel Venn raised £300 in the vicinity of Windsor 'for the relief of the garrison'. Although intermittent payments continued, 'drunken mutinies' against the governor were reported in 1643–1644. Nevertheless, the hardships and discontent experienced by the garrison's soldiers continued, and, on 26 February 1644, their officers were compelled to submit the following petition to the Speaker:

We the commanders in Windsor Castle of the regiment of Colonel Venn hereunder subscribed, with the several sums due to us, being confident of you care for your good and safety of the whole Kingdom and every part thereof, emboldens us to make our redress to you of the dangerous condition of the castle and garrison stands in, without a present supply, these 18 months by the assistance of the Almighty we have been instrumental by our persons, our purses and credits, for the safety of this place, in keeping our regiment strong and able ever it has been and is at this present near good men not doubting but that our endeavours herein would have been very acceptable which we are zealous of in that we are not looked upon with that favourable aspect which other commanders have in this public service, if this place by the wisdom of the State be not conceived of that concernment for the safety of the Kingdom in part, and the City of London in especial, or that it be our unhappiness to be under-valued, we know not for what, except it be in that we are citizens, we humbly desire our great arrears to be made us good, and that we may return to the City or be employed abroad, or be made capable to keep our regiment from disbanding here, which without a present considerable supply is not in our power to help, we have used all possible means by petitions to both Houses of Parliament, the Militia and Common Council of London … we do must humbly entreat you will be pleased to entreat the honourable House of Commons with our condition, having none else that does own us for payment. Our Colonel we contend has much business, and cannot be so sensible of our present wants, as we with our poor soldiers that have suffered much and have not food to eat, nor clothes to wear.

---

115 *CJ*, III, p. 85.

[Arrears declared in the document owing to each company]:
Lieutenant Colonel John Bradley £1301 19s. 10d.
Sergeant Major Thomas Buxton £959 19s. 4d.
Captain Henry Saunders £848 2s. 8d.
Captain John Gawthorpe £712 1s. 3d.
Captain Joseph Symond £844 1s. 8d.
Captain Richard Lane £692 13s. 4d.
Captain John Barkstead £819 16s. 4d.
Captain William Stackhouse £816 2s. 9d.
Captain Phillip Purchon £750 18s.
Total: £7,705 14s. 3d. Besides what is due to the Colonel and his company, the gunners, matrosses, and divers other officers of the regiment.[116]

On 16 November 1644, the Committee of Both Kingdoms wrote to Venn:

> Your letters concerning the mutiny of your soldiers have been received by us, and we are very sorry that they should have been so unmindful of their duty as not to have manifested their grievances in a fair way, but, on the contrary, behaved themselves in so insolent a manner to their commander-in-chief. We have written to your officers to contribute their endeavours for quieting of that distemper, and shall be further careful to settle you in the peaceable command of that garrison.

Thus, 300 men from the London Trained Bands commanded by Captains Hammond and Wilkes were quickly sent from the capital on 16 November for 'suppressing the mutineers' and to secure the castle. The sum of £100 weekly for a fortnight was allowed to the trained bandsmen as wages from the monthly Parliamentary assessment of Middlesex. They were refused entry, however, and, by then, any uprisings appear to have subsided, although eventually seven mutineers were singled out and sent to London for punishment.[117] Throughout 1644, Colonel John Venn strove to raise funds for the Parliamentarian war effort, including the garrison of Windsor, which he commanded, his own regiment, and in general. As a member of the Committee for the Advance of Money, he elicited loans from Parliament, and, in March 1644, he warned the Commons that the garrison was 'ready to disband for want of pay'. Venn's appeal was supported by the Speaker 'with much vehemency', prompting the release of £2,000 from the Excise.[118] By June 1644, the commissioned officers and men of Venn's regiment were in arrears by £11,220 16s. 6d.[119] During November, the newsbook *The Weekly Account* reported that, before any further monies were received from central sources, 'some discontent did arise for want of pay and upon misdemeanor of one of the garrison was committed to prison and was set at liberty by the rest without order, which done the difference was ended'.[120]

---

116 Bodl. Lib., Ms Tanner 62/3, f. 580r.
117 *CSPD 1644–1645*, pp. 126–28; *LJ*, VI, p. 66.
118 *CJ*, III, pp. 388, 420, 422; *LJ*, VI, p. 397.
119 TNA, SP28/126/1, f. 41v.
120 *The Weekly Account*, 13–20 November 1644. TT, E81[2].

Although the soldiers were irregularly paid, resulting in hardship and poor discipline, the root of the problem in 1643–1644 lay in the undependable supply of money to the soldiers from central sources. Thus, Parliament placed the blame on Venn and used London-based newsbooks to insinuate that his poor treatment of his men had led to the various rebellions. Nevertheless, the garrison accounts suggest otherwise and confirm that Venn was highly concerned for the material welfare of his garrison, in addition to investing substantial amounts of money in supplying, victualling, and clothing it. Parliament got its way, and, because of the continuing costs involved in funding and supplying the garrison, Parliament ordered a reduction of Windsor garrison on 29 October 1644 to the new Establishment of 200 soldiers, with officers in two companies, in addition to gunners and others. Those to remain were to be 'chosen out of the soldiers and officers now in the castle, by the said colonel', perhaps affording them the opportunity to rid the garrison of any potential mutineers.[121] Accordingly, though the soldiers remained 'in great want', the commissioned and non-commissioned officers of the garrison, as well as certain others, were placed on half pay.

Table 3 'Upon report from the Committee of Both Kingdoms, it is ordered that this Establishment of Windsor Castle following, shall stand *pro tempore*'

	Weekly Full Pay			Weekly Half Pay		
	£	s.	d.	£	s.	d.
Colonel at 45s. per day	15	15	0	7	17	6
1 captain at 15s. per day	5	5	0	2	12	6
2 lieutenants at 4s. per day	2	16	0	2	16	0
2 ensigns at 3s. per day	2	2	0	2	2	0
5 sergeants at 18d. per day	2	12	6	2	12	6
5 corporals at 12d. per day	1	15	0	1	15	0
5 drummers at 12d. per day	1	15	0	1	15	0
12 gunners at 2s. per day	8	8	0	8	8	0
12 matrosses at 12d. per day	4	4	0	4	4	0
1 minister at 8s. per day	2	16	0	2	16	0
His man at 8d. per day	0	4	8	0	4	8
1 marshal at 5s. per day	1	15	0	1	15	0
1 gunsmith 1s. 6d. per day	0	10	6	0	10	6
1 armourer at 1s. 6d. per day	0	10	6	0	10	6
1 surgeon at 4s. per day	1	8	0	1	8	0
His man at 8d. per day	0	4	8	0	4	8

An adjustment to the Establishment occurred soon afterwards, however. On 11 January 1645, the Committee of Both Kingdoms rebuked Venn:

> We have been informed that there is not the full number of 200 in your garrison according to the appointment, and that those who are there present are very

---
121 *CJ*, III, pp. 681–82; *CSPD 1644–1645*, p. 73.

negligent and remiss in the performance of their duty. We have taken into consideration the strengthening of your garrison, and intend that it be increased to 400, consisting of 4 companies, for which an establishment will be drawn up and reported to the Houses. In the meantime, you are to look diligently to your charge, and see that the soldiers be more vigilant in performance of their duty. We recommend it to you in an especial manner that you take into your garrison such soldiers as are fit to discharge that duty and trust, and not raw countrymen.[122]

Colonel John Venn resigned as governor of Windsor Castle due to the Self-Denying Ordinance, which began on 3 April 1645 and disqualified MPs and peers from holding military commands, though with an option of being reappointed if circumstances require it. He was replaced by Colonel Christopher Whichcote. Although this officer was not as politically prominent as Venn, he was from a mercantile background and had served successively in the Green Regiment of the London Trained Bands, the White Regiment, under Colonel Isaac Penington, and the Green Regiment of London Auxiliaries. In 1644, he was commander of a London brigade serving in the Earl of Essex's march to the West and fought at Lostwithiel in the August.[123] Whichcote, however, inherited from his predecessor the task of acquiring money to pay the soldiers of the Windsor garrison, in addition to munitions and victuals. On 13 May 1645, the Committee of Both Kingdoms ordered, 'concerning the garrison of Windsor shall stand good to the new governor as to the number of 400 soldiers in 4 companies, with their officers, and that the establishment be prepared to that purpose'.

Forty horses were to be raised from Oxfordshire, Berkshire, and Buckinghamshire 'to serve for mounting dragoons, and the charge to maintain them be fixed at 12d. per day', whereas two fatts of match were to be 'sent thither for the use of the garrison, and to be for a store available upon all occasions'. Moreover, 50 snaphaunce muskets were supplied for the use of the garrison, and it was deemed that 'there shall be provided a constant magazine of a month's provision for the garrison, to be always ready in case of any straitening of Windsor Castle'.[124] Generally, snaphaunces had clear advantages over matchlocks where safety was concerned because they reduced the danger of accidental powder explosions and the weapon was also more economical, avoiding the requirement for large quantities of match. In February 1648, the Commonwealth government agreed to send 1,000 snaphaunces to Dublin, 'if they are in store, both for the sparing of match and for the better carrying on of the many services for which they are more proper'.[125] In terms of the consumption of match, including amongst garrison soldiers, on 30 May 1643, Sir William Savile, the Royalist governor of Sheffield, advised his deputy, 'For the match you write for, I shall send you some, but I put you in mind once more to use your snaphaunce pieces to keep

---

122 *CSPD 1644–1645*, p. 247.
123 TNA, SP28/18, ff. 67r., 370r.; *CSPD 1644*, pp. 513–15.
124 *CSPD 1644–1645*, p. 485.
125 HMC, *Ormonde*, II, pp. 142–43.

sentry with. They will save our match'.[126] One remedy for this was to issue a limited number of snaphaunces to each company for them to use on guard duty. Every 20 musketeers were issued a snaphaunce musket at Stafford in December 1644, 'for want of muskets with firelocks upon the guards in this garrison there has been much match spent'. Likewise, the governor, Colonel Simon Rugeley, was still requesting these weapons two months later, 'in regard the garrison is short of match be pleased to lend the snaphaunces [from the Earl of Denbigh's magazine] to save the said match'.[127]

In July 1645, with the assistance of the Corporation of London, Colonel Whichcote secured £400 for the pay of the garrison, with a further quantity of match. He reported to Parliament that there were merely 200 soldiers at Windsor, 'part of them very aged and unserviceable', and requested an additional 50 cavalry and 400 infantry to guard the castle.[128] His appeals were partly answered in October–November 1645. When Windsor was threatened by the Royalist garrison at Donnington Castle, 'a company of Middlesex foot which has orders to march thither for its better security' was dispatched. These were withdrawn soon afterwards, however, when the threat subsided.[129] On 23 February 1646, Parliament ordered that the 'new works about Windsor Castle be slighted'.[130]

---

126 W. D. Macray (ed.), *Beaumont Papers: Letters Relating to the Family of Beaumont of Whitley, Yorkshire* (London: Nichols and Sons, 1884), p. 70.
127 D. H. Pennington and I. A. Roots (eds and intro.), *The Committee at Stafford, 1643-1645* (Manchester: Manchester University Press, 1957), pp. 230, 256, 296.
128 *CJ*, IV, p. 197.
129 *CSPD 1645–1647*, pp. 212, 217–18, 232, 234, 239.
130 *LJ*, IX, p. 95.

Chapter 2

'A place strongly fortified': The Royalist Garrison of Reading

Following the indecisive clash at Edgehill on 23 October 1642, Charles I seized the initiative by advancing towards London. The King's army promptly captured Banbury and Broughton, and, on 29 October, he re-entered Oxford. On 1 November, news reached the town of Reading that a body of Royalist cavalry was heading from Abingdon, a move that caused the small detachment of Parliamentarian defenders of the town to flee. Dominating the route to the West and sitting on the convergence of the Thames and Kennet, Reading was an important artery for the transport of military equipment and material from London to Parliament's forces, as well as Oxford and the Thames Valley area for the Royalist armies. On 3 November, the King himself was in Reading, but, although the church bells rang dutifully to mark his arrival and brief stay, the town council and the local landowning families had divided loyalties. Charles I, however, was determined to garrison the place and remained there until a line was drawn round the town and the fortifications were well-advanced. He left soon afterwards and reached Maidenhead on 6 November. The next day, a large mounted force under Prince Rupert attacked the town and castle at Windsor, but the Parliamentarian garrison there under Colonel John Venn repulsed it.

Keeping ahead the main body of Charles I's army, Rupert advanced with his horse to Maidenhead and from there pillaged Staines and Egham on the outskirts of London. Critically, on 12–13 November 1642, Parliamentarian troops under the command of the Earl of Essex, and elements the London Trained Bands, blocked the Royalist advance on London at Brentford and Turnham Green. When the King with his army advanced towards the capital, he left behind in the form of a garrison two cavalry regiments – Sir Arthur Aston's and Sir Thomas Aston's – and six foot regiments, being Sir Edward Fitton's, Colonel Richard Fielding's, Colonel Richard Bolles', Sir Thomas Lunsford's, Sir Thomas Salusbury's, and Colonel Charles Gerard's; the first four had served together previously as part of the brigade commanded by Fielding at Edgehill. These were augmented by the time of the Parliamentarian siege of April 1643 by the addition of Lord Belasyse's regiment, though Sir Thomas Aston's cavalry had left for Shropshire. But, instead of holding a permanent

'A PLACE STRONGLY FORTIFIED': THE ROYALIST GARRISON OF READING

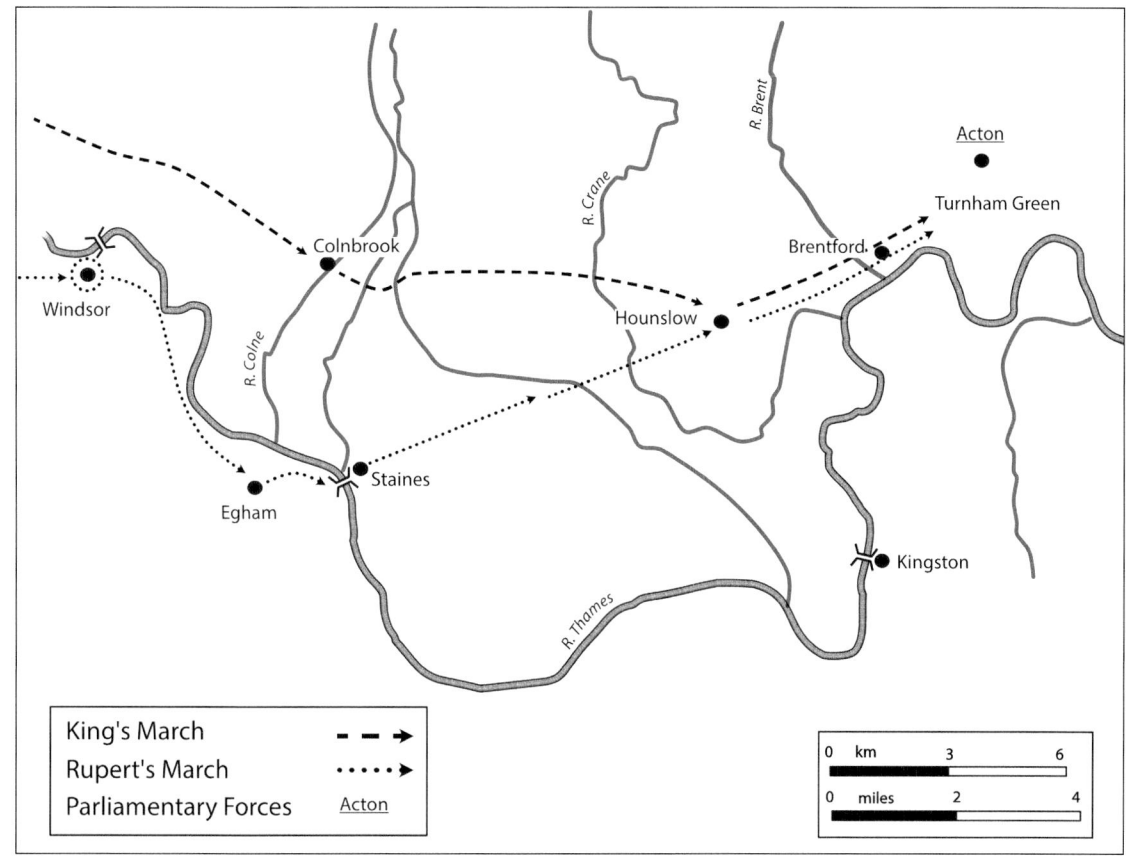

Map 2 The Royalist advance towards London, autumn 1642.

military force, Reading became the principal garrison of the foot regiments of the Oxford Army until its surrender and evacuation in April 1643 and, for a period of the following year, a large part of the Royalist infantry.

Nonetheless, on 14 April 1644, a regiment of trained band auxiliaries was raised in Reading under the command of the High Sheriff of Berkshire, Colonel Richard Neville. He served previously in the Earl of Caernarvon's regiment of horse and replaced Caernarvon as colonel following his death at the First Battle of Newbury. According to a set of propositions for the establishment of the Reading regiment, there was to be a lieutenant colonel, two captains, and three ensigns, with 100 pikes issued to the soldiers (although the latter entry is struck though in the document).[1] However, the Royalists withdrew from Reading in May 1644, demolishing the fortifications and transferring to Oxford, where Neville's regiment continued to serve the King until the surrender of that city in July 1646.[2] The Royalists raised a number of similar units in garrisons, such as Oxford, Bristol, and Chester. In support of the Chester city volunteer regiment, commanded by Colonel Francis Gamull, the residents were mobilised periodically when the need arose. On 5 June 1643, an order was issued 'for all citizens of Chester, not enlisted in Colonel

---

1   BL, Ms Harley 6802, ff. 88r., 143r., 198v.
2   TNA, SP23/191/818.

49

Gamull's regiment, to assemble on the morrow at the Roodee at noon, then, and there to be enlisted, and put under such commanders as the mayor and governor appoint'. Moreover, the order was given on 12 December 'For all the citizens on alarm being given to repair to the High Cross, and put themselves under the aldermen appointed to command them; the armed citizens bringing their armour with them, and the unarmed citizens coming prepared to receive halberds and such other weapons as are stored up for them in the Pentice'.[3]

On 19 November 1642, a Royal army arrived at Reading, the small Parliamentarian garrison that had occupied the town having departed a few days previously upon the news of the King's retreat from Turnham Green. Three days later, Sir Arthur Aston, a Catholic officer of considerable military experience, was appointed governor. His commission stated:

> Charles, by the grace of God King of England, Scotland, France and Ireland, Defender of the Faith, etc. To Our trusted and welbeloved Sir Arthur Aston, Knight, Sergeant Major General of the Horse of Our army Greeting. Whereas We have thought fit for the defence and security of Our good town of Reading in Our county of Berkshire, to settle and appoint therein a governor with such number of soldiers as may on all occasions be of force to defend Our said town and the inhabitants thereof, and likewise other of Our good subjects of Our said county of Berkshire against any attempts that be made against them, by the traitorous proceedings of the Earl of Essex and his adherents, constitute and appoint you governor of Our said town of Reading, and of all such forces, both of foot and Horse, as shall either be left in garrison of Our said town or shall be sent or commanded thither for your assistance, and better defence of the same, hereby willing and requiring you immediately to take into your charge and command, the government of Our said town, and of all both officers and soldiers in garrison there, and to dispose and govern them therein, as you shall find best for your service the security and defence of that Our town, straightly commanding and charging all colonels, lieutenant colonels, sergeant majors, captains of both foot and Horse, and all other inferior officers and soldiers of the said garrison, you to obey and serve as governor.[4]

Aston was unpopular among his soldiers and the inhabitants of Reading alike. Additionally, a London-based Parliamentarian source remarked upon his religious activities, 'There is mass constantly in the town in several places … the minister of the town was put out of his house on Saturday last and a Papist, one Mr Plowden was put into it'.[5] As the staunchly Royalist Earl of Clarendon wrote, Sir Arthur Aston 'had the fortune to be very much esteemed where he was not known and greatly detested where he was … [and] lost much reputation there in respect of his nature and manners, not of his soldiery, which stood as it did before'.[6]

---

3 HMC, *Eighth Report, App. I* (London: HMSO, 1881), p. 384.
4 BRO, R/Z10/11.
5 *Most Happy Newes*. TT, E85[30].
6 Macray (ed.), *History of the Rebellion*, VII, p. 106.

'A PLACE STRONGLY FORTIFIED': THE ROYALIST GARRISON OF READING

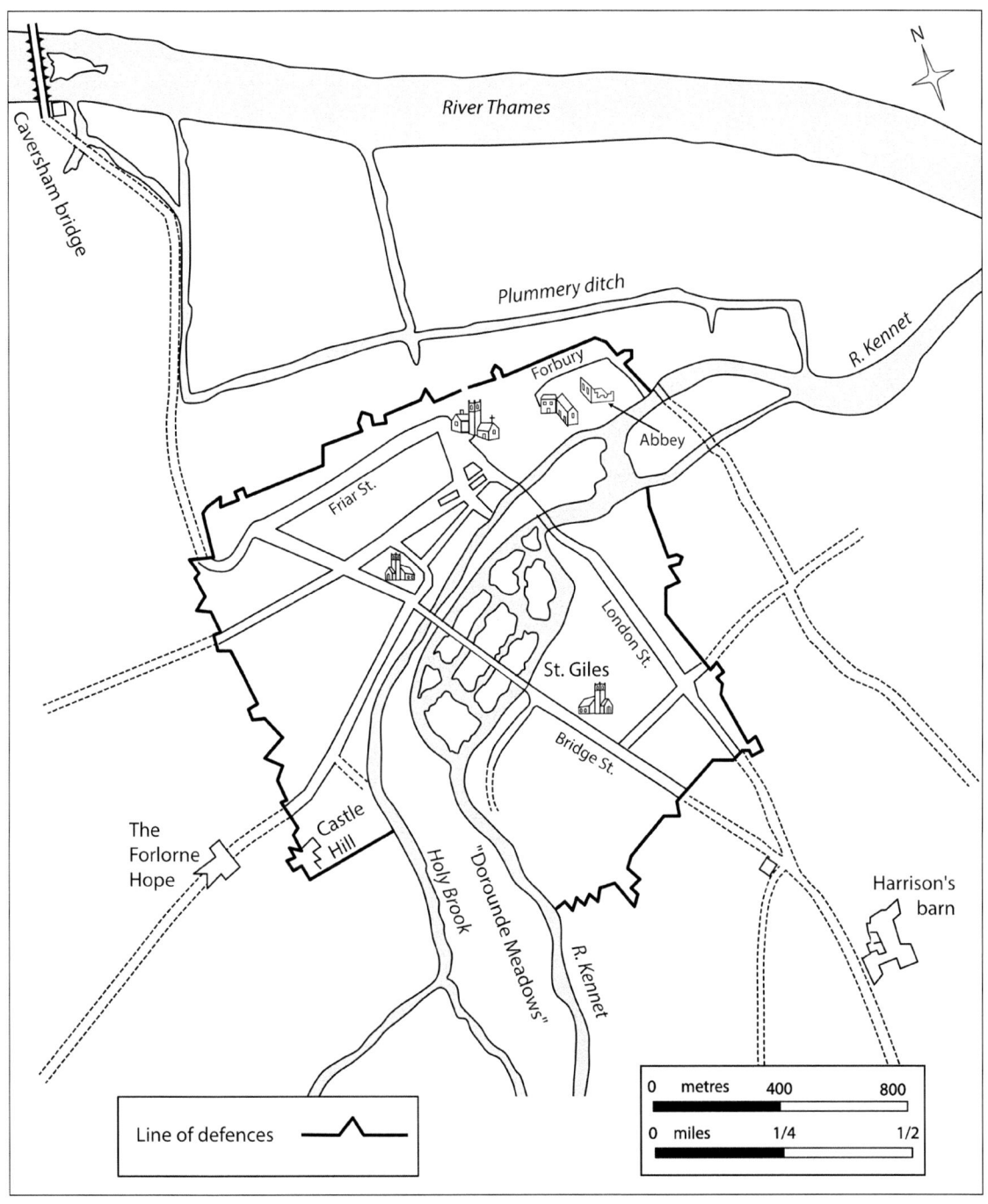

Map 3 Reading in the 1640s.

Unlike at Windsor and Wallingford, which possessed medieval castles and walls, there were almost no fortifications at Reading before hostilities began. In December 1642, Aston employed forced civilian labour alongside his soldiers and began the construction of a defensive line of ditches with a raised earthen rampart stretching between a series of bastions or redoubts (projecting features built at an angle to the line of fortifications, in order at provide defensive fire in several directions). These were located at Castle Hill,

51

Greyfriars, Abbey Bridge, and Whitley Hill on the southwestern Berkshire bank of the river. Parliamentarian accounts of the siege of Reading in April 1643 mention that the town was 'a place strongly fortified, with a deep ditch around, and strong works near and remote, he marched a compass of 7 miles extraordinary, as if he had intended Oxford, by means which he got the west and weakest side of the town, and possessed himself of a hedge and ditch' and that 'we made our approaches that night, taking some advantages of the hedges and ditches unslighted by the enemy'.[7] Moreover, bridges, barges, and mills within the town were apparently ruined in order to deny their use to the enemy, while major roads out of Reading were torn up, and bales of wool were commandeered from the town's merchants and used to bolster the town's defences to enhance their ability to absorb cannon shot. By comparison, in 1643, Thomas Dennis, who had been elected mayor of the city in September 1642, was employed in 'exchanging that part of the fortification which was allotted to the city of Oxford'.[8] He also provided tools and shovels for the work, issued warrants to press workmen, paid them for their labour, contracted for timber and other materials, and levied the recruitment of soldiers in the garrison.

Throughout the period of his governorship, Sir Arthur Aston pursued multiple objectives – on the one hand maintaining a garrison and fortifications at Reading, whilst on the other utilising the resources of the town and its inhabitants to support the King's main forces in the field. Nevertheless, the garrison experienced an uncomfortable relationship with the town's population, who were required to accommodate and feed the soldiers. Aston's harsh discipline may have caused some resentment and perhaps mutiny among the garrison, because, on 12 December 1642, three soldiers were executed. Some lowering of morale among the officers and men is suggested by a letter from Sir John Byron, who commanded the cavalry at Reading and was impatient of inactivity when Rupert and other Royalist leaders were actively engaged. Two days before the executions, Bryon wrote to him:

> The time prefixed for the stay of my regiment in this town will be expired on Friday next, at which time, I humbly desire, according to your Highness's promise, to be relieved; not for any impatience in myself, or unwillingness to undergo anything that may be for his Majesty's service, but to avoid the certain ruin of my regiment, which, for want of accommodation here, and all things necessary for the subsistence of men, hath been very hardly kept from breaking forth into a mutiny, and doth daily diminish, notwithstanding the best care I can take for the preservation of it … Neither will it be requisite that above two or three troops at the most be sent hither, the number we have now being greater than can be fed or lodged with any convenience in this town.[9]

---

[7] *Speciall Passages*, 18–25 April 1643. TT, E116[41]; *The third Intelligence From Reading. Dated from His Excellency His Quarters Before Reading, April 26. at night* (London: Samuel Gellibrand, 1643). TT, E99[29].

[8] TNA, SP19/133/27.

[9] Eliot Warburton, *Memoirs of Prince Rupert, and the Cavaliers* (London: Richard Bentley, 1849), p. 76.

The governor, Sir Arthur Aston, also arrested and hanged a London merchant, claiming that he was a Parliamentarian spy, causing A Perfect diurnall to report for 30 December:

> The House of Commons has taken into serious consideration the death of Master Boyes, who was wrongly executed by martial law by Colonel Aston, a great Papist in the King's army at Reading, about 10 days since, he being a citizen in London, and a great dealer in strong waters and other commodities, and went down into the country as usually he did used to do every year about this time, to receive and gather up such money as was due to him for commodities, and at Reading he was apprehended and hanged, but the causers thereof will have time to repent it, for spilling the blood of such a man.[10]

On 8 December 1642, Prince Rupert had informed Sir Arthur Aston, 'I received your letter and am glad to hear that your works are so well forward. My troops are ready to come to you; therefore, if you have need of any, send me or Lieutenant General Wilmot word of it, and you shall see them when you judge fitting'.[11] A 'statement of accounts of disbursements relating to the King's stay in Reading with his army', probably compiled in early 1643, includes payments for bread and cheese sent by the town to troops at Henley-on-Thames and Bagshot, for providing cloth for soldiers, in addition to firewood, victuals, and lights for the court of guard, and for furnishing labourers to work on the fortifications, especially those at Forebury. To compound the situation, all trade with London was prohibited – particularly onerous, given Reading's dependency on the clothing trade and the enduring economic impoverishment of the town due to competition from northern manufacturers. Sir Arthur Aston also pressed townsmen and others from the local area into a Reading regiment, but these recruits soon deserted. How they went about this in a garrison town remains unclear, although the guard posts and military patrols may not have been overly vigilant.

Similarly, the mayor and aldermen of the town were compelled to provide a loan 'for the maintenance of the King's garrison', which at the time comprised 2,000 foot and a regiment of horse.[12] Needless to say, these required accommodation, victuals, clothing, horses, and other supplies, in addition to pay. One such contribution, made in March 1643, involved the Reading Corporation mortgaging the town's lands for 99 years as security for a loan of £600 by the alderman and brewer Thomas Harrison, to supply the garrison. Harrison later argued that he was lent the money as he was an adherent to the King's cause and that the Royalist officers had forced the corporation to provide such assurance.[13] The tanner William Braxton later testified to the Berkshire Sequestration Committee that, in 1643, he was a commissioner 'when Reading was a garrison for the late King, and levied money for him'. He was evidently a loyalist because he claimed to have

---

10   *Perfect diurnall*, 26 December 1642–2 January 1643. TT, E239[9].
11   BL, Ms Add. 18980, f. 20r.
12   BRO, R/Z3/28; R/Z3/35; R/Z3/36; R/Z3/39; R/Z3/42.
13   BRO, R/Z7/4.

reported another resident, Henry Hamblin, to Sir Jacob Astley, as he was 'an enemy, and deserted the garrison because he would not serve the King, on which Hamblin was apprehended, and kept in prison for some days'. Braxton further swore that he would serve Charles I 'as far as his life and estate went, and forced his servant to be a soldier in the garrison'.[14] Such cases as these illustrate the choices faced by some inhabitants caused by the occupation of the town – its corporation and dwellers being mostly predisposed to the Parliamentarian cause – by Royalist troops.

On 3 January 1643, Aston had demanded an additional £2,000 and, with characteristic harshness, supplied the corporation, at Charles I's command, with a list of men who had refused to pay the first loan and hence were to be taxed double for the second.[15] Out of desperation, on 6 January, the town corporation petitioned the King, requesting:

> to be herein excused, for they are altogether unable, by reason of their great payments, burdens and losses, which they have already and do daily undergo, since the first advancement of his Majesty's army to the town. Nor can we boast ourselves safe from the army of the Earl of Essex, his soldiers divers times putting us to great affrights, lest they should by the example of the cavaliers plunder and pillage us, though they be kept in better order.[16]

Their answer – a somewhat tardy one – came on 6 February, 'If my Lord of Essex approach the town, and besiege it, his Majesty hopes the garrison within it are sufficient to defend and make the said town good against those forces that shall beleaguer it, to the security of themselves and the inhabitants'. Hence, the King demanded supplies and money by force, aggravating the local population, which transformed into an alliance against the Royalist cause. Nonetheless, on 4 February 1643, Sir Edward Nicholas, one of the King's most astute and loyal advisers, informed him, 'Sir Arthur Aston is left quiet at Reading, only the Roundhead garrison at Henley "troubles his markets."'[17] A Parliamentarian newsbook reported on 15 February:

> [the] townsmen of Reading are very willing and forward to the endangering of both their lives and fortunes to assist Parliamentary forces ... The town is engaged instead of finding 1 horse for the Parliament, they must be constrained to find 2 for the King, and pay double both in money and in plate, and that for non-payment of taxes they are imprisoned and those men that are gone they imprison their wives in their stead.[18]

Exactions inflicted upon town populations, either by garrisons, externally, or both, were not confined to Reading. On 16 October 1643, the mayor of

---

14 Mary A. E. Green (ed.), *Calendar of the Proceedings of the Committee for Advance of Money, 1642-1656* (London: HMSO, 1888), II, p. 1002.
15 BRO, R/Z3/31; R/Z3/33.
16 BRO, R/Z3/33.
17 Warburton, *Memoirs*, II, p. 116.
18 *Perfect diurnall*, 13–19 February 1643. TT, E240[19].

Oxford sought advice 'touching the finishing of our [city] regiment, showing to them that he and his brethren have endeavoured to take of Sir Nicholas Selwyn our intended colonel and his major, and to procure a colonel of our own body but cannot yet prevail and are uncertain whether they can prevail or no'. Subsequently, in June 1644, the following proclamation was issued by the mayor and council:

> Whereas by an order bearing date the 8th of this instant June, it was ordered, that all the inhabitants and persons resident within this city, should at their perils within 7 days after the date thereof, provide and lay in for their families, 3 months' provision of corn and other victuals. Now that there may be a full execution of that resolution, it is ordered, that Mr Vice Chancellor appoint honest and fit persons on Monday next to search, examine, and view the several colleges and halls, and certify this board in writing, what provisions of victuals is there made by the several persons and families inhabiting in the said colleges and halls, with the names of the persons, and number of the families, that the proportion of provision may be judged. And Mr Thomas Nevill, Mr William Loving, Alderman Charles, and Captain Bowman are likewise appointed the same day to search, examine, and view the provisions laid in by the several inhabitants of what degree soever, of and in this city or suburbs thereof. And to certify us the number of the persons within the several families and what provisions are laid in for the support of the said families, according to the former order, that all those who neglect to conform themselves to the directions aforesaid may be put out of the town as persons justly to be suspected, which shall be strictly put in practice.[19]

A substantial stock of munitions for the garrison of Reading was placed under Aston's command, and an officer for the magazine was chosen. The arsenal was in the converted ancient grammar school, with its headmaster being expelled as a delinquent. Reading's magazine was the most important outside Oxford, the King's wartime capital, and was supplemented throughout the winter of 1642–1643. The Reading garrison was initially supplied with two minions and two demiculverins, whilst, on 24 November 1642, the magazine contained 3,000lbs of powder, one-and-a-half tons of match, and one-and-a-half tons of musket shot. The next day, a further 1,000lbs of powder was delivered by the King's train of artillery.[20] Over the following week, large quantities of ordnance, ammunition, and specialist personnel also arrived at Reading to strengthen the military capacity of its garrison. This included a further eight pieces of artillery – two demi-culverins, one saker, two 3lb Spanish guns, two 3lb Dutch guns, and a bastard falcon – and the arrival of seven gunners and 12 matrosses under the authority of Mr Betts, four conductors, three carpenters, and a blacksmith.[21] On 9 December, Charles I ordered Sir John Hayden, his lieutenant of the Ordnance, to deliver to

---

19 M. G. Hobson and H. E. Slater (eds), *Oxford Council Acts 1626-1665* (Oxford: Clarendon Press, 1933), pp. 91, 140.
20 TNA, WO55/457/60, ff. 17r.–18r.
21 TNA, WO55/423, ff. 148r.–v.; WO55/457/60, ff. 15r., 17r.; WO55/457/62, ff. 16r.–17v.

Reading '50 bundles of match, some bullet moulds, and as many offensive arms for 2 troops of horse as you have in your custody'.

The next day, two snaphaunce carbines, four carbines without locks, 18 swords, six sword belts, and 13 carbine belts were received 'for the use of Colonel [Arthur] Aston's regiment of horse'. Supplies to the garrison of weapons and accoutrements continued, for, on 15 December 1642, 300 pikes and 100 halberds were reassigned from the Royalist garrison at Abingdon to Reading.[22] Nevertheless, there was some debate among the King's council of war at Oxford as to whether to abandon the latter town, but it is clear that, by the time that the Earl of Essex began military operations against Reading in April 1643, both the town's fortifications and the sustainment of its garrison were sufficiently advanced. Sir Arthur Aston had received a commission from Prince Rupert on 17 March as captain of an independent company of dragoons and, by his authority, was appointed 'general under his Majesty of all his Majesty's forces of horse, as well as all troops of horse, cuirassiers, dragoons and carabiniers of all and all manner of horse forces':

> captain of a free company of dragoons, consisting of 100 men to remain and constantly with your regiment of Horse as an auxiliary company to the same, which company you are presently to raise and levy in many parts of his Majesty's Kingdom of England and the dominion of Wales of such as will willingly and voluntarily serve for his Majesty's pay, for the defence of the true Protestant Religion, his Majesty's person, the two Houses of Parliament and their instant privileges, and the proprieties of his subjects … And yourself likewise diligently to observe and expedite such orders and directions as you shall, from time to time, receive from Myself and all other superior officers of his Majesty's army to whom of right you are, or may be, subordinate, according to the Discipline of War.[23]

Aston's dragoon formation may have counted amongst its ranks men of foreign birth who possessed considerable military experience. Rupert's own dragoons were evidently part of, or attached to, Sir Arthur Aston's cavalry regiment in January 1643. By this time, however, the Earl of Essex had begun devising plans for an advance on Reading and carried out a surprise assault on the Royalist outpost at Henley-on-Thames on 21 January. This was easily achieved, and the garrison expelled, yet the King reacted by ordering a counterattack. Nevertheless, in the confusion, one of Rupert's dragoons shot and killed Sergeant Major Holby of Aston's horse, triggering the failure of the enterprise. Sir Arthur Aston was so disgusted by the conduct of the soldier that he sent him and his comrades back to the Prince at Reading, as he wanted rid of them.[24] Aston duly wrote to Rupert:

> With all the expedition possibly I could I have sent these dragoons after you, I beseech God send your Highness better success than I had with them, for they

---

22 TNA, WO55/423, ff. 36r., 38r., 41v., 230r.
23 BRO, R/Z10/12.
24 *Mercurius Aulicus*, 22–28 January 1643. TT, E244[20].

and my horsemen did most shamefully lose the bravest design at Henley that ever was undertaken since my coming to this army, and lost it not but gave the victory away when they had already possession of all that they went for, and with it I lost as brave an officer as I ever hope to command in this kingdom. May it please your Highness I am so extremely dejected at this business that I do wish with all my heart that either I had some German soldiers to command, or that I could infuse some German courage into them, for your English common soldiers are so poor and base that I could never have a greater affliction light upon me than to be put to command any of them I beseech your Highness to present my humble services unto Lieutenant General Wilmot, I am loath to repeat my disasters too often or else I would have written also unto him, whom I know will suffer in this thought with me.[25]

The episode at Henley was confirmed on 24 January 1643 by Nicholas, who reported from Oxford:

I would not suffer this bearer to pass without this tender of my respects and duty. Sir Arthur Aston understanding of some forces come into Henley, sent thither a party Friday night under the command of the Sergeant Major of his Horse, Mr Holby, they entered the town and possessed themselves of the ordnance in the market place, but, by an unfortunate shot out of a window Sergeant Major Holby being slain, the dragoons [of Rupert's regiment, commanded by Captain Sir Thomas Hooper] ran away and the Horse did little better, notwithstanding the earnest[ness] of their officers and so they lost the effect of their own pains and hazard. The rebels do approach towards Aylesbury.[26]

However, on 2 February 1643, Thomas, Lord Wentworth succeeded Aston as sergeant major general of the Oxford Army's dragoons. During the first winter of the war, the infantry regiments of the King's Oxford Army foot were quartered in that city, in addition to a ring of defensive strongholds surrounding it, predominantly Reading, Abingdon, Wallingford, Banbury, and Brill.

Letters deposited in the William Salt Library at Stafford show that, during the early months of 1643, the governor of Reading, Sir Arthur Aston, and other Royalist officers provided Prince Rupert with intelligence reports about the military situation in the Thames Valley area, in addition to pleading him for re-enforcements. On 1 March, Aston notified Rupert that he would counter any Parliamentarian movements in the areas around Wargrave, Twyford, and Henley and was 'reconnoitering passages over the River Lodden'. The former also implored the Prince to ask his uncle to send money to pay his troops in Reading. Recruitment remained a perennial issue amongst civil war armies. Rates of desertion and side-changing were particularly high among Sir William Waller's forces in the West in spring 1644, although 'to depart from the colours', whether on the march or in battle, in theory meant the death

---

25   William A. Day (ed.), *The Pythouse Papers: Correspondence Concerning the Civil War* (London: Bickers and Sons, 1879), pp. 12–13.
26   BL, Ms Add. 18980, f. 16r.

GARRISONS AND GARRISON WARFARE IN THE BRITISH CIVIL WARS, 1638-1653

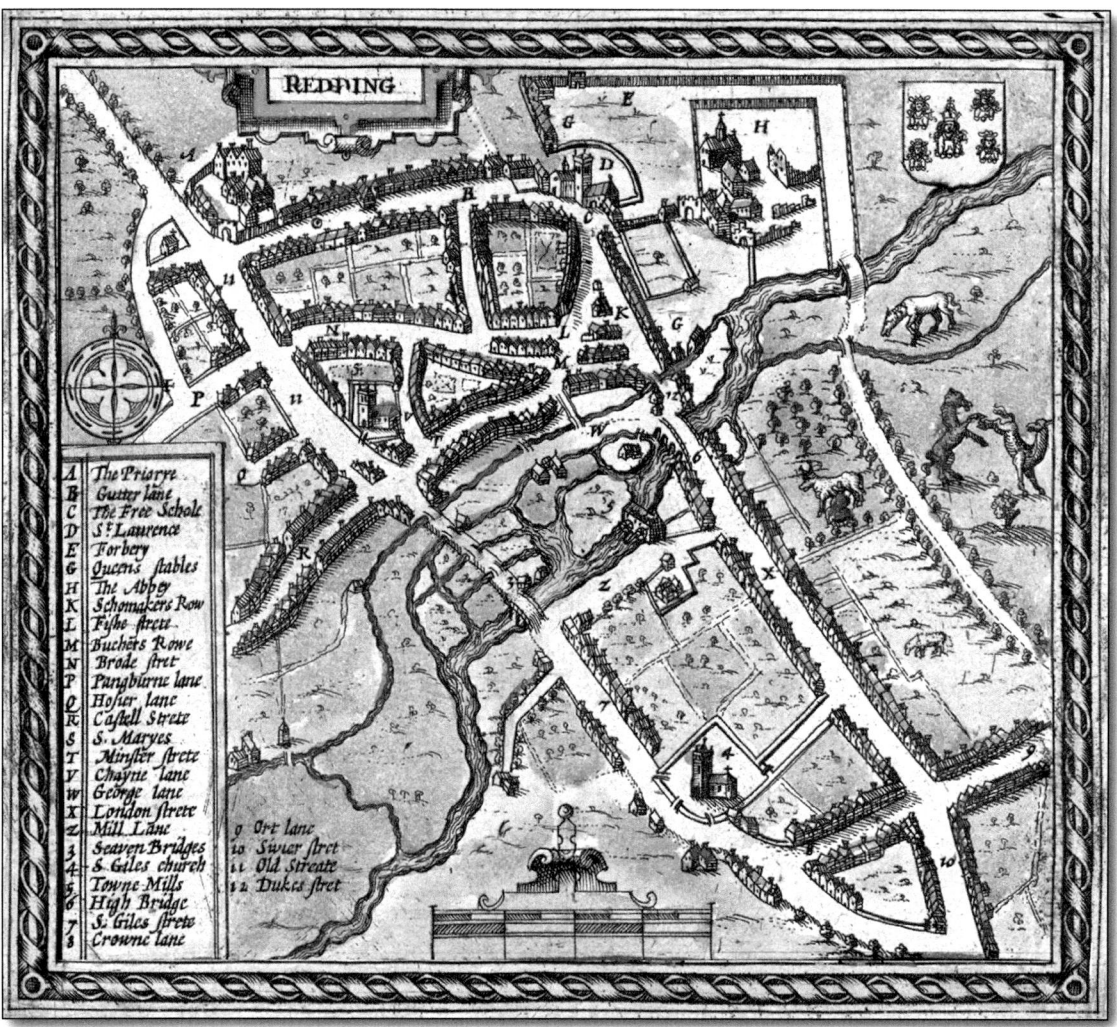

Map of Reading by John Speed (1611).

penalty for the guilty. Moreover, the Parliamentarian forces in Cheshire were bolstered by soldiers from the English army in Ireland who had changed sides after the Battle of Nantwich and the siege of Liverpool in 1644.

Perhaps as many as 600 of the 1,500 soldiers captured on 25 January took service with Sir William Brereton's army, perhaps including those of two firelock companies. Brereton later described his dragoons 'which were soldiers in Ireland' as 'very serviceable' and 'well-accommodated'. He also informed Lord Leven on 22 May 1645, 'I can bring no more foot than one regiment and some choice dragoons – firelocks which were soldiers in Ireland lately mounted'.[27] Following Rupert's capture of Cirencester in February 1643, 1,000 soldiers of the garrison were taken prisoner. Some refused to serve the King and were made to work on the fortifications at Oxford. However, 140 of the most unreliable were put into the garrison at Reading, where five soldiers

---

27 BL, Ms Add. 11331, f. 142v.

were placed in each company, in return for five of the best being retained for field duty. Nonetheless, Sir Arthur Aston was unenthusiastic and allegedly 'sent to the King that he needed not to have sent him more enemies, for he had enough already'.[28]

On 15 March 1643, a Parliamentarian scout reported that, at Reading, 'A garrison of 1,500 are so sick and lame that the commanders are fain upon training days to supply their places'. Correspondingly, a fortnight later, the same source mentioned, 'They would not withstand more than 2 hours for want of powder, arms and other ammunition'.[29] On 19 March, Sir Arthur Aston had warned Prince Rupert that Parliamentarian forces were preparing a major assault on the town. He reported that the garrison possessed far fewer soldiers than the officers had claimed in the musters and bade the Prince to persuade King to 'forward me 1,000 more foot, or result will be disastrous'. Sir Arthur Aston further requested 'the removal of useless, troublesome unarmed men from this garrison' and suggested the sending out of Sir John Byron's regiment of horse to forage for provisions. Lastly, in a letter written at Oxford on 20 April 1643, Secretary Sir Edward Nicholas repeatedly urged Rupert to come quickly to prevent the fall of besieged Reading. He added:

> Sir Arthur Aston was incapacitated by a chimney-brick which struck his head, he was delirious until trepanned last night. This has encouraged the rebels to besiege them more closely. The officers have demanded more ammunition, but sending it through a 15,000-strong army will be very difficult. It were much better if the county of Stafford, than the town of Reading were lost as things now stand.[30]

After a period of convalescence, in August 1643, Aston was appointed governor of Oxford. Later in the year, Sir Arthur Aston raised his own regiment of foot in the city, which formed part of the garrison of Oxford, although he was injured in a riding accident and replaced as governor in autumn 1644 by Sir Henry Gage.

On 13 April 1643, the Earl of Essex and his main field (or 'old') army – consisting of 16,000 foot and 3,000 horse, with a train of artillery supplied from the Tower and other Parliamentarian magazines – departed Windsor and marched west. His original force contained the infantry regiments commanded by Colonel Thomas Ballard, Colonel Henry Chomley, Colonel William Constable, the Earl of Essex, Colonel John Hampden, Colonel John Meldrum, the Earl of Peterborough, Lord Robartes, and Lord Rochford. There were five regiments raised as new, those being Colonel Harry Barclay's, Colonel James Holborne's, Colonel John Holmstead's, Colonel George Langham's, and Sir Philip Skippon's.[31] These were sustained by the issue of large quantities of munitions. Hence, on 11 March, the Purveyor General of the Train had directed 37 loads of ammunition, whilst, five days

---

28 DRO, 1392M/L 1644/22.
29 *Perfect diurnall*, 22–26 March 1643. TT, E239[14]; 3–9 April 1643. TT, E202[29].
30 WSL, Mss Salt 477/3-4, 564.
31 Christopher L. Scott and Alan Turton, *Hey for Old Robin! The Campaigns and Armies of The Earl of Essex during the First Civil War, 1642–44* (Solihull: Helion & Co., 2017), p. 70.

later, 11 loads containing powder, match, and musket shot were sent from Windsor via Thames transport.[32] During their march, Essex was reinforced by a brigade of the London Trained Bands and part of the fledgling Eastern Association army under Lord Grey, which had been recruited in the eastern counties during the winter. When Essex arrived before Reading on 15 April 1643, under the cover of darkness, he immediately called for the surrender of the town. According to a Parliamentarian account:

> my Lord suddenly wheeling about came before Reading, he summoned the town for the King and Parliament, but Aston the governor (a Papist, and one that is guilty of divers murders) answered very resolutely, he would keep the town or starve in it, my Lord sent to them to have the women and children let out, which he refused, my Lord seeing that the town must be caried by the gun and spade, and not by words.

The writer continued:

> The town is very strongly fortified, many outworks, commanded by some main bulwarks, more inward, the garrison 3,000 or more, besides the townsmen, there are near 22 pieces of ordnance, to tell you the particular quarters of each regiment were useless to you, being you know not the town, only in general thus, my Lord encamped on the west side of the town, between Redding and Oxford, the better to hinder any aid that should come from thence to the town, he also took care to secure the river, that no relief should come that way, then fell wee presently to work with the spade, to intrench our quarters, which work was carried on with more facility and speed then could be expected, the soldiers (herein right soldiers being willing to fight with the spade as well as the sword) successively relieving one another, night and day, the next work was to view the ground, for to make our approaches, to which purpose 8 went out, of which number the all worthy [Sergeant] Major Skippon was one the enemy perceiving our intention, laboured by their shot, and by setting some barns on fire, that by the smoke that so they might hinder them but yet they did their work, and God kept them safe, only 1, a mean officer received a shot.[33]

However, the Royalist newsbook *Mercurius Aulicus* reported with some bravado:

> it was advertised this day from Reading, the Earl of Essex having drawn together all his forces and called all the bridges over the River Loddon (which he had formerly broke down) to be set up again, was marched with all his army towards that town, intending to assault the same, and that he was already come within sight of their works, to the great joy of all the garrison, who have long desired to see his Excellency, and try the metal of his soldiers, whose brave exploits are so well talked of in the weekly pamphlets, though not heard of otherwise.[34]

---

32 TNA, SP28/140/4, f. 40v.
33 *Good and true newes from Redding, Being an exact relation of the proceedings of his Excellence the Earl of Essex, since he advanced from Windsore* (London: J. G., 1643). TT, E99[2].
34 *Mercurius Aulicus*, 9–15 April 1643. TT, E246[10].

Charles I, safe at Oxford, was startled at Essex's immediate attack against Reading. On 16 April, he wrote to Rupert, who was then at Lichfield:

> Nephew, I thought it most necessary to advertise you, that the rebels have attacked Reading; not to recall you, though I could be content you were here, but to desire you to hasten northward, that you may send the powder and matches which I have sent for to the Earl of Newcastle, for I may be distressed for want of such munition. I write not this to make you raise your siege, but that you lose no more time in it than you must needs.

The following day, when the seriousness of the situation became clear, the King decided to recall him, writing:

> … lest that our letter should miscarry, we have thought it necessary, considering how much it imports us to use our utmost endeavours to repel the great forces of the rebels now before Reading, by this express to second our former letters sent to you, desiring you to use all possible diligence to come away with so much of the forces there as may with the security of those parties be spared.

Moreover, on 19 April 1643, Charles I's secretary, Sir Edward Nicholas, urged, 'I assure your Highness it is the opinion here, that if (Prince Rupert come not speedily, Reading will be lost. Sir Arthur Aston is past hope of relief.) Reading is so closely begirt as we can get no news from thence.'[35]

After spending 16 April bombarding Reading's fortifications, the next day, Essex sent another demand for the garrison's surrender. Aston agreed to yield if he and his soldiers were permitted to march out unmolested to rejoin the King at Oxford, but the Earl declined, as he had come 'for the men, not the town barely'.[36] Perhaps more ominous a sight for the defenders was the appearance during the next few days of an additional 4,000–5,000 men from the Eastern Association army, a major re-enforcement that enabled Essex to fully encompass the town. Further reports of the siege of Reading, undertaken between 14 and 26 April 1643, spoke of the presence of Royalist dragoons – probably Sir Arthur Aston's own and those of Sir Thomas Aston – but, although the former's cavalry regiment formed part of the garrison, Sir Thomas' horse had left the area by that time.[37] Sir Robert Howard's small regiment, possibly the '2 troops of dragoons' listed as being part of the garrison of Reading in December 1642 and again in February 1643, had been sent to the Welsh borders the following month.[38]

By 15 April, the garrison was critically low on supplies, and Parliamentarian reports were noting smugly:

---

35 Warburton, *Memoirs*, II, pp. 165–66, 171–74.
36 John Vicars, *Magnalia Dei Anglicana. Or, England's Parliamentary Chronicle* (London: J. Rothwell, Tho. Vnderhill, 1646). TT, E247[32].
37 *Victory Proclaymed, in an exact relation of the proceedings of the Parliament Forces in their Siege before Reading from April 15 to 27* (London: Benjamin Allen, 1643). TT, E100[4]; *third Intelligence From Reading*. TT, E99[29]; *Perfect diurnall*, 3–10 June 1643. TT, E239[18].
38 BRO, R/Z10/2; R/Z10/4; DRO, 1392M/L 1644/22.

we understand the state of it, to be full of wants, both of provision and ammunition; the Welshmen have already feasted with a horse or 2, and those lean ones, in regard that horsemeat have much failed of late, which occasioned an endeavour of the horse to go away on Saturday night; but they were stopped by the foot. So likewise for their ammunition, they want powder, but bullets more, shooting very seldom, and very strange shot, as stones, and suchlike they were short of powder and ammunition.[39]

Essex's rapid advance on Reading had caught the garrison on the hop, while the Royalist reaction was slow and uncertain. One Parliamentarian report noted that the Earl's troops 'intercepted a servant of Sir Lew Dyves', who told them of the garrison's short supply of powder and of how 'the supply was prevented by some troops of horse'.[40] The mention of 'Welshmen' among the Royalist troops at Reading is noteworthy. Many English and Welsh troops who had been dispatched to Ireland in the months between the outbreaks of the Irish Rebellion in 1641 returned, and, during the British Civil Wars, Wales was considered the 'nursery of the King's infantry'. Four infantry regiments of the garrison were raised either wholly or partly from Welsh recruits.

Moreover, Colonel Richard Bolles' regiment contained a significant quantity of Irishmen within its ranks. In March 1643, Sir Samuel Luke was informed by a spy of his that the 'greatest part' of the Royalist soldiers in Reading was 'Welsh and Irish', and similar reports – particularly the London-based writers of Parliamentarian newsbooks – reflected a bias against Welsh identity and language, in addition to 'a tendency by Parliamentarian intelligencers to assume that every group of enemy soldiers who did not speak English were as likely to be Irish, as thy were to be Welsh (or, indeed, Cornish)'.[41] Furthermore, among the 900 Royalist prisoners taken by Sir William Waller's forces at Alton on 13 December 1643 were substantial numbers of Colonel Bolles' soldiers. As *The Weekly Account* related, 'the whole regiment consisted most of Welsh (and which is very strange) they were all very well habited, which put our soldiers presently upon exchange for hats, coats, cloaks, doublets, etc., which the enemy (by reason of the present danger they were in) told our men that they would exchange with all their hearts'.[42] According to Clarendon, Bolles' regiment was among the Royalist units on the receiving end of Parliamentarian bombardments at Reading on 18 April 1643:

They [the besiegers] had many batteries, from whence they shot their cannon into the town and upon their line at a near distance, but without any considerable execution, there being fewer lost by that service than will be believed, and but one man of note, Lieutenant Colonel D'Ewes, a young man of notable courage and

---

39 *The Second intelligence from Reading. Dated from His Excellency his quarters before Reading, 24 April* (London: Samuel Gellibrand, 1643). TT, E99[19].
40 *The Last Joyful Intelligence from his Excellency his Quarters at Reading, since the surrendering of the town* (London: Thomas Watson, 1643). TT, E100[5].
41 Mark Stoyle, *Soldier and Strangers: An Ethnic History of the English Civil War* (New Haven, CT: Yale University Press, 2005), p. 55.
42 *Weekly Account*, 20 December 1643. TT, E250[13].

vivacity, who had his leg shot off by a cannon bullet, of which he speedily and cheerfully died.[43]

Clarendon was mistaken, however – his officer did not lose his leg but received a leg wound and possibly died of blood poisoning.

Some civil war petitions submitted by military veterans and their widows during the 1660s demonstrate the kinds of non-fatal injury that soldiers of the period could receive in battle and sieges, such as that of Reading in April 1643. Hence, at the quarter sessions held at Ruthin, Denbighshire, Anne Jones, the widow of John Thomas of Llangollen, testified that he 'was a soldier in his late Majesty's service under the command of Sergeant Major John Edwards in the late unhappy wars; that the said John Thomas died in his said Majesty's service in Reading, leaving behind him his said widow without any subsistence, she being constrained ever since her husband's decease to live upon charity'. Likewise, Edward Morris of Henfache, 'a poor maimed soldier', stated that he was:

> a soldier for his late Majesty Charles the First of ever blessed memory in the late unhappy war, wherein your petitioner behaved himself valiant, loyal and trusty, never disserting his said Majesty nor his service, being first listed in Sir Thomas Salusbury's Regiment and in his own company therein. And then in the said service, your petitioner was at the several battles at Edgehill, Banbury, and Brentford, in which your petitioner was grievously hurt and shot in the thigh at Reading.

At the quarter sessions for Wrexham Parish, the following certificate was issued in July 1660:

> These are to certify all whom it may concern that Rowland Prytherch of the county of Denbigh in the principality of Wales came into his Majesty's service about 12 months since [sic]; and that he continued in the service of a common soldier under the command of Captain Robinson in Colonel Salusbury's Regiment until the siege of Reading, where he was shot with a cannon bullet in defence thereof, whereby he has quite lost the use of one of his hands.[44]

Furthermore, at the Wiltshire Quarter Sessions, Captain Joseph Smith of Marlborough implored that he:

> has been a faithful servant to the Parliament ever since these unnatural differences began and has received divers wounds in their service. And at the siege of Reading, he was dangerously shot through the thigh and on the foot, with which wounds and others he has lain several times under the surgeon's and others' hands, to his extraordinary cost and charges, at his father's house in Marlborough and at Bath. And he has lost the use of his limbs and sustained great loss by the enemy, he having bought 16 or 17 horse and arms at his own charge to serve

---

43 Macray (ed.), *History of the Rebellion*, VII, p. 26.
44 NLW, Chirk Castle Mss B35A/16; B16C/41; B86/95.

the Parliament. And his father being often plundered and robbed by them is not able to relieve your petitioner (if willing). Your petitioner further shows that with those dangerous wounds he received, he was conceived to be dead and so made him uncapable of receiving his arrears.[45]

Intelligence-gathering and information had an important role in the British Civil Wars and were available to both sides. In normal operational terms, deserters, prisoners, and the interception of messengers provided sources of military intelligence, even if this was sometimes unreliable. According to John Cruso, writing in 1632, scouts 'must be choice men, valiant, vigilant, and discreet such as neither fear nor misconceit can easily distract. They must see that with their own eyes which they inform, the least error of theirs misleading the whole body'.[46] Similarly, John Vernon recommended that spies should be amply remunerated, 'which will cause them to expose themselves unto all hazards and dangers to give intelligence'.[47] Trumpeters and drummers were also an indispensable part of armies. They acted like heralds, in that they negotiated with enemies, discussed prisoners, delivered terms of surrender, or acted as messengers. They might also pass on intelligence information on enemy troop movements, numbers, and the like. The Parliamentarian lawyer Bulstrode Whitelocke described how a spy 'taken by the Parliament soldiers at Reading, was tortured into confession by having lighted matches put to his fingers', whereas it was reported that, before the Royalist garrison surrendered in April 1643, the governor employed a female double-agent 'to good effect', he believing 'the advantage he received was greater than she could carry to the enemy'.[48]

Although the King and Prince Rupert led a relieving force out of Oxford, along the north side of the Thames, Reading fell to the Earl of Essex after a 10-day siege on 26 April 1643. As the Royalists approached Caversham, they were drawn into a heavy firefight and forced back, sustaining 100 dead and significantly more wounded. Furthermore, in his memoirs, produced after 1660, Richard Atkyns – a former officer in Prince Maurice's regiment cavalry, who participated in the siege of Reading – remembered seeing troops ordered to attack the Parliamentarians defending a barn 'drop like ripe fruit in a strong wind and never see their enemies; for they had made loopholes through the walls that they had the full bodies of the assailants for their mark, as they came down a plain field, but the assailants saw nothing to shoot at but mud walls'. Even when most of the relieving force was withdrawn, Atkyns and his soldiers remained perilously close to these defences, 'more like a flock of sheep than a party of horse'.[49]

---

45 WSHC, A1/110A/64.
46 John Cruso, *Militarie Instructions for the Cavallrie* (Cambridge: Cambridge University, 1632), p. 60.
47 John Vernon, *The Young Horseman, or, the Honest Plain-Dealing Cavalier* (London: Andrew Coe, 1644), p. 41.
48 Bulstrode Whitelocke, *Memorials of the English Affairs* (London: Nathaniel Ponder, 1682), p. 114; Macray (ed.), *History of the Rebellion*, VII, p. 42.
49 Peter Young and Norman Tucker (eds), *Military Memoirs of the Civil War: Richard Atkyns and John Gwyn* (London: Longmans, 1967), pp. 10–11.

'A PLACE STRONGLY FORTIFIED': THE ROYALIST GARRISON OF READING

Various Parliamentarian reports of the siege of the town were published in London, the quantity no doubt a reflection of the importance of such operations and possible outcome. One account, entitled 'A true relation of the siege of Reading, from the first to the last', informed its readers:

> Fifteenth [of] April late at night we sat down before Reading, being Saturday at night, the next morning by sun rising the fight began very hot both by them and us, and so continued all that day and night, after that fight somewhat abated, but held on with much temperance, for on their side it appeared afterwards, it was because they were necessitated through want of powder, which the enemy supplied by a barge in the night, and put in 3 or 400 men, but this was a little quantity, for on Friday night last they attempted to relieve it by the same way with 1,500 men, but with 500 of ours we beat them back again, so that they missed of their ends then. At the Lord's Day at night, we sent out a party of horse, and beat up their quarters at Dorchester, where lay a regiment of horse, and another of foot, where we took 100 horse and 50 foot, and killed some without any loss at all. Then on Tuesday morning Reading men hung our their white flag for a parley, and we sent them 3 hostages and they sent us 3, to treat about the yielding up of the town, and as they have ever done while they were treating, the King came up with all his forces both horse and foot, and dragoons, and cannons on the other side of the water, where we had but 1 regiment of foot, and fell in upon them and gave them 4 cannon shot, and a whole pile of shot before our men knew it, notwithstanding the great order of all things to preserve our men, that it no more unto them than awaken them, so as they roused like lions, for though the King's forces had the hill and this great advantage, yet our men soon got it from them, and whether it was the storm, or our bullets (for there was a great one) they were in 3 hours routed, and had 100 men, some of their chief commanders slain and 400 wounded, and we took 300 arms, and pursued them, so that they retreated faster than they came on, and we lost but 6 men. And this day the forces of Reading are to yield up the town and march away with their colours flying, and I hope that we shall not now be long from Oxford, for we are about 20,000 foot and horse, and there we expect to meet Sir William Waller's, my Lord Grey's, and Sir John Gell's forces, which consists of 7 or 8,000 men.[50]

Perhaps the most detailed report of the siege is that sent by Colonels Philip Stapleton, John Hampden, and Arthur Goodwin of Essex's army to the Speaker on 27 April 1643:

> After [marching] 10 miles on Saturday 15 April, we made our approaches that night, taking some advantages of the hedges and ditches unslighted by the enemy. On Sunday we sat down before the town, battered with our ordnance, and played it with our small shot all that day, in which the governor received a hurt upon the head, which rendered him unfit for further service, we had very warm work, and hot returns from the town. On Monday we advanced our approaches as far as they could. On Tuesday in the night the King sent in a relief of men and ammunition, which we could not prevent by reason of the situation of the town, and their

---

50 *Victory Proclaymed*. TT, E100[4].

advantages of barges which we could not command, being wholly engaged on Berkshire side. On Monday last we sent out a party of horse and dragoons as far as Dorchester, which did beat up the enemy's quarters, routed their horse and foot, killed and took many prisoners. On Tuesday morning last the enemy did beat a parley, and accordingly came out to treat, and in the interim while business was depending, the King's army appeared for their relief, and fell on with their artillery, foot and horse, upon our guards on Oxfordshire side, but having roundly received after above an hour's fight, the enemy was routed with the loss of above 100 men, and 300 arms. The King, Prince Charles, Prince Rupert, Prince Maurice, and the generals being all in the field, that night our capitulation was concluded. And now his Excellency being very tender of the town that they should not be plundering, and as careful that the soldiers might received due encouragement, has appointed 12s. per man for an extraordinary, and so we advancing to take possession, for the consequence of which success I doubt not but the wiser and well-minded will see reason to think and thank God, the business having a blessing in it of a great, and growing constitution. If a short survey be but taken of the considerable circumstances, being rendered with so little loss of blood in so short a time, and the King resolved to relieve it. Not to mention the 10 pieces of cannon they relinquished, nor the restitution of the Western clothes taken from our friends.[51]

During the siege, both sides were immobilised by what was probably typhus or 'camp fever' – a disease caused by a bacterium hosted by the human body louse, and therefore associated with dirty and overcrowded conditions, and spread mainly by armies marching across the countryside and living in filthy and unhygienic conditions. This was often exacerbated by malnutrition and exceptionally cold weather. Some 1,200 soldiers arrived in Oxford in April 1643 from Reading, bringing infections with them, while, the following year, 16 carloads of sick troops arrived from Abingdon, increasing an ever-growing ailing and wounded population.[52] Following the surrender of the Reading garrison, what remained of the infantry regiments, most of whom belonged to the Oxford Army, then quitted the town. But they, in addition to the Royalist garrisons of Abingdon, Brill, and Woodstock, were subsequently mustered at a hutted encampment on Culham Hill, near Abingdon, in readiness for the commencement of the King's summer campaign.

Here, the officers of the various foot regiments protested at the shortages of bandoliers and other fighting equipment for their soldiers. Hence, a batch of 250 collars was included in one delivery of arms on 22 May, and, five days later, a council of war ordered as many powder bags as were complete to be directed to the army.[53] Sir Arthur Aston, though, relinquished command of the Reading garrison after being hit on the head by a roof tile dislodged by cannon fire while inspecting one of the courts of guard in the line of

---

51 *Third Intelligence From Reading*. TT, E99[29].
52 Eric Gruber von Arni, *Justice to the Maimed Soldier: Nursing, Medical Care and Welfare for Sick and Wounded Soldiers and Their Families during the English Civil Wars and Interregnum, 1642–1660* (Aldershot: Ashgate, 2001), pp. 19, 26; Roger Gilboy, 'Crisis Mortality in Civil War Oxford, 1642-1646', *Oxoniensia*, 82 (2017), p. 100.
53 BL, Ms Harley 6804, ff. 92v.–93r.

fortifications.[54] Upon the surrender of the Reading garrison, Aston was carried out first, according to one report, 'in a horse litter covered with red and lined with white, after him both coaches and wagons, and then horse and foot beat a march and so departed with their colours flying towards Oxford'.[55] The governorship passed to Colonel Richard Fielding, a professional soldier who had served in the Scots Wars. He sensed that there would be no relief for the garrison and straightaway informed Charles I that, unless he was relieved within a week, the town must be surrendered.

Articles of Surrender of the Garrison of Reading to the Earl of Essex, 26 April 1643 (*The Last Joyful Intelligence from his Excellency his Quarters at Reading, since the surrendering of the town*) (London: Thomas Watson, 1643). TT, E100[5])

1. That the governor, commanders, and soldiers, both horse and foot, may march out with flying colours, arms, and 4 pieces of ordnance, ammunition, bag and baggage, lighted match, bullet in mouth, drum beating, and trumpet sounding.
2. That they shall have free passage to his Majesty's city of Oxford, without any interruption of any forces under the command of his Excellency the Earl of Essex, provided the said governor, commanders, and soldiers, use no hostility until the come to Oxford.
3. That what persons soever are accidently come to this own, and shut up by siege, may have liberty to pass without interruption; such persons only excepted, as have run away from the army under the command of the Earl of Essex.
4. That they might have 50 carriages for baggage, sick, and hurt men, and that they not out of the town of Reading and such goods and commodities as have been taken from the western carriers, and brought into Reading.
5. That the inhabitants of the town of Reading may not be prejudiced in their estate or persons, either by plundering or imprisonment; and that those who will leave the town may leave free, and passage, and safely to go to what place they will, with their goods, within the space of 6 weeks after the surrender of the said town.
6. That the garrison of Reading shall quit the said town by 12 of the clock tomorrow in the morning; that timely notice shall be given to his Excellency when they begin to march, that a guard may be provided for their security. That at the time when the garrison begins to march out of the post towards Caversham Bridge, there shall be a post open at Newbury way, for my Lord General to pass into the town.

Richard Fielding
John Belasyse
Richard Bell
Edward Villiers
Anthony Thelwall
Theophilus Gilby
George Bond

---

54 *Mercurius Aulicus*, 16–22 April 1643. TT, E246[16].
55 *Last Joyful Intelligence*. TT, E100[5].

Sir Jacob Astley, governor of Reading, 1643-1644.

Although the damage caused to Royalist morale would prove enormous, the immediate benefit of the surrender of the town and garrison of Reading in terms of Parliamentarian military strategy is more difficult to assess. Sickness, exacerbated by chronic desertion, had devastated the Earl of Essex's army and consequently prevented any immediate follow-up strategic operations. For the next couple of months, there was stalemate in the Thames Valley area, and, although Essex's forced moved around the eastern vicinity of Oxford, he could not bring the King to battle because he was too weak to attack the Parliamentarians, having consumed most of his ammunition whilst attempting to relieve Reading. When that town's garrison capitulated, the Earl of Essex's council of war were said to be 'in fear of a general defection' when Parliament failed to honour its promise to pay his troops the sum of 12s. apiece from sparing the town from plunder. Additionally, discovered among the Reading soldiers were deserters from his own forces when it capitulated.

These had taken advantage of a Royal proclamation of 18 April 1643, which offered his soldiers a pardon if they defected. The men were duly court-marshalled and hanged, although Clarendon later wrote, 'I have not known the King more afflicted than he was with that clause [Article 3] which he called no less than giving up those poor men, who, out of their conscience of their rebellion, had betaken themselves to his protection, to be massacred and murdered by the rebels who they had deserted'.[56] The new Royalist governor, Colonel Fielding, claimed that he endeavoured to change Essex's decision, but, once the surrendered garrison reached Oxford, some of the soldiers accused him of a 'treacherous liaison' with the enemy, for which the Royalist officer was court-marshalled. The King, though, declared his conduct to be 'most prejudicial to his service and derogatory to his honour'.[57] Fielding was condemned to death but not executed, however. In 1644, he was created lieutenant general of the King's artillery under the command of Sir Ralph Hopton.[58]

During the Earl of Essex's Reading campaign in April 1643, he deployed a combined mounted force of cavalry and dragoons as a reconnaissance in force, to assess the strength and intentions of the King's army at Oxford. As one Parliamentarian newsbook reported:

---

56 Macray (ed.), *History of the Rebellion*, III, pp. 24–25.
57 *His Majesties Proclamation and Declaration Concerning a Clause in One of the Late Articles at Reading* (Oxford: Leonard Lichfield, 1643). TT, E669[13].
58 BRO, D/EZ179/1.

> That very night [23 April 1643] we sent a party of horse under the command of Colonel Middleton, and a regiment of dragoons under the command of Colonel Melve, to pursue Prince Rupert and make discovery of the enemy, who in the night time marched towards Dorchester [on Thames], where a great party of the enemy was quartered, and with intention only to give them alarm, but the scouts that were abroad were took, their sentinels slain, and our forces entered the town, killed forty at least, of which there were 8 commanders slain in one house, who discharged pistols out of windows against our men, yet without hurry, we took 140 horses, some of £50 price, and divers prisoners, some officers, and harbingers to the King, and plundered a little, and so retreated.[59]

The Lord General's letter to the Speaker of the House of Commons, written on 24 April 1643, read (in part):

> I hold it my duty to acquaint the Parliament with some passages that happened yesterday morning, and this last night: In the morning, about two of the clock, Captain Carr that commands Sir William Balfour's troop, with two troops more, being upon the guard at Caversham, to take care that no provisions should be put into the town, the General Ruthven, with some 2,500 horse and dragoons, namely, seven regiments of Horse, and two or three hundred dragoons, surprised two sentinels; but, having the alarm, our troops charged with 40 Horse, and so retreated to Colonel Barclay's regiment, that was drawn over the bridge. The enemy charging, the musketeers gave fire (having Colonel Holborne with his musketeers) so resolutely, that they wheeled about and went away, our few Horse following them three miles, their intention was to put in 40 barrels of powder. That evening, I sent out Colonel Middleton and Colonel Meldrum with horse, and Colonel Melve with 4 troops of his dragoons, to find out the enemy; they fell in about eleven at night at Dorchester, where the King's Lifeguard of foot lay, and the King's Standard, which they knew not of till afterwards. If the soldiers could have been kept from plundering, they might have done much more; but, there being four troops of horse there, besides the regiment, and in danger of having Wallingford cut the passage between them and us, they only routed most of that regiment, took the captain-lieutenant to the guards, one other lieutenant, two of the King's harbingers, 40 prisoners, 150 Horse, one cornet, which they say was Sir Thomas Aston's.[60]

On 6 June 1643, the Earl of Essex led a large part of his army from Reading northwards to the area around Thame (not far from the Parliamentarian garrison of Aylesbury), with the intention of penetrating closer to the King's defences at Oxford. Essex, though, was dreadfully short of horses and saddlery, many of his soldiers were sick, and morale among the army was particularly low. Sir Lewis Dyve, who commanded a regiment of foot in the Oxford Army, reported to Prince Rupert on 9 June:

---

59 *Kingdomes Weekly*, 25–27 May 1643. TT, E75[17].
60 *LJ*, VI, p. 17.

I have now certain intelligence brought me from Reading that the Earl of Essex marched away this morning with all the force he had towards Henley. The baggage and his rear are not yet come thither: after the baggage there were ten troops of horse to march, which had not all past [Caversham] bridge when the messenger which brought me this news came out of Reading. The chief cause of their moving is supposed to be for fresh quarters, and for the relief of their sick, which die in great abundance: four hundred of them were sent this day in barges for London, and great numbers remain behind unable to stir, and many who have the use of their legs employ them in running away from the misery that follows their army. They are certainly in great confusion, and are possessed with marvellous fears, which your Highness knows best how to make advantage of.[61]

Rupert slipped out of Oxford on 17 June intending to maul enemy quarters in the area and to seize a convoy of money sent for the payment of the Earl of Essex's troops. The next day, Rupert inflicted a severe setback upon a body of Parliamentarian cavalry and dragoons near the Oxfordshire village of Chalgrove.

Arms and Ammunition

Besides, issues of arms and ammunition to Royalist forces at a distance from Oxford and Reading are more difficult to determine. In November 1642, 1cwt of powder, match, and bullet was issued to Colonel Ralph Dutton's Royalist regiment of foot from the Oxford magazine. In order to safeguard the convoy delivering these items, 80 horses were brought to Reading, which, as the governor reported, 'I am to mount musketeers upon there, 1lb of powder, with match and shot [provided to each soldier] accordingly'.[62] In November 1642, the newly appointed governor of Reading and colonel general of dragoons to the Oxford Army, Sir Arthur Aston, ordered Sir Edward Grey's regiment to be furnished with 12 bundles of match, four barrels of powder, two barrels of musket bullets, and two of carbine shot.[63] On 23 April 1643, it was reported by a Royalist source that supplies of powder and ammunition had recently arrived safely in Reading:

> It was advertised this day, that the rebels lying before Reading, having notice (as they have very good intelligence) of certain provisions of powder and ammunition, which were sent from Oxford by his Majesty to be conveyed into the town, had so filled up the ways with their troops of horse, and lined the hedges on both sides (where they were to pass) with their musketeers, that his Majesty's forces sent along for the convoy of it, had almost fallen into the danger ere they were aware: that they possibly might have received some notable loss, but that the most noble and valiant Earl of Carnarvon with some troops of Horse faced a whole regiment of the rebels, and made a stand until his Majesty's foot with the ammunition, were got off in safety.[64]

---

61   Warburton, *Memoirs*, II, p. 202.
62   TNA, WO55/423, f. 142v.
63   TNA, WO55/423, ff. 211r.–v.
64   *Mercurius Aulicus*, 23–28 April 1643. TT, E246[19].

The only known journal of receipts of stores into a Royalist garrison during the British Civil Wars is that belonging to Reading.[65] Kept by officials of the magazine there under the command of Henry Sherburne, the brother of the commissary Edward Sherburne, it principally records the delivery arms, ordnance, ammunition, tools, and other stores brought in between 4 October 1643 and 11 April 1644 from Oxford. It also includes receipts of items from local craftsmen and townspeople. The broader context of this document is the Royalist reoccupation of Reading following the town's evacuation by Parliamentarian forces after the First Battle of Newbury on 3 October 1643. On 28 October, the King issued a proclamation ordering the inhabitants of Reading who had left the town for London to return home by the following December, on pain of confiscation of their houses and goods in Reading.[66]

Table 4 A Selection of Receipts of Arms, Munitions, and Other Stores into 'his Majesty's Magazine at Reading' (TNA, WO55/1661/4)

4 October 1643	Arms remaining in the magazine at our coming to town:	
	Head pieces	120
	Gorgets	10
	Back pieces	100
	Breast pieces	118
	Tassets for breast pieces	410
	New pikes un-headed	164
4 October 1643	Received from Oxford powder, match, and shot, and to attend 4 brass pieces of ordnance assigned for [Reading] by order of the Right Honourable Lord Percy:	
	Roundshot of iron for 2 6lb pieces	100
	Roundshot of iron for 2 3lb pieces	100
	Cartouches of powder remaining in the pieces' lockers	28
	Match	11cwt
	Budge barrels	2
4 October 1643	Materials:	
	Shovels	120
	Spades	110
	Pickaxes	24
	Hoes	26
	Axes	10
	Hedging bills	9
	Covered wagons	2
	Carts	1
	Tumbrels	1
	Ammunition for the foot:	
	Powder	30cwt
	Match	30cwt
	Musket shot	30cwt
6 October 1643	Received out of the church of St Lawrence at Reading:	
	Powder	1cwt 10lbs

---

65 TNA, WO55/1661/4.
66 BRO, R/Z10/6.

	Match	1cwt
	Musket shot	3cwt
8 October 1643	Received from Sir James Pennyman:	
	Powder	300cwt
	Small bundle of match	1
13 October 1643	Received from Sergeant Major Collings of Colonel Dutton's regiment:	
	Powder	2cwt
	Musket shot	2cwt
14 October 1643	The townsmen's arms received into his Majesty's magazine:	
	Head pieces	52
	Gorgets	1
	Breast pieces	31
	Back pieces	31
	Muskets	8
	Musket barrels	2
	Bandoliers	8
	Halberds	1
	Pike staves	2
	Brown bills	2
18 October 1643	Received from Nicholas Ashmore of Reading, his Majesty's matchmaker:	
	Match	2cwt 1lb
24 October 1643	Received arms from Oxford by warrant of the Right Honourable Lord Percy:	
	Muskets fixed	60
	Powder bags with girdles and hangers	60
	Long pikes	200

In the absence of documentary evidence to the contrary, the Bristol manufacturer and contractor Thomas Bushell was probably the most important supplier of clothing to the King's armies. In March 1643, he fitted out the infantry foot regiments (and possibly the dragoons) of the Oxford Army with caps, cassocks, breeches, and stockings 'at reasonable rates to be delivered at Oxford, and at the delivery to receive ready money, or a bill of exchange to be paid at London, the choice to be left to them who provided the clothes'. A testimony to Bushell's service, dated 12 June 1643, in addition to a later petition from him, mentions, 'your clothing our Life Guard and 3 regiments more, with suits, stockings, shoes, and monteros which we were ready in the field'.[67] By 15 July, the Oxford scholar Anthony Wood could record, 'upon the next, viz. Saturday all the common soldiers then at Oxford were new appareled, some all in red, coats, breeches, and monteros, and some all in blue'. Shortly afterwards, a Parliamentarian spy reported to Sir Samuel Luke, 'they have clothed all their foot soldiers in red and blue, having all of them monteros, coats and breeches'.[68] Monteros were round peaked caps constructed of panels of woollen cloth with a skirt running around the edge that could fold down for protection in bad weather.

---

67 TNA, SP16/494, f. 16v.; SP28/251, f. 209r.
68 Andrew Clark (ed.), *The Life and Times of Anthony Wood, Antiquary, of Oxford, 1632–1695, Described by Himself* (Oxford: Clarendon Press, 1891–1892), I, p. 103; H. B. Tibbutt (ed.), *The Letter Books of Sir Samuel Luke, 1644-45* (London: HMSO, 1963), p. 119.

Whilst at Oxford on 13 November 1643, Prince Rupert wrote to the Sheriff of Merionethshire about the arrival of troops from Ireland and the need to supply them with clothing:

> Many of the soldiers there being English Protestants are coming over to and are daily expected to land in some of the counties of North Wales. Rebellious subjects were the promoters of the rebellion in Ireland, and now they untruly charge the King on the occasion of the coming over of the soldiers, with bringing over the Irish rebels. Since the rebels have lately forced their passage over Holt Bridge and obstructed all the ways to Chester, orders have been given to the soldiers from Ireland to repair to those parts (of North Wales) for succour. The county of Merioneth having been freed of many burdens which other counties have sustained in the paying and free billeting of soldiers, the King's will and command is that there be provided, at the charge of the county, cloaks, shoes, stockings, and apparel sufficient for 500 men, and likewise victuals for 4,000 men for fifteen days, or money sufficient for the same use to be brought forthwith to Conwy where a magazine has been provided.[69]

More troops that came over from Ireland were supplied with clothing by Bushell whilst in the West Country. Thomas Piggott, a Royalist colonel of a yellow-coated infantry regiment, later testified:

> in the year 1643 there landed out of Ireland (for his Majesty's service in this Kingdom) the Lord of Inchiquin's regiment of foot (to which I was then major) and Sir Charles Vavasour's, Sir John Paulett's, Sir William St Leger's, Colonel Mynne's regiments of foot with part of the Lord Kerry's and part of the Lord Broghill's regiments of foot likewise, the soldiers of all which regiments were clothed at and from Bristol by Mr Thomas Bushell to the great content and satisfaction of both officers and soldiers of each regiment, and for which I never know heard that he was paid or satisfied in any part; my cause of knowledge of all this is, that I received about a 1,000 suits of clothes of him for my own regiment, and did so most of the other regiments receive their clothes, and did (afterwards) often see them march in them.[70]

Royalist armies were likewise supplied by clothiers from the West Country and the Thames Valley area. The narrative of John Ashe, the West Country clothier and Parliamentarian deputy lieutenant for Somerset, was reprinted in pamphlet form from a letter he wrote to the Speaker. In March 1643, the Royalist's chief newsbook, *Mercurius Aulicus*, reported the governor of Reading's seizure of Ashe's supplies for London:

> Certain news also came this day, that Sir Arthur Aston had seized on seven cartloads, one wain-load and 24 horse-loads of broad fine cloth, amounting in the whole to 380 cloths, and that in many of the packs were found some belts and bandoleers, and great store of match, and a considerable sum of money. All

---

69   NLW, Clenennau Letters and Papers 539.
70   BL, Ms Harley 6833, f. 100r.

of which were sent towards London from one Mr Ashe, the greatest clothier in the kingdom, as it is conceived, but of so turbulent a spirit and so pernicious a practitioner in the maintaining and fomenting of this rebellion, that he stands excepted by his Majesty amongst some others, out of his Majesty's general pardon for the county of Somerset.[71]

Soon afterwards, the clothing tradesmen of Reading petitioned Charles I, 'requesting that the cloths seized by Sir Arthur Aston may be kept in safe custody until they and the inhabitants of Somerset, Devon, Wiltshire and Gloucestershire have procured safe conduct from Parliament for the transport of their goods to London'. The appeal included the claim that Reading 'is an ancient clothing town solely consisting of the traffic and trade with London, which your petitioners did enjoy until your Majesty made the town of Reading a garrison town'.[72] Reading, which had been garrisoned for the King in late October 1642, had been a clothing town since the Middle Ages, although its declining economic prosperity was not assisted by Charles I's refusal to allow manufacturers to sell their goods in London. Although the writer of *A Catalogue of the Taverns in Ten Shires about London* (1636) stated, 'Reading is the prime and principal town in this county of Berkshire, for fair buildings, large streets for clothing and other blessings', the governing charter of the borough was granted by Charles I on 17 December 1638, but the decline in the prosperity of the town followed this event with astonishing swiftness.[73] This was partly caused by a rapid deterioration in the fortunes of the local cloth trade, which faced increased competition not only from northern and West Country manufacturers but also from the self-serving members of the corporation.

A 'petition from the mayor and burgesses to James I's commissioners for grievances, relating to the unemployment due to the decline of clothmaking in Reading', dated about 1623, foreshadowed the situation:

> Due to a sudden decay of clothing in our town many poor families, men, women and children who had their means and livelihood from the work of the clothier, to which only they have been trained, are now for want of work exposed to great misery, and have in woeful manner complained to your petitioners expostulating with them why they did not now as in former times furnish the poor people of the town with work. Their answer is they cannot because they have not that sale for their cloth as heretofore, they have had which causes them to make a less quantity of cloth; and so by consequence theirs is a necessity of the failing of work to the poor.[74]

Hence, the clothiers attributed the inability to sell cloth to 'the small number of merchants to whom they are limited to sell their clothes', and the inability to transport their cloth as cheaply as northern merchants:

---

71 *Mercurius Aulicus*, 1–7 March 1643. TT, E244[16].
72 BRO, R/Z3/36.
73 John Taylor, *A Catalogue of the Taverns in Ten Shires about London* (London: Henry Gosson, 1636), unpag.
74 BRO, R/Z3/24.

who have also recently altered the size of their cloths from twelve yards to the same length as Reading cloth and sell it under the name of Reading cloth. They might be restored to their former position and supply the poor with work if merchants of white cloth were required to purchase at least one coloured cloth for every ten white ones, as the manufacture of one coloured cloth requires as much labour, and yields as much profit to the King, as six white ones. This would relieve many hundreds of poor people distressed for want of work [who are] ready to perish, and relief of whom will be insupportable for the town.

Payments made during the Royalist occupation of Reading in October 1642 include those for bread and cheese to be sent to Charles I at Henley-on-Thames and Bagshot, making soldiers' uniforms, wood and lights for the court of guard, the sum of £2,000 loaned to the King for the maintenance of the army, fortifying the town, as well as victuals for horses and soldiers provided by the inhabitants of the town and not paid for.[75] On 4 November, from Oxford, Charles I informed the mayor and aldermen of his permission to the clothiers of Reading to continue in their trade and vowed to take no more garments from them without payment, provided that they send none to London. An earlier order to the inhabitants 'to bring to the town hall all their arms and armour' for the use of Royalist troops appears to have resulted in limited success, however, as they needed to be reminded that, unless it was adhered to by 1:00 p.m. on 7 November, 'any house in which such weapons are discovered thereafter shall be immediately given unto the soldiers to plunder'.[76] Similarly, on 5 November 1642, the King and the council of war took steps towards a good supply of clothing for the soldiers, as winter approached. As a sizeable part of the Royal army lay in quarters at Reading, cloth was brought in from Abingdon, enough, at two-and-a-half yards a suit, for over 2,500 men.[77]

It is evident, nevertheless, that significant quantities of clothing continued to be produced in Reading for the King's soldiers. On 8 November, 16 days after the Battle of Edgehill, Charles I issued a warrant to the mayor to impress all the tailors within a six-mile radius of the town to employ them in making clothing for the soldiers of the Oxford Army. The following day, the King ordered the tailors and merchants of Reading to supply 1,000 suits of clothes, the town of Abingdon having sent the mayor 137 cloths (sufficient to make 1,644 suits). The sum of £1,500, being the cost of 'dying, drying and making cloth into suits for the King's soldiers, the cloth (valued at £1,000) having been freely given by the borough', was levied on the population. However, as this erroneous figure was found to be impossible to raise, the entire county of Berkshire petitioned Charles I to be permitted to shoulder the burden.[78] In addition to this, on 12 November, a further warrant was issued to the mayor and aldermen authorising them to 'take up [requisition] such carts, boats or barges as shall be most convenient' to deliver the clothes and victuals

---

75   BRO, R/Z3/28.
76   BRO, R/Z6/1/5; R/Z6/1/19.
77   BL, Ms Harley 6851, f. 219r.
78   BRO, R/Z3/27/1–7; R/Z3/29; R/Z3/38/1.

to be provided by the town for the King's army throughout the county of Berkshire.[79] Moreover, in 1643, the Oxford mercer and mayor, Thomas Dennis, contracted with a local draper to supply 'coats and clothes, and other necessaries' to the King's army, although the documentation provides few other details, such as quantities, prices, or colour.[80] On 7 April 1643, Dennis and the councillors were called together at Charles I's court at Christ Church concerning the establishment of a garrison at Oxford. Wood reported that, when the King and Queen came to Oxford on 14 July, 'Mr Dennis, the mayor of the town, accompanied only with his mace bearer on horseback, brought his Majesty into Christ Church, the mayor in scarlet, bearing the mace upon his own shoulder, riding with Garter the chief of the heralds, etc., but no other of the town came with him, and of the University there rode none at all'.[81]

According to a list of the locations of the various elements of the Oxford Army, produced on 7 December 1642, Colonel Richard Fielding's tertia was quartered at Reading, although individual units, at least, departed soon afterwards:

> Sir Arthur Aston's regiment of horse
> Sir Thomas Aston's regiment of horse
> Sir John Byron's regiment of horse
> two unnamed troops of dragoons.[82]

Sir Arthur Aston's cavalry regiment was raised in late 1642, and, during the period of his governorship of Reading, the unit formed part of the garrison. On 20 November 1642, Aston commissioned Sir Walter Pye as lieutenant colonel of the regiment. Three days later, Aston's troopers received '60 complete arms, back and breast, and 53 head pieces'.[83] George Boncle served at lieutenant colonel and took command of the regiment when Sir Arthur Aston was created governor of Oxford in 1643.

The commission issued by the King to Sir Thomas Aston on 3 October 1642 authorised him to 'impress, raise, enroll, and retain 1 regiment of 500 horse as colonel of them to command, arm, discipline, train, and order in warlike manner'. Aston had clearly established his regiment some time before this date. Sir Thomas Aston initially raised two cavalry troops from his estate in Cheshire, and various townships in the locality, whilst those commanded by Sir William Radcliffe and Captain Prestwich (described by Sir Thomas as 'not raised by me but brought in') were recruited in Lancashire. By late 1642, the regiment contained nine troops. Sir Thomas Aston's cavalry regiment returned to Cheshire from its quarters in Reading in January 1643, although they were overwhelmed at Nantwich by Sir William Brereton's Parliamentarian forces.[84] In November 1642, Sir Thomas Aston's regiment

---

79 BRO, R/Z6/1/3.
80 TNA, SP19/133/27.
81 Clark (ed.), *Life and Times*, I, pp. 103–04.
82 BRO, R/Z10/2.
83 BL, Ms Add. 18980, f. 8v.; TNA, WO55/423/50/2.
84 *Cheshire's Successe since their pious and truly valiant Colonel, Sir William Brereton, Baronet, came to their rescue, &c.* (London: Thomas Vnderhill, 1643). TT, E94[6].

Ruins of Reading Abbey, which were incorporated into the town's fortifications. (Photo by Paul Wright)

received 60 arms, 28 corslets, and five helmets from the magazine at Oxford.[85] By the time his regiment fought at Edgehill on 23 October 1642, it numbered 150 troopers, besides commissioned and non-commissioned officers, and, in October 1643, whilst quartered in Wiltshire, it consisted of 300 men in seven, exclusive of officers, although this is likely to have included dragoons.[86]

When at Oxford on 19 November 1642, Prince Rupert, the King's nephew and commander of the cavalry in the Oxford Army, had referred to the issuing of commissions to colonels of regiments, 'Many commissions are given out, but no money, to raise the regiments of horse. Sir Arthur Aston, the governor of Reading, has one; Sir [William] Pye has a commission to be his lieutenant-colonel for raising a troop upon his own charge. Sir Thomas Aston raises a regiment, and some others also to ten or twelve new regiments'.[87] Little is known of the composition of Sir John Byron's regiment of horse, although he was raising troopers from late July 1642 after receiving £5,000 'mounting money' (also known as 'advance money', possibly the £140 received by troop captains in the Earl of Essex's army and other Parliamentarian forces in 1642) from the Marquis of Worcester. Byron's regiment fielded six troops

---

85   TNA, WO55/423/51/2.
86   WSHC, X3/119, unf.
87   Warburton, *Memoirs*, II, p. 69.

at Edgehill, where it led a cavalry brigade that included Sir Thomas Aston's, although its stay in Reading was a brief one, it leaving for Burford on 10 December 1642 or soon afterwards.[88] In January 1644, whilst operating in Wiltshire, Sir John Byron's cavalry regiment mustered 280 troops, besides commissioned and non-commissioned officers.[89]

Table 5 Foot Regiments in the Garrison of Reading, April 1644 (BL, Ms Add. 986, ff. 79r.–82v.)

	Capts	Lts	Ens	Gents	Sgts	Cpls	Dmrs	Sldrs	[Total]
Colonel Anthony Thelwall's	5	8	7	7	15	20	7	127	196
Sir John Owen's	3	3	4	4	8	12	5	106	145
Sir George Lisle's	6	7	8	7	17	22	14	189	270
Sir James Pennyman's	11	10	11	11	23	33	20	360	479
Sir Theophilus Gilby's	9	10	11	11	22	30	14	268	375
Sir Charles Lloyd's	8	9	10	10	20	28	16	308	409
Colonel Stephen Hawkins'	9	9	9	10	19	29	19	171	275
Sir Edward Stradling's	8	9	10	10	21	29	18	246	351
Sir Bernard Astley's	7	7	8	8	14	18	9	146	217
Sir Thomas Blackwell's	4	4	4	2	6	5	5	56	86
Colonel William Eure's	3	4	3	3	5	9	5	59	91
Sir Henry Vaughan's	6	6	5	6	13	17	12	195	260
Total of the muster								2,231	3,154
							Sir Bernard Astley, Governor		

Symonds also provided some weekly pay rates for the infantry serving in the garrison, being a week's pay for three captains £7 17s. 6d.; three lieutenants £4 4s.; three ensigns £3 3s.; six sergeants £3 3s.; three gentlemen of the arms £1 11s. 6d.; six drummers £2 2s.; nine corporals £3 3s.; and 200 common soldiers £40. With the addition of Colonel Charles Gerard's and Sir Henry Bard's regiments of foot of the Oxford garrison, these units from the Reading garrison formed the tertia commanded by Colonel George Lisle for the Battle of Cheriton on 29 March 1644, although a composite regiment of about 1,000 musketeers had previously drawn from the Reading regiments as an advance guard. Towards the end of the action, these troops lined the hedgerows to cover the retreat of the defeated Royalist army, before the perhaps 12–13 regiments reverted to their quarters at Reading.[90] On 4 April, the Committee of Both Kingdoms informed Sir Henry Vane senior that:

> My Lord General has received letters which he has communicated to the Committee assuring from eye-witnesses that the King is drawing his forces together, and the rendezvous is appointed at Marlborough on Saturday next. The garrison is all marched out of Reading, and the report is that they will presently

---

88 Whitelocke, *Memorials*, pp. 102–03.
89 WSHC, X3/119, unf.
90 *A Fuller Relation of the Victory obtained at Alsford, 28 March, by the Parliaments forces* (London: Laurence Blaiklock, 1644). TT, E40[1]; Tibbutt (ed.), *Letter Books*, pp. 266, 268.

face Sir William Waller again and do their utmost to recover their losses, by which you will see the great necessity of all expedition to be made in the dispatching away of those additional forces that are appointed to be sent to [Waller].[91]

Colonel Anthony Thelwall's Regiment

The regiment was originally raised by Sir Edward Fitton of Gawsworth, Cheshire. Fitton was one of 11 colonels to be commissioned by the King in Wales and the Marches in the summer and autumn of 1642. Both Earl Rivers and he raised infantry regiments in Cheshire and Flintshire, their captains being gentry relatives and tenants, while a few formed a cadre of 'foreign' veterans. Both units fought at Edgehill and participated in the assault on Brentford and Turnham Green in November 1642.[92] During the following month, Fitton's regiment entered the garrison at Reading. Sir Edward Fitton was killed whilst leading his regiment during the storming of Bristol on 26 July 1643 and was succeeded as colonel by Anthony Thelwall, who had previously served as lieutenant colonel of the unit.

Company commanders in 1642–1644 were:

Sir Edward Fitton/Colonel Anthony Thelwall (Captain Lieutenant Alcockley; superseded by Captain Lieutenant Davenport, who was killed at Bristol.)
Sergeant Major Urian Leigh
Captain Claver
Captain William Davenport
Captain Thomas Green
Captain Charles Leigh
Captain Henry Leigh
Captain Peter Leigh
Captain Peter Mainwaring
Captain Thomas Minshull.

Sir John Owen's Regiment

In summer 1642, Owen was commissioned by the King to form a regiment of foot from the three counties of Gwynedd. However, it was not ready for field service until the operations around Oxford in May 1643. The regiment took part in the siege of Bristol, during which Owen received a wound in the face, and the First Battle of Newbury on 20 September 1643, in addition to the Royalist campaign in Cornwall in 1644. At Culham Camp on 24 May, it had eight companies, but, by the time of Symonds' list (see previously), there were only four, and it is possible that the others had been sent back to Wales as the core of a new regiment that was being raised there.

---

91   *CSPD 1644*, p. 95.
92   Bodl. Lib., Ms Ashmole 830, ff. 292r.–293v.

Company commanders were:

Colonel John Owen
Lieutenant Colonel Roger Burgess
Sergeant Major Hugh Hookes
Captain John Brynkir
Captain William Brynkir
Captain Richard Thomas
Captain Rowland Vaughan.

Sir George Lisle's Regiment

The regiment was raised by William, Lord Paget in Staffordshire in 1642 and taken over by Colonel Richard Bolles, who led it at Edgehill. In December 1643, Bolles was killed at Alton and was succeded by the veteran officer, Sir George Lisle.
Company commanders were:

Colonel Richard Bolles/Sir George Lisle
Lieutenant Colonel Edward Littleton
Sergeant Major Robert Skerrow
Captain Thomas Corbet
Captain Rugeley Littleton
Captain Thomas Pocklington
Captain John Taylor
Captain John Tichborne
Captain Thomas Smith
Captain Humphrey Whitgrave.

Sir William Pennyman's Regiment

The regiment was formed from the Yorkshire Trained Bands in 1642 by Sir William Pennyman, command of the regiment passing to his cousin Sir James upon his death at Oxford on 22 August 1643. Although Pennyman's was quartered in Shropshire, where Sir William acted as governor of Bridgnorth, in autumn 1642, the regiment served in most of the operations undertaken by the Oxford Army, including the Battle of Edgehill, the storm of Brentford, and stalemate of Turnham Green, before entering the garrison of Oxford in late December.
Company commanders were:

Sir William Pennyman/Sir James Pennyman
Lieutenant Colonel George Symms
Sergeant Major ??
Captain John Beverly
Captain John Jackson

Captain Mallory
Captain Anthony Norton
Captain Richard Page
Captain William Pennyman
Captain John Simpson.

Sir Theophilus Gilby's Regiment

The regiment was originally raised by John, Lord Belasyse in Nottinghamshire and Yorkshire in 1642. Belasyse was sent to command Royalist forces in Yorkshire in 1644, and command of his Oxford Army regiment passed to Sir Theophilus Gilby.

Company commanders were:

Lord Belasyse/Sir Theophilus Gilby (Captain Lieutenant Humphrey Baine)
Lieutenant Colonel Henry Darcy
Sergeant Major William Booth
Captain Henry Bellingham
Captain Thomas Booth
Captain David Gore
Captain Doyley Gower
Captain Thomas Monck
Captain John Pollock
Captain Alphonso Thweng
Captain William Trueman
Captain John Wolverston.

Sir Charles Lloyd's Regiment

Established as Sir Thomas Salusbury's regiment of foot in 1642 with recruits from Denbighshire and Flintshire, the unit was quartered in Shropshire before entering into the Oxford Army.

Company commanders were:

Sir Charles Lloyd
Lieutenant Colonel Edward Tyrwhyt
Sergeant Major ??
Captain Robert Challoner
Captain Garraway
Captain Hugh Jones
Captain Ellis Price
Captain Francis Williams
Captain Roger Williams
Captain Robinson.

Colonel Stephen Hawkins' Regiment

Lieutenant Colonel Hawkins took command of Sir Ralph Dutton's regiment on 6 December 1643.[93] Dutton had recruited heavily for the regiment in Gloucestershire in 1642, before it undertook service in the King's Oxford Army and the garrisoning of Greenland House.

Company commanders were:

Colonel Stephen Hawkins (Captain Lieutenant Thomas Atkins)
Lieutenant Colonel Palmer
Sergeant Major Charles Kirke
Captain William Atkins
Captain Thomas Cardinal
Captain George Grimes
Captain Fane Hack
Captain Hopkins
Captain Thomas Hull
Captain William Humphreville
Captain John Jauncy
Captain Charles Morris.

Sir Edward Stradling's Regiment

Raised originally in Glamorgan, the regiment fought at Edgehill (where Sir Edward was captured, and his lieutenant colonel, William Herbert, was killed) and Turnham Green, and it entered the Reading garrison on 9 December 1642.

Company commanders were:

Sir Edward Stradling
Lieutenant Colonel John Stradling (replaced Herbert, having acted previously as the regiment's sergeant major)
Sergeant Major Carne
Captain Bussey
Captain Edward Carne
Captain Hopkin Dawkins
Captain Oliver Hardwick
Captain Edward Morgan
Captain William Price
Captain Henry Vaughan.

---

93   BL, Ms Harley 6852, f. 253v.

Sir Bernard Astley's Regiment

Raised in Herefordshire in 1642 by Colonel Richard Fielding, the regiment fought at the Battle of Edgehill in the brigade led by Fielding himself. On 13 November, the unit was present at the standoff at Turnham Green, and, on 9 December, it became part of the Reading garrison. Following the fall of Reading and Fielding's court-martial in April–May 1643, the unit passed to Sir Jacob Astley. On 12 January 1644, the following warrant was issued in the King's name to Lieutenant Colonel Coningsby and Captain Coningsby of Colonel Fielding's regiment:

> Our will and pleasure [that] we are hereby graciously pleased to give you and either of you your free leave and service to be absent from either of your charges and commands under the regiment of our trusty and welbeloved Colonel Richard Fielding and to repair in to the county of Hereford to recruit and complete your companies and to return to your charges in our army with such numbers as you shall get before the first day of February next. And for your doing this shall be your warrant.[94]

Company commanders were:

Colonel Richard Fielding
Lieutenant Colonel Robert Coningsby
Sergeant Major Toby Bowes
Captain Coningsby
Captain Jackson
Captain La Warr
Captain Thimbleby
Captain Whalley.

Sir Thomas Blackwell's Regiment

The regiment was raised in Nottinghamshire in early 1643 and served as part of the Oxford Army (including being quartered at Reading in 1644). In August 1643, it participated in the Royalist attack on Gloucester, a Parliamentarian observer reporting on 12 August 1643, 'The same night the enemy making an approach in Barton Street, our cannon killed 6 of them, whereof 1 was a lieutenant colonel, and another a captain of the Queen's black regiment under Colonel Blackwell'.[95] This evidently small unit probably merged with other understrength regiments in November 1644, and Blackwell became one of the infantry officers who joined the Northern Horse.

---

94 BL, Ms Harley 6802, f. 9v.
95 *A Briefe and exact relation of the most material remarkable passages that hapned in the late well formed (and as valiantly defended) Siege laid before the City of Glocester* (London: Thomas Vnderhill, 1643). TT, E67[31]. The term 'black regiment' is likely to refer to its standards.

Company commanders were:

Colonel Sir Thomas Blackwell
Lieutenant Colonel Richard Meridel
Lieutenant Thomas Buttman
Ensign Ferdinand Babington
Ensign Charles Martin.

Colonel William Eure's Regiment

The regiment was formed in Northern England in 1643 and served with the Oxford Army foot.
Company commanders were:

Colonel William Eure
Lieutenant Colonel William Martin
Sergeant Major Emanuel Gilby
Captain Thomas Barner
Captain William Metcalfe
Captain John Plumpton
Captain Henry Pullen.

Sir Henry Vaughan's Regiment

The regiment was raised in Cardiganshire and Carmarthenshire in December 1642, then joined the King's army at Oxford the following month, where Henry Vaughan senior was knighted by the King. Vaughan was sergeant major general of the Royalist forces in Pembrokeshire from 1643 until he was defeated by Major General Rowland Laugharne in February 1644. Vaughan returned to Oxford and was captured at Naseby on 14 June 1645.
Company commanders were:

Colonel Sir Henry Vaughan senior
Colonel Henry Vaughan junior
Lieutenant Colonel Williams
Sergeant Major Gwyn
Captain John Floyd
Captain David Gwyn
Captain Thomas Jones
Captain William Marychurch
Captain William Sheales.

In March 1644, the magazine at Reading was emptied to the supplying the King's regiments for the Cheriton campaign. This caused Sir John Owen, the deputy governor of the garrison, to write to Henry, Lord Percy, the King's general of artillery, on 5 April 1644:

The great proportions of ammunition, lately drawn forth of this garrison, occasion our present address unto [you] for a supply, not knowing how sudden need we may have thereof. We most humbly therefore desire your Lordship with all convenient speed to send us 2,000lbs of match, 2,000lbs of musket shot, and 100 round shot for minion. In the expense whereof we shall employ our care in his Majesty's service.[96]

On 6 April, the King ordered the Reading Corporation to maintain 'a sufficient number of townsmen to pass on duties and keep watches during the absence of that part of the garrison which is gone to the Lord Hopton'.[97] This brought speedy results, for, on 16 April 1644, such munitions were brought from Reading from the King's arsenal at Oxford. These supplies were augmented by another issue made to the garrison four days later.

A warrant was issued to 'forthwith cause to be sent to Reading for the use and service of our garrison there the several kinds and quantities of ammunition following, viz.: 44 barrels of gunpowder; 250 round shot for minions; 4,000 of musket bullet; and 26cwt of match'. The supply of these consignments was paralleled by the delivery on 26 April 1644 of 10 barrels of powder; 1,000lbs of musket shot; 1,500lbs of match; 100 muskets; and 200 pikes to the Berkshire garrison of Wallingford, commanded by Colonel Thomas Blagge, which had also been denuded of weapons and ammunition for the same military operation.[98] Upon the return of the Reading regiments from Cheriton, the governor also attempted to replace some of the weapons and equipment lost during the fighting by issuing a proclamation the townspeople on 11 April. However, this brought in only 32 muskets, 43 pikes, six swords, six staff weapons, and 18 pieces of armour. It is likely that this poor response was down to a previous gathering of private arms, in addition to a reluctance to assist the garrison following a series of grievances articulated by the local population.[99]

The King's forces re-entered Reading, which had been abandoned by Parliament after the Battle of Newbury on 3 October 1643. On the same day, it was ordered that 'every householder shall forfeit 1s. for each day he fails to work at the bulwarks' and that all labourers would receive 8d. per day for their work on the fortifications. It was also resolved by the town's corporation that 'Sir Jacob Astley, the governor, should have £7 per week for his allowance, which is to be levied by a tax upon the inhabitants'.[100] A week later, three Royalist infantry regiments marched from Oxford, Wallingford, and Abingdon through Dorchester to Reading, and, with funding and the supply of provisions secured for the oncoming winter months, the newly reconstituted garrison, now under the command of Sir Jacob Astley, was estimated by Parliamentarian scouts to have increased

---

96 Bodl. Lib., Ms Rawlinson D395, f. 185r.
97 J. M. Guilding (ed.), *Reading Records: Diary of the Corporation* (London: J. Parker, 1892–1896), IV, p. 107.
98 TNA, WO55/423, ff. 293v.–294r., 299r., 301v.
99 TNA, WO55/1661/4; BL, Ms Harley 6804, ff. 182r.–183v.
100 Guilding (ed.), *Reading Records*, IV, pp. 90–91.

to more than 4,000 horse and foot.[101] Astley was a professional soldier whose considerable military service on the Continent and the Bishops' Wars brought him prominence during the fighting of 1642. He acted as governor of Reading from September 1643 to May 1644. Furthermore, he was sergeant major general of the King's Oxford Army and led the infantry in most of its campaigns.

On 24 October 1643, a conductor of the train of artillery of the Oxford Army, Robert Horne, received orders to convey 60 muskets, 60 powder bags with girdles and hangars for them, and 200 long pikes into the magazine at Reading.[102] Yet Astley was chronically short of pay and victuals for his men, and the inhabitants were constantly distressed by the activities of the governor of Wallingford, who attempted to claim 'the money for fortifying' the town and castle there.[103] The system of assessments in Berkshire and Oxfordshire was ineffective, something that increasingly created friction among both civilians and troops over the continuing Royalist demands for the maintenance of the garrisons in the region. On 13 January 1644, Sir Jacob Astley reported that, because of the loss of trade and the cost of fortifying the town, the citizens of Reading were unable to pay the contribution and that the local townships assigned to him brought in little income.[104] This is evident from two other letters written by Astley to Prince Rupert a couple of days earlier. Thus, Sir Jacob Astley complained:

> After many solicitations by letters and messengers sent for better payment of this garrison, and to be provided with men, armes, and ammunition for the good ordering and defence of this place, I have received no comfort at all. So that in little time our extremities must trust the soldiers either to disband, or mutiny, or plunder, and then the fault thereof will be laid to my charge. God send the King more money to go throw with his great work in hand, and me free from blame and imputation, that ever will remain.

To compound the issue, Prince Maurice's cavalry regiment had recently entered Reading. This caused Astley, as governor, to protest that his appearance 'so impoverished' the town that he was obliged to quarter the regiment in the adjacent villages, he having just received a petition from '"his friends, the mayor and corporation" against further demands upon them for some time'.[105] By comparison, Maurice's appearance in Royalist-held Chester in mid-February 1645 actually weakened the garrison because, upon his departure, he took with him the experienced troops under Byron, who had come out of Ireland. Similarly, he was accused by the local Parliamentarian forces and civilians of 'plundering and impoverishing the country extremely'.[106]

---

101 Tibbutt (ed.), *Letter Books*, p. 166.
102 TNA, WO55/459, f. 540r.
103 Guilding (ed.), *Reading Records*, IV, p. 84.
104 Bodl. Lib., Ms Firth C6, ff. 44r.–46v.
105 Warburton, *Memoirs*, II, pp. 359–60.
106 CRO, DDX/428, ff. 4r.–5r., 32r.–v.

By comparison, the consequences of plundering local communities were particularly heavy in Worcestershire, wherein the local population was obliged to bear the expense of maintaining and quartering many Royalist garrisons, including Worcester itself and Hartlebury Castle, the latter of which was garrisoned for the King by 120 men under the command of Captain William Sandys in 1644. Among others, these are characterised by the 'several losses and damages sustained by Mr John Freemen of Kidderminster in the county of Worcestershire since the unhappy wars between the King and Parliament'.[107] Hence, Freeman claimed, amongst other things, that, in October 1642, 'Prince Rupert's soldiers plundered £40-worth of plate, and of household stuff about the value of £40'; six tons of firewood was taken by Sir William Russell, worth £150, in addition to three horses to the value of £20; he was robbed 'by the cavaliers 4 horses to the damage of £50 at the least'. His overall losses – verified by Parliamentary committee in 1646 – amounted to £990, of which £400 had been 'suffered by them the cavaliers by reason of the loss of his trade, having a wife and 8 children to maintain'.

On 3 March 1644, Charles I dispatched orders to Sir Jacob Astley, 'governor of Reading town and garrison', for the preparation of the town in the event of a further siege. He was to command the inhabitants to provide themselves with three months' supply of victuals for their own families and a 'fitting proportion' for the poor. Astley was also to take care that a good quantity of salt was received in the magazine, whereas collections were to be made from the local area and other places 'not in contribution', including 'as much corn, peas and wheat as possible, and enough bacon for the town for 3 months'. Likewise, if enemy forces approached, Astley was to have much of the corn supplied by local parishes brought into the town and stored for the use of the inhabitants and the garrison. He would provide satisfaction to the suppliers and pay for victuals consumed by the garrison if they brought them in voluntarily and sold it at reasonable rates. The King further informed Sir Jacob Astley that he had ordered his Commissary of the Victuals to furnish 200–300lbs of cheese to be stored at Reading and to assist him in providing other foodstuffs. Furthermore, there had been '6 pieces of mounted ordnance, 700 muskets, and a good proportion of ammunition' directed from Oxford to Reading, and Astley was commanded to cause all the unfixed arms in the garrison to be repaired. Similarly, he was to send frequent parties and scouts to discover any Parliamentarian troop movements and to prevent any supplies of corn or provisions being carried to London. A postscript promised a week's pay for the soldiers of the garrison by the following night.[108]

How much of this was carried out remains unclear, though among the sizeable consignments of arms and munitions imported from Amsterdam for the use of the King's armies in late February and early March 1644 were 300 muskets and 300 bandoliers earmarked for Sir Jacob Astley's regiment at Reading. Concerning their useability, Captain John Strachan, Charles I's agent at Weymouth, reported the poor condition of arms and ammunition received at ports in the West, in that of 'the muskets, there are about 1,000 of

---
107 TNA, SP19/133/41.
108 BRO, R/Z3/34.

them, I am assured they are of 3 or 4 score sundry bores, some pistol bores, some carbine bores, some little fowling pieces, and all the old trash that could be rapt together'.[109] There were also considerable doubts expressed about the serviceability of the garrison's ordnance at Reading, in addition to a lack of pay for the gunners. Hence, on 9 March 1644, the keeper of the garrison's magazine reported to Lord Percy at Oxford:

> That proportion of the cannon and ammunition I have received, and have landed the cannon, and mounted 2 of them., the other 6 I have not, as yet, but shall by the first, I thought fit, to inform your Lordship and that there are many defects here, which will be a let to the speedy mounting of the rest, as axtrees, axtree bands, and much ironwork, which indeed may be here, but not without present monies. I beseech your Lordship to take some speedy course for it, otherwise the service will be retarded, things are so difficult to accrue without it. I request your Lordship to consider those ministers of the Train that are here, who for want of pay suffer exceedingly and that your Lordship would be mindful of the expense, that I have been at in providing such things, as have been necessary for this garrison, indeed it will be fitting, with some impressed monies were had, since the carriages for the cannon here are very much out of frame, and no man will work without present monies.[110]

With the creation of a new Parliamentarian army commanded by Major General Richard Browne and recruited in London, the Royalists in the Thames Valley region were placed firmly on the back foot, and, by the end of May 1644, the town and garrison at Wallingford alone blocked Parliament's main approach to Oxford. On 14 April, Sir Edward Nicholas wrote to the Earl of Forth, Lord General of the King's forces:

> I have this day received certain advertisement from several hands of very good credit that the rebels of London are resolved to levy all the forces they can possibly and fall on this city or Reading, and that they are now actually and vigorously in hand with their levies and preparations to this purpose. Their rendezvous is Aylesbury, where they say they will be next Friday, and the Earl of Manchester is also to join with the Earl of Essex in this rebellious design. There are between 2,000 and 3,000 foot of the [Tower] Hamlets and auxiliaries at Kingston, whence they are to march towards Waller tomorrow. Waller's two regiments of Londoners are returned back to that rebellious city.

Six days later, Nicholas informed 'Sir Jacob Astley, or his deputy-governor':

> I have private notice from a very good hand that 3,000 men are sent out from London who march in the night and have marched already two nights, their design being for Reading, which they hope by surprisal and a party within the town to carry suddenly. Wherefore his Majesty commands that you keep good scouts abroad night and day to watch these rebels' motions, and that you be

---

109   TNA, WO55/423, ff. 211r.–v.; Bodl. Lib., Ms Rawlinson D395, ff. 114r.–118v.
110   Bodl. Lib., Ms Rawlinson D395, ff. 119v.–120r.

vigilant to discover what intelligence they hold or what party is affected to them in Reading, that so, by your timely discoveries of both, and securing of such as you find treacherous within, so great a mischief to his Majesty's affairs may be prevented. What is further to be done upon this information for the safety of Reading is left to your circumspection.[111]

Soon afterwards, the council of war at Oxford decided that the fortifications at Reading should be dismantled and all outlying garrisons recalled to the city. Although the town remained in use as a supply hub and place for quartering troops for Parliament's forces, in March 1645, Reading became the headquarters, principal magazine, and logistical centre for the fledgling New Model Army commanded by Sir Thomas Fairfax. It was here that, during the first few weeks of April 1645, a significant proportion of the infantry regiments of the armies of the Earl of Essex and the Earl of Manchester were reduced. On 3 April, Fairfax departed London for Windsor, and, the following day, £7,000 was conveyed to the town, while another £3,000 went to Reading 'towards the payment of 14 days' pay to such officers and soldiers as shall appear in the muster rolls, under the hands of such person or persons as shall be appointed to take the muster and listed under my command there'.[112] Reading's role as a major magazine for the sustainment of the New Model would continue into 1646.

---

111 *CSPD 1644*, pp. 117, 128.
112 TNA, SP28/29/1, ff. 4r., 23r., 168r.

Chapter 3

'A frontline fortress': The Parliamentarian Garrison of Aylesbury

On 9 January 1643, the newsbook *A Perfect diurnall of the passages of Parliament* reported:

> From Aylesbury in Buckinghamshire it is informed that the town is very strongly fortified, and that there are 6 pieces or ordnance and a strong garrison of men, Colonel Bulstrode his regiment, some other forces being there, that the King's forces continue still at Brill near unto Aylesbury, but dare not march any further this way in the country for that more of the Parliament's forces are quartered at Wendover, Missenden, Wickham, and other towns thereabouts, which carry themselves very orderly, do no harm where they come, and paying very justly for the things they have.[1]

The Buckinghamshire town of Aylesbury was a major part of Parliament's defence against Royalist threats from Oxford, particularly after the Earl of Essex abandoned Thame in June 1643, fell back to Aylesbury, and then relocated his headquarters to Great Brickhill, leaving Aylesbury as the frontline stronghold. Located on a major route through the Chilterns to London, it also guarded the Eastern Counties, which were strong supporters of Parliament.

On 17 June 1642, a petition was presented to Parliament by the 'captains, officers, and soldiers, of the Trained Bands and volunteers of the county of Buckinghamshire', mustered at Aylesbury, desiring a new Lord Lieutenant and returning thanks for the Ordinance for the Militia. Lord Paget was subsequently replaced by Lord Wharton, alongside a committee of reliable local gentleman, who began recruiting local forces for Parliament, using Aylesbury as the centre of operations.[2] The correspondence of Nehemiah Wharton, a sergeant in Colonel Denzil Holles' infantry regiment, records

---

1 *Perfect diurnall*, 9–15 January 1643. TT, E240[14].
2 *CJ*, II, p. 638.

that, as the London regiments went through Buckinghamshire in October 1642 during their march to Northamptonshire, they discovered the towns of Amersham, Wendover, and Aylesbury strongly sympathetic to their cause. He also mentioned, however, that, before Aylesbury, the companies of his regiment practiced skirmishing, resulting in the death of a local woman, who was killed when a musketeer failed to remove the scouring stick from his musket before firing.[3] Royalist troops from Oxfordshire quickly engaged in foraging for supplies and currency in Buckinghamshire. On 16 September, a small action occurred near Aylesbury, causing the King's forces to retreat beyond Oxford.

The Parliamentarian dragoon regiment commanded by Colonel John Seton was recruited partly in London from veterans from the Netherlands, where he had previously served, and completed by 30 November 1642.[4] Despite Parliament's order of 6 August 'that all the soldiers shall have delivered unto them at their first marching, coats, shoes, shirts and caps in all to the value of 17s. for every man', some of the regiments left the city without their clothing issue.[5] It is difficult to know whether this included any of the dragoons in Essex's army, however. Although still in the early weeks of the conflict, Seton's officers and soldiers appear to have undertaken the tasks and operational methods that would later become synonymous with the dragoons of both sides. Colonel Seton was sent from London to Oxford to demonstrate Parliamentarian authority. Thus, according to one Parliamentarian newsbook, on Thursday, 8 September:

> Captain Lee, Captain Stackhouse, and Captain Mason, towards the evening marched out of the City of London with two pieces of ordnance, and wagons of ammunition to Acton, and there took up their quarter that night. Captain Wilson with his company marching after them in the night rode to Uxbridge and quartered his men there, Acton not being able to contain them; and Colonel [John] Brown with his dragoons being to march the same way, wanting lodging there at Acton, crossed over from Acton [and] rode to Brentford to quarter there.

On the following day, the writer continued, 'Captain Wilson marched from Uxbridge and quartered at Amersham, and in that afternoon drew his men into a body, and exercised them, and Captain Lee, Captain Mason, and the company of Captain Stackhouse did lodge at Chalfont St Peter, with their ordnance and ammunition'. On 10 September, Wilson's company marched to Aylesbury, 'and there in the way met divers cavaliers that were conveyed up in carts towards London, being taken in the north, and guarded up by the High Sheriff's men of Buckinghamshire'. However:

---

3   Stuart Peachey, *The Edgehill Campaign and the Letters of Nehemiah Wharton* (Leigh-on-Sea: Partizan Press, 1989), p. 7.
4   TNA, SP28/44, f. 62r.; SP28/4, ff. 359r., 361v.; SP28/5, ff. 115r., 204v.–206v., 334r., 340v., 452r.; SP28/7, ff. 92r.–v., 452r.
5   *CSPD 1642*, p. 367.

> Captain Wilson hearing that they were coming drew up his men into a broad place in the rode that so they might have room to pass by his troop; and passing on further he drew up his men in battalia in a great cornfield on this side [of] Wendover, and so exercised his men on horseback, to see how his men could do execution on horseback if they should be set upon in a place that might be disadvantageous to them on foot; at last, having exercised his men, and hearing the other companies and the ordnance were coming he set forward towards Aylesbury, and half a mile on this side the town made a stand, that so all four companies might march into the town together, where they were received with much acclamation. Colonel Browne's dragoons coming about two hours after, there being no room in the town, they were constrained to go further to lodge themselves.[6]

Two days later, Captain Lee's dragoons continued to Amersham, where they guarded a wagon containing money en route to Aylesbury. Similarly, Captain Mason's company marched to Missenden, upon which they searched the property of a suspected delinquent.

Parliament had recognised that the town of Aylesbury required defending. Colonel Henry Bulstrode was authorised on 21 October 1642 'to raise all the forces within the 3 hundreds of Chiltern'. On 12 November, he was appointed governor of Aylesbury, with additional command of the local trained bands. Ten days later, he mustered the new regiment in Aylesbury.[7] Moreover, the Parliamentary committee there had been established 'for the better managing of the affairs of the county of Buckinghamshire, the more effectual execution of the orders and ordinances of Parliament, and the better paying of soldiers belonging to the garrison of Aylesbury'. It was also responsible to the treasurer of Buckinghamshire, 'unto whom all money collected in the said county, also the money allowed out of any other counties for the maintenance of the said garrison, shall be paid and delivered'. In efforts to reinforce the garrison, Bulstrode alerted Wharton with his concerns that the town could not be held against a Royalist attack. Wharton had commanded a foot regiment that had absconded at Edgehill and was disbanded in November 1642. On 30 October 1642, he informed Bulstrode:

> It grieves my heart that your county should be put into such great distraction. My lords have considered of your letter, and are very desirous to do anything for the preservation of your county. They conceive it most of the service of the county and the safety of yourselves, and the forces now raised, that you retire a little nearer to Uxbridge, which is appointed to be the rendezvous for a convoy of great strength, to be sent down with diverse things to my Lord Essex, in which if you think good to fall in, and to join unto my Lord Essex his army, the State will entertain you, and allow such pay as all other officers and soldiers have.

From the governor of Aylesbury's perspective, this could not have been particularly heartening.

---

6   *True Relation of the late proceedings of the London Dragoneers.* TT, E118[39].
7   *LJ*, VII, pp. 696, 700.

Nevertheless, Colonel John Hampden, a Buckinghamshire gentleman who had raised and led a regiment from the county in the Earl of Essex's army during the Edgehill Campaign, wrote from Northampton on 31 October in a more encouraging fashion, 'to my noble friends, Colonel Bulstrode, Captain Grenville, Captain Tyrrell, Captain West, or any of them: Gents, the army is now at Northampton, moving every day nearer to you. If you disband not, we may be a mutual succor to each other, but if you do disperse, you make yourselves and your country a prey'. The next day, Hampden added:

> We cannot be ready to march till tomorrow, and then, I believe, we shall. I desire you will be pleased to send to me again, as soon as you can, to the army, that we may know what posture you are in, and when you will hear which way we go. You may do me a favour to certify me what you may hear of the King's forces, for I believe your intelligence is better from Oxford and those parts as ours can be.[8]

On 1 November 1642, a skirmish or minor military action occurred at Aylesbury, in which part of Hampden's regiment of foot, Colonel Thomas Grantham's regiment, and six troops of Parliamentarian cavalry under the command of Sir William Balfour, the Earl of Essex's lieutenant general of the horse, participated. Aylesbury's garrison had been temporarily moved to a location from which to screen the main force, thereby leaving the town exposed to enemy occupation and plundering by a substantial Royalist raiding party. Although the sequence of events, outcome, and importance of the encounter has been the subject of debate, the only contemporary account of the alleged battle is the somewhat biased and propagandist Parliamentarian newsbook *Good and Joyfull Newes Out of Buckinghamshire, being a True and Exact Relation*.[9] A second account, produced on 19 December 1642 and entitled *Abingtons and Alisburies Present Miseries*, contains much less hyperbole and a more accurate view of events, yet, nevertheless, the writer highlights various Royalist atrocities, both within the town and elsewhere.[10] Given the possibility that both narratives relate to the same event, there are disparities in the numbers on each side and the levels of plundering within the town of Aylesbury.

The writer of *Good and Joyfull Newes* related that:

> the next morning their horse drew towards us, almost within cannon shot, and we expected every hour when they would fall upon the town, and our horse drew into the field towards them, and the forlorn hopes fire 1 upon the other, but they being much too strong in horse for us, we drew our horse into the town, preparing for their assault, but whilst we looked for their approach, they drew away towards evening on Tuesday.

---

8 George Nugent, *Some Memorials of John Hampden, His Party and His Times* (London: Chapman and Hall, 1854), pp. 306–07.
9 *Good and Joyfull Newes Out of Buckinghamshire, being a True and Exact Relation etc.* (London: Francis Wright, 1642). TT, E126[99].
10 *Abingtons and Alisburies Present Miseries etc.* (London: Rich Herne, 1642). TT, E128[33].

Once they got into Aylesbury, however, the Royalists reportedly pillaged the town and 'spoiled and tore into pieces the inside of divers fair houses, and besides the corn they spent upon their horses, they spoiled and split upon the ground, and threw it about the fields, and what goods they could not carry away, they cut in pieces, and threw about the fields and highways as they went'. According to the second account, 1,000 cavalry under Wilmot reached Aylesbury, where they accommodated themselves in 'the best inns and houses of quality'. It was also contended that these unwanted guests were received by the townspeople only through fear of retaliation. Moreover, upon hearing of the presence of the Royalists, the local trained bandsmen rushed to the town's defence from the adjacent countryside. Some 600 Royalist cavalry subsequently retreated, leaving another 400 surrounded in the marketplace, where they were 'assaulted so hotly that they tumbled above a score of their horses'.

In December 1642, Lord Wentworth led a considerable Royalist mounted force through Thame, to strike at Aylesbury. But, finding the place strongly fortified by batteries to the north and west, and a redoubt, and not wanting to engage in a siege, he withdrew to Wycombe, where heavy fighting followed.[11] During the first week of January 1643, a newsbook reported, 'From Aylesbury in Buckinghamshire it is informed that the town is very strongly fortified, and that there is 6 pieces of ordinance and a strong garrison of men, Colonel Bulstrode, his regiment and some other forces being there'.[12] These troops were confident enough to reconnoitre enemy outposts around Oxford. Colonel Arthur Goodwin, commander of a cavalry regiment in the Earl of Essex's army and who had seen action at Brentford and Turnham Green, was appointed as commander-in-chief of Buckinghamshire in January 1643. He undertook a night assault on Piddington on 17 January and:

> with his troop of horse in Buckinghamshire had taken a troop of horse of the King's, being the second troop that the King had at a small town within 2 or 3 miles of Brill in that county, and that without any loss, falling upon them in the night and took the whole troop, being 60 horse with their riders and arms, and all the officers belonging to the said troop, except the captain, who went the day before to Oxford to the King.[13]

The closest Parliamentarian garrison to Brill was at Aylesbury, and it was here that Goodwin concentrated the infantry regiments of Colonels Henry Bulstrode, John Holmstead, and Thomas Tyrell, in addition to his own regiment of horse and Colonel John Browne's dragoons. He was determined to eradicate Royalist opposition in the area and left Aylesbury in late January 1643 with his own horse, Homestead's foot, and Browne's dragoon regiment. These arrived before the village of Brill on 27 January; however, Goodwin's

---

11 *A Glorious and Happy Victory obtained by the Volunteers of Buckingham, Bedford, Hariford, Cambridge, Huntingdon and Northamptonshire against Lord Wentworth nere Alesbury and Wickham* (London: I. H. and J. Wright, 1642). TT, E129[17].
12 *Perfect diurnall*, 2–9 January 1643. TT, E240[14].
13 *Perfect diurnall*, 16–23 January 1643. TT, E240[21].

attack failed to make adequate progress against the stout fortifications put up by the garrison. One source reported:

> The fight continued 2 hours, the Parliament's forces not giving way on one side in all that time, but at last the wind, and so the smoke being so in the face of them, which was made greater by wet straw which the enemy set on fire, they retreated, which the enemy perceiving made out after them in great triumph, pursuing them 4 miles with their horse.[14]

The King had reinforced the garrison the day before the attack, and Colonel John Hampden had been unable, due to the poor condition of the roads, to bring up more artillery than two sakers. Tellingly also, on 9 February, Essex wrote to Goodwin, 'I have received letters from Aylesbury … importing Prince Rupert's arrival at Brill the last night which I much doubt, but that which most troubles me is that they write that they are not able to defend the garrison alone 1 day'.[15]

Another important Royalist garrison in Buckinghamshire was located at Boarstall House, some 12 miles to the west of Aylesbury and 26 miles from Oxford. Fortified in late 1643 to protect the King's headquarters at Oxford, it was, however, evacuated during the following April–May when the Royalists decided to abandon Reading and other outward garrisons. The Parliamentarian forces, including, in 1646, the New Model Army, were evidently frustrated by the Boarstall garrison. Sir Thomas Fairfax, the New Model's commander-in-chief, was urged by the Committee of Both Kingdoms on 4 May:

> although it be but a very small thing, hath yet much infested the country, both by levying contribution and by plunder, wherein they have been more than ordinarily active. We therefore recommend it to you now while your forces are in those parts to take some effective course for the reducing of that garrison, whereby you will bring a very great ease to those parts which have long groaned under the oppression thereof.[16]

The garrison, effective at harassing enemy forces, also provided the King's regiments at Oxford with provisions, such as ammunition, when required.

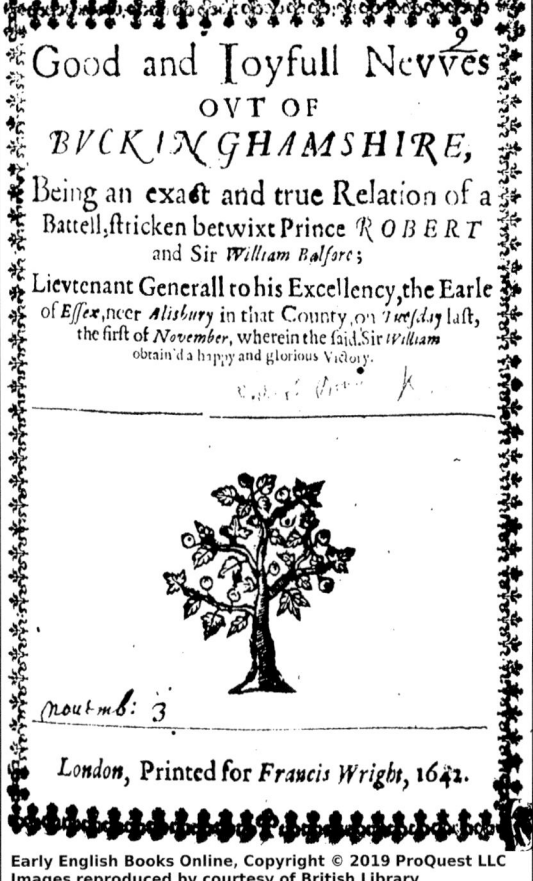

Good and Joyfull Newes Out of Buckinghamshire. TT, E126[99]

---

14 *The Latest Intelligence of Prince Rupert's Proceedings in Northamptonshire and Also Colonel Goodwin's at Brill* (London: Publisher unknown, 1643). TT, E88[3].
15 Bodl. Lib., Ms Carte 103, f. 100r.
16 *CSPD 1645–1647*, p. 432.

Clarendon thought the Boarstall garrison particularly effective, because it 'did very near support itself by the contribution it drew from Buckinghamshire, besides the prey it frequently took from the very neighbourhood of Aylesbury'.[17] On 12 March 1645, Sir Edward Nicholas wrote to the governor, Sir William Campion:

> Whereas we have daily occasion to use great quantity of tow, hemp, and flax, for the making of match, and understanding that the country which lies under command of your garrison, will yield considerable supplies of each kind, we do hereby require you forthwith to cause diligent inquiry to be made for all such hemp, flax, tow, and other materials fit for the making of match, as lies within your reach and power. And what you shall find remain in the custody of, or belonging either to well or ill-affected persons, to seize and take to our use, and to send ye same by a safe convoy to this our city of Oxford.

On 28 October 1644, Campion had been commissioned by the King as governor of Boarstall and authorised to take command 'of all the horse and foot belonging to the garrison at Borstall'. Likewise, Campion was informed by Charles I at Oxford on 14 December:

> for the better fortifying of Borstall House, that the church and other houses adjoining to the same should be pulled down. Our will and pleasure therefore is, and we do hereby require and authorise you to take down the said church, and all such houses as you shall conceive may prove prejudicial to the security of that our garrison. And we do further give you full power and authority to cut down such trees near the said garrison as you shall find needful for the making of palisades and other necessaries for the use and defence of the same. For the doing whereof, this shall be your sufficient warrant.[18]

The condition of the fortifications at Boarstall was noticed by Richard Symonds, who passed through the place on Thursday, 28 August 1645, on his way to Oxford. He recalled, 'This day we marched to Borstall House, belonging to the Lady Denhara. Sir William Campion is governor, there is a palisade, or rather a stockade, without the graff; a deep graff and wide, full of water; a palisade above the false bray another 6 or 7 feet above that, near the top of the curtain'.[19]

On 19 March 1643, the Royalist Sir John Culpeper, informed by his spies within Aylesbury, wrote to Prince Rupert from Oxford, describing the condition of the garrison:

> According to the intimation I received from your Highness I sent several spies into Aylesbury; the 1 of them brought me here the last night at 10 of the clock

---

17 Macray (ed.), *History of the Rebellion*, III, p. 361.
18 ESRO, DAN4/1/50; DAN4/1/38; DAN4/1/42.
19 Charles E. Long (ed.), *Diary of the Marches of the Royal Army during the Great Civil War; Kept by Richard Symonds*, Chetham Society, Old Series, 74 (Westminster: J. B. Nichols and Sons, 1859), p. 231.

this paper enclosed, which was sent from a very good hand in the town yesterday at 11 in the morning. If the tawny regiment should be in the town I presume the business will be full of difficulty. If your forces should fall upon them in their march or probably both the works (the breaking of them, and the reducing of the town) will be easy. But your Highness will best judge of these particulars near the place. I shall only presume to offer to you that if you look upon the town, a general offer of a pardon both to officers, soldiers and burgers, with the promise to the one of the continuance of their entertainment (upon security of their loyalty by taking the protestation) and to the other of security from plundering (upon fit expression of their affections by a sum of money) may much advance the work in hand, by freeing them from despair and dividing them amongst themselves.[20]

A few days later, a Parliamentarian deserter informed his captors that Aylesbury was manned only by a garrison of 700–800 men. On 13 March, a Royalist force from nearby Brill had advanced towards the town. Although the record is incomplete, such an estimate of the strength of the garrison appears to correlate with known aggregated figures. Colonel Henry Bulstrode's regiment was raised on 10 November 1642 as per its Establishment of 800 common soldiers, exclusive of commissioned and non-commissioned officers; on 12 December, the unit mustered 717 soldiers at Aylesbury, whereas 613 were present on 21 April 1644.[21] When Colonel Francis Martin's regiment entered the garrison in August 1643, it comprised 71 commissioned and non-commissioned officers and 130 private sentinels in six companies, in addition to the sum of £200 from Parliament with which to recruit the regiment.[22] The figures for Colonel Thomas Tyrell's regiment and other garrison troops, such as gunners and matrosses, are unknown.

Nevertheless, the Aylesbury garrison was quickly reinforced by troops from Wycombe and Beaconsfield, and any confrontation was avoided. But, soon afterwards, another incursion, supported by six heavy cannon, marched on Thame, causing all the Parliamentarian troops in the area to withdraw inside Aylesbury's fortifications.[23] The ensuing military operations were recounted at length by the senior military officers of the garrison – Colonels Henry Bulstrode, Arthur Goodwin, John Hampden, and Thomas Tyrrell – in *Two letters of great consequence to the House of Commons*, from which below is an extract:

We hold it convenient to give you a true relation of the passages concerning the King's forces, and their appearance against the town. On Saturday last they marched from Oxford and those parts, and on Monday all their forces were drawn near to this town, within 1 mile or 2 miles of the place, and showed as if they would have fallen upon us that day, but they spent that day in viewing the town, where to make their best assault, and interposing between us and the Chiltern parts of

---

20 F. G. Lee, 'A Letter of Sir John Culpeper to Prince Rupert, Informing Him of the State of the Aylesbury Garrison 1643', *Records of Buckinghamshire*, 3:3 (1864), pp. 99–101.
21 TNA, SP28/49/259, unf.
22 *CSPD 1644*, p. 132.
23 *Perfect diurnall*, 27 March–3 April 1643. TT, E247[9].

our country, to hinder their assistance to us, where we had several skirmishes without any loss ... on Monday night the whole forces quartered within a mile or 2 of this town, and the next morning drew towards us, almost within cannon shot, and the forlorn hopes fired 1 upon the other often, but they being much too strong in horse for us, we drew our horse into the town, preparing for their assault, but whilst we looked for their approach, they drew away towards evening on the Tuesday, and instead of soldiers they turned sheep stealers, for they have plundered all the towns hereabouts ...[24]

As elsewhere during the British Civil Wars, garrisoning a town necessitated more than military troops and fortifications. The long-term payment, victualling, and quartering of soldiers, in addition to exercising control over an area sufficiently extensive for foraging and taxation to support – in some cases – large quantities of men and animals, were vital. About the beginning of November 1642, Richard Grenville, sheriff of Buckinghamshire, deputy lieutenant, and member of the county committee, received the sum of £40, being:

> subscription money of several persons, upon the propositions of Parliament dated in June 1642, for bringing in of money, horse, arms, etc., which £40 I received of him towards the payment of soldiers then raising in the county, according to command received from the Parliament about this time, whereby the deputy lieutenants were commanded to raise 400 foot and 60 horse, and to pay them by such means as they should think fit.[25]

On 30 March 1643, the Buckinghamshire Committee informed the Commons that 'they did by virtue of the ordinance of both Houses, of 29 November, raised monies within that county monthly for the pay of the county soldiers within the garrison of Aylesbury, and have for the making of fortifications there', apportioning £200 from the county's weekly assessment of £425 to maintain both the soldiers and the town's defences.[26] Frequent military operations and raids in the Buckinghamshire area, however, kept the Aylesbury garrison on constant alert.

During the evening of 17 June 1643, Prince Rupert led a raiding force comprising 1,000 horse, 500 dragoons, and 500 foot from Oxford with the aim of intercepting a Parliamentarian convoy and generally harassed any enemy outposts to the southeast of Oxford. In the early hours of the following day, Rupert's forces overran some enemy quarters at Postcombe and Chinnor, and, in the ensuing struggle, the Parliamentarian troops were overwhelmed, losing around 200 casualties. According to *A True Relation of a Great Fight Between the Kings Forces and the Parliaments, at Chinner neer Tame on Saturday last*:

---

24 *Two letters of great consequence to the House of Commons: the one from Alisbury in Buckinghamshire, dated March 22. 1642. and signed by Col: Arthur Goodwyn: Col: Bulstrode: Col: Hampden: Tho: Terrill: Esq; the other from Sir William Brereton to a member of the House of Commons* (London: Edw. Husbands, 1642). TT, E94[2].
25 TNA, SP28/149/2, f. 145v.
26 *CJ*, III, p. 24; *LJ*, V, p. 719.

Robert Devereux, Earl of Essex, Captain-General and Chief Commander of the Parliamentarian army (1591-1646)

> Within lay some 200 dragoons of Sir Samuel Luke's Bedfordshire regiment, under their Sergeant Major Edwards. These, though, but new levied men, yet had already actually appeared in rebellion as being of that strong party, which the day before had marched out against Islip … Almost all their horses and arms were taken, with three of Sir Samuel Luke's dragoon cornets. Their field or ground was black, with one, two, three, four, or five bibles, bossed and buffed, depainted in them.[27]

The Parliamentarian reaction to the raid was swift. As Essex's letter from Thame to the Speaker of the House of Commons – written on 19 June, partly to disguise the extent of the subsequent Parliamentarian setback at Chalgrove – details:

> Sir Philip Stapleton, who had the watch here that night at Thame, when he discovered the fire there, to know the occasion of it, he likewise sent one troop of dragoons under the command of Captain Dundas, who came up to them. There were likewise some few of Colonel Melve's dragoons that came up to them: at length our men pressed them so near, that being in a large pasture ground they drew up, and notwithstanding the inequality of the numbers, we not having above 300 Horse, our men charged them very gallantly, and slew divers of them; but while they were in fight, the enemy being so very strong, kept a body of Horse for his reserve, and with that body wheeled about and charged our men in the rear, so that being encompassed and overborne with multitude, they broke and fled, though it was not very far.

The primary Royalist account of the fight, generally thought to have been written by Prince Rupert's engineer, Bernard de Gomme, provides a detailed picture of events and, in particular, the deployment of dragoons:

> His Highness was now making halt in Chalgrove cornfield, about a mile and a half short of Chiselhampton Bridge. Just at this time (being now about nine o'clock) we discerned several great bodies of the rebels' Horse and dragoons, coming down Golder Hill towards us from Easington and Tame, who (together with those that had before skirmished with our rear) drew down to the bottom of a great close, or pasture, ordering themselves there among the trees beyond a great hedge, which parted that close from our field … [There] marched some 350 under my Lord Wentworth, their sergeant-major-general, drawn altogether out of his lordship's own troop, Prince Rupert's regiment, commanded by Colonel Innes, Sir Robert Howard's and Colonel Washington's regiments … the van of this great party was a lesser party commanded by Sergeant-Major Legge, made up of the Prince of Wales his regiment, under Lieutenant Colonel Lisle. These marched like a forlorn hope, a distance before the greater party.[28]

---

27 *A True Relation of a Great Fight Between the Kings Forces and the Parliaments, at Chinner neer Tame on Saturday last* (London: B. A., 1643). TT, E55[11].
28 *His Highnesse Prince Ruperts Late Beating up the Rebels Quarters At Post-comb and Chinner in Oxfordshire. And his Victory in Chalgrove Field, on Sunday morning June 18, 1643* (Oxford: Leonard Lichfield, 1643).

Table 6 Payments for the Maintenance and Quartering of the Garrison of Aylesbury, 1646 (TNA, SP28/126/1, ff. 157v.–187v.)

	£	s.	d.
Paid to Sergeant Major Egleton for himself, officers, and soldiers of Colonel Bulstrode's regiment according to a muster taken 27 [no month given] instant	425	17	2
Paid to the gunners and matrosses belonging to the garrison of Aylesbury according to a muster taken 27 [no month given] instant	28	14	0
Paid to John Kemp for 3 weeks' pay due to Robert Booth for looking to the magazine of wood in Aylesbury and for other duties	1	3	0
Paid to Edward Hargood for ironwork for the use of the garrison of Aylesbury	1	1	7
Paid to Mr Cooke, minister of Hardwick for quartering Captain Wray and his soldiers	1	11	0
Paid to John Millett in full for 4 weeks' pay	1	0	0
Paid to Walter Huntley, Robert Woodley and Richard Ireland for the inhabitants of Hambleden for quartering Captain Robert Aldridge's soldiers	70	0	0
Paid to the inhabitants of Halton for quartering soldiers belonging to the garrison of Aylesbury, and for the carriage of wood to the garrison	63	1	6
Paid to the inhabitants of Lane End for quartering soldiers belonging to the garrison of Aylesbury, and for the carriage of wood to the garrison	7	13	6
Paid to the inhabitants of Wichendon for quartering Sergeant Major Shilbourne's soldiers	2	9	6
Paid to Richard Heywood for candles for the garrison	26	7	9
Paid to Captain Edmund Phipps in part of £907 3s. 6d. due to him and his troopers for victuals for the use of the troop	122	5	9
Paid to Captain Phipps which he paid formerly for 14 horses for his troop	35	0	0
Paid to Captain Phipps for pay for his troop	123	0	0
Paid to George Forty for the inhabitants of Wotton Underwood for hay and provender for Sergeant Major Shilbourne's troop, and for 12 days' work at the fortifications at Brill, and for spades and shovels sent thither	13	17	11
Paid to Sergeant Major Egleton in full for 24 days' pay for himself, and the officers and soldiers of Colonel Bulstrode's regiment, together with the mayor of the town, according to a muster taken 11 July 1646 instant	422	19	6
Paid to Robert Jackman, gunsmith, for mending and dressing of Colonel Bulstrode's soldiers' arms	1	0	1
Paid to Thomas Shilbourne's man for cleaning the drawbridge of the garrison of Aylesbury for 4 weeks	0	8	0
Paid to Captain-Lieutenant Aldridge for 7 days' pay for himself, 1 sergeant, 3 corporals and 27 soldiers which guarded the magazine and artillery of the garrison	9	5	6
Paid to Silvester Whitnall, trumpeter to Sergeant Major Shilbourne's troop in full for 4 weeks' pay	4	4	0
Paid to Ensign Francis Russell for 7 weeks' pay for himself, officers and soldiers which were at Boarstall House	45	5	0
Paid to Sergeant Major Shilbourne in full, with £124 1s. 8d. for 47 horse bridles and saddles of the State, and pay for his troop	716	5	3
Paid in full for 14 days' pay for the officers and soldiers of Colonel Bulstrode's regiment	487	16	11
Paid to Matthew Durer, blacksmith, for shoeing and branding Sergeant Major Shilbourne's, Captain John Deverill's and Captain Phipps' troop horses	1	14	10

The journals of Sir Samuel Luke record that, during August 1643, the Royalists vigorously recruited dragoons and appropriated horses within four miles of Aylesbury, and, probably because of this and more generally continuing dangers, on 13 September, the garrison was granted the weekly payment of £600 from the Buckinghamshire, Hertfordshire, and Bedfordshire assessments for its maintenance. Some weeks later, the sum of £1,000 was allotted out of sequestration revenues to pay the soldiers.[29]

---

29 Tibbutt (ed.), *Letter Books*, pp. 132–34; *LJ*, III, p. 262.

Colonel Henry Bulstrode's Regiment of Foot

The original company commanders were:

> Colonel Henry Bulstrode – company under Captain Lieutenant Severinus Durfey
> Lieutenant Colonel Adam Cunningham
> Sergeant Major unknown or not appointed
> Captain Hall
> Captain Richard Fortescue (later sergeant major and lieutenant colonel, and colonel of a regiment of foot in the New Model Army)
> Captain Thomas Bulstrode
> Captain Hornigold
> Captain Kirtle
> Captain Ralph Williams.

Colonel Francis Martin's Regiment of Foot

The regiment was originally raised for service in Ireland by Colonel Thomas Ballard, before being transferred to the Earl of Essex's army. Ballard departed from the regiment in August 1643, and command passed to its lieutenant colonel, Francis Martin. In spring 1644, Martin and part of the regiment served in the garrison of Aylesbury until its disbandment in autumn or winter 1645–1646. This deployment led to major changes among the company officers, with all but the new colonel himself largely being replaced with officers from Colonel George Langham's regiment.

Company commanders were:

> Colonel Francis Martin
> Lieutenant Colonel Thomas Clark
> Sergeant Major Edward Hooke
> Captain John Collingwood
> Captain William Harrison
> Captain Edward Huson
> Captain Henry Langham
> Captain John Wheatley.

Colonel Thomas Tyrell's Regiment of Foot

Tyrell acted as treasurer at Aylesbury in 1642 to early 1643, and, by 5 July 1643, he took command of Colonel John Hampden's Buckinghamshire regiment of foot in Essex's army. A pay warrant of 7 December 1643 refers to 'Colonel Thomas Tyrell, colonel of the green regiment late of Colonel Hampden', the 'green' probably denoting the colour of its standards.[30] Tyrell appears to have

---

30 TNA, SP28/11, f. 261r.

exercised command of both this regiment and a smaller unit at Aylesbury until at least May 1644, when the lieutenant colonel of his garrison regiment, John Mosely, became the sergeant major of the former regiment of Hampden. In the accounts submitted by Tyrell to the Buckinghamshire County Committee in 1646, he excluded his command in Essex's army and accounted merely for his disbursements in that county. Hence, he claimed pay as colonel from 7 April 1643 to late May 1644 in a garrison regiment at Aylesbury. Evidently, the regiment was recruited in Aylesbury, possibly as a new, or partially new, unit raised from various local units, such as Bulstrode's pre-existing regiment in the garrison. Furthermore, Tyrell included payments 'to the country [*recte* county] captains, being Captain Mosely, Captain Deverell, Captain Theed, Captain Smith, and Captain Field'.[31]

Company commanders were:

Colonel Thomas Tyrell
Lieutenant Colonel John Mosely
Captain John Topcliffe
Captain Thomas Hartley
Captain Mosely
Captain Deverell
Captain Theed
Captain Smith
Captain Field.

Sir John Wittrough's Regiment of Foot

Commanded in the field by Lieutenant Colonel Thomas Sadler, the regiment was raised in Herefordshire. It served at the siege of Reading as part of the Earl of Essex's forces in April 1643, before joining the Aylesbury garrison the following month, and was there until at least January 1644. In February 1645, it was reduced into Colonel Thomas Ayloffe's regiment.

Colonel Arthur Goodwin's Regiment of Horse

Goodwin was MP for Buckinghamshire, where his regiment was raised in 1642. As part of the Earl of Essex's army, it served in various operations, including Edgehill, the sieges of Reading and Gloucester, and the First Battle of Newbury. The unit was disbanded in May 1643, on Goodwin's death.

Troop commanders in October 1642 were:

Colonel Arthur Goodwin
Sergeant Major Sigismund Alexander
Captain Rovery Vivers

---

31   TNA, SP28/127/7, ff. 65r.–67v.

Captain Thomas Sanders
Captain Richard Grenville
Captain Philip, Lord Wharton.

Dragoons

When Colonel Edward Aldrich acted as Parliamentarian governor of Aylesbury between August 1643 and May 1644, the garrison possessed a small number of both horse and dragoons under his command. One such unit was the dragoon company of Captain Edmund Phipps, who commanded the unit from 3 August 1643 to 13 May 1644. On 16 November 1643, 59 dragoons and 10 commissioned and non-commissioned officers mustered for duty.[32]

The continued vulnerability of the Aylesbury garrison was illustrated in January 1644, when Royalist attack plans to seize it were uncovered. This led to the governor, Colonel Martin, being financially rewarded by Parliament and the arrears of his troops' being paid. Moreover, on 29 January, the Lord Admiral ordered five cannon, 20 barrels of powder, and 300 shot to be delivered to Aylesbury from the Ordnance Office stores in London.[33] Even so, further pay shortages afflicted the garrison. In March 1644, £3,000 was provided by the Court of Wards and Liveries, whilst a Parliamentary committee discussed how to raise a further £1,000. On 25 April, Sir Henry Mildmay, commissioner for militia for Middlesex and for assessment for Essex, was ordered to facilitate enough money to enable the garrison of Aylesbury to march out to rendezvous with the Earl of Essex's expedition to the West. However, a few weeks later, it was reported to the Lord General that 'most of the soldiers of the garrison of Aylesbury have deserted it, and to desire to take some speedy course for the safety and preservation of that town'. In response to this crisis, the sum of £1,250 was ordered to be supplied to the garrison, and, on 6 May 1644, the treasurer of the Bedfordshire County Committee was directed to forward an additional £1,500 to the Aylesbury soldiers.[34] On 25 May, the Committee of Both Kingdoms wrote to Essex, warning him that 'Colonel Martin's regiment at Aylesbury is in so great want of pay that they are like to disband, which regiment being with the Establishment of his Excellency's army, they thought fit to represent this to him, and that the Town of Aylesbury, in the absence of their governor, is in great disorder'.[35]

On 19 June 1644, Sir Walter Earle, the lieutenant general of the Ordnance, was ordered to issue 30 barrels of powder to Aylesbury, and, the next day, it was ordered that Colonel Martin should receive £300 for pay for his officers, soldiers, and gunners. But external military dangers remained, because, on 4 April, Sir Samuel Luke reported, 'I hear the enemy is abroad and fell into Aylesbury horse quarters yesterday with 200 horse'. Similarly, on 26 June,

---

32 TNA, SP28/253A, f. 106v.; SP28/266/1, f. 73r.
33 *CJ*, III, pp. 378–79.
34 *CJ*, III, pp. 469, 477, 481.
35 *CSPD 1644*, p. 168.

Major General Richard Browne informed the Committee of Both Kingdoms, 'I received intelligence from 2 of the Hertfordshire Committee from their scouts, that the enemy sat before Aylesbury and were playing with their guns upon it'.[36] At the end of May, Martin again requested Parliament to supply weapons and ammunition to the garrison. This appeal appears to have received a favourable response, for, on 6 June, the Commons ordered the delivery of 20 barrels of powder, 200 pikes, 400 muskets, and 400 swords to Aylesbury from the public stores.[37] Additionally, on 13 August 1644, Lieutenant Colonel Owen Rowe, one of the chief agents for the Committee of Safety and supplier of arms and ammunition to the Earl of Essex's army, in addition to other forces, distributed collars of 400 bandoliers 'for the service of Aylesbury' out of the Ordnance Office stores.[38]

Nonetheless, despite such receipts of military equipment, the ill-disciplined behaviour of the garrison continued and ultimately led to the dismissal of the governor on 11 November 1644, to be replaced first by Colonel Charles Fleetwood – commander of a regiment of horse in the Eastern Association army and later a cavalry officer in the New Model Army – and then by Colonel Thomas Bulstrode. Reporting upon the change of governors and the general situation at Aylesbury, on 21 January 1645, the Royalist governor of Boarstall, Colonel William Campion, wrote to Prince Rupert:

> Sir, I have certain intelligence that Martin is put out of Aylesbury and a Scotchman is in his place, whose name I cannot yet learn. He is come with Manchester's horse, of which a troop is quartered at Wadsdon, another at Quainton, and 2 more at Upper Winchington, the other at Nether Winchington, the rest I understand lie backward near Aylesbury, your Highness shall hear more from me very suddenly. I humbly desire that those things necessary for this garrison which were granted mee might not be longer detained for if this weather hold I shall expect a storm, which if it happen I hope to give a good accompt, as far as can be expected from so slender a proportion of ammunition and shall ever remain, your most faithful servant.[39]

The 'Scotchman' in question was Sergeant Major General Lawrence Crawford, who also commanded a regiment of foot in Essex's army; he was appointed governor in December 1644 and was replaced by Colonel Francis Martin in the following February.[40]

On 24 September 1645, the Committee of Both Kingdoms wrote to Major General Richard Browne, 'Being informed that there is like to be some disorder at Aylesbury betwixt the 2 regiments of Colonel Martin and Colonel Fleetwood, which may prove dangerous if not speedily prevented, we desire you to go thither in person and take care for preventing of further danger

---

36 Tibbutt (ed.), *Letter Books*, p. 230; *CSPD 1644*, p. 279.
37 *CJ*, III, p. 545; IV, p. 165.
38 TNA, WO55/1646, unf.; *CSPD 1644*, p. 422.
39 BL, Ms Add. 18982, f. 20r.
40 *LJ*, VII, p. 692.

that might otherwise fall upon that town through their dissension'. Troops from the Aylesbury garrison continued to assist in military operations in the greater area of Buckinghamshire and its borders. For instance, in October 1645, 200 soldiers were sent to the siege of Basing House, whereas Colonel Martin's infantry regiment was 'appointed with other forces for the reduction of Donnington Castle'; Colonel Fleetwood was thus ordered to take his own regiment and 'in their absence to take care of the security of Aylesbury garrison'.[41] On 31 January 1646, martial law was proclaimed in the town, while, in June, the Commons received a petition from the residents of Aylesbury complaining about the soldiers' poor conduct. Although Parliament commanded the dismantling of the town's fortifications and the demobilisation of the garrison on 11 June, the same issues persisted, because, two months later, a further order was given that those garrison soldiers who were not willing to go to Ireland should be disbanded.[42]

Despite the numerous documentary references to the garrison of Aylesbury's pay, equipment, personnel, and military activities during its lengthy occupation of the town, few refer to the type and location of fortifications.

Table 7 Payments Due for Work on the Fortifications of the Garrison of Aylesbury, April–July 1646 (TNA, SP28/126/1; SP28/221)

	£	s.	d.
To William Delafield to pay the soldiers and other workmen employed in repairing of the works of the garrison of Aylesbury	29	4	3
To William Delafield, gunner, by the appointment of Edward Withers, gentleman of ordinance in the garrison of Aylesbury in full of 14 days' pay for himself, gunners, and matrosses in the said garrison	37	2	0
To William Delafield in full of 14 days' pay for the gentleman, ordinance gunners, and matrosses in the said garrison	28	14	0
To William Delafield for to pay the soldiers and other workmen employed in repairing of the works of the garrison of Aylesbury	32	18	7
For carts and teams that worked at the fortifications, 19 days at 4s. a day	3	16	0
Due to Henry North for making of 11½ poles [pole = five-and-a-half yards or approximately five metres] of the parapet in the new battery [fortified earthwork for artillery] at 10s. a pole	5	15	0
Due to Thomas Alinson for making of 4½ poles of the parapet next to the Friarage battery and finding carts himself is to have 15s. a pole	3	7	6
Due to William Rutland for enlarging the graff [ditch or trench] round the Friarage battery, 17½ poles at 7s. 6d. pole	6	10	9
Due to Frances Parnes the younger for 3 days' work at 10d. a day for 5 days that his men worked with him for 10d. a day	0	6	8
Due to Thomas Whittaker for intrenching of 7½ poles in the graff next to Oxford Gate at 14s. the pole	5	5	0
Due unto 2 men for filling of cart 20 days at 18d. a day	0	15	8
Due to Thomas Alinson for making up of a breach at Walton turnpike [moveable spiked barriers across a road as a defence, mainly against attacks by horsemen]	0	4	0
Due to John Swaine for work done in the graft and upon the parapet next to Bierton battery 9½ poles at 11s. the pole	5	4	6
Due to William Delafield for 20 days' work at 12d. a day	0	0	0

---

41 *CSPD 1645–1647*, pp. 157, 204–05.
42 *CJ*, IV, pp. 423, 573, 615, 633.

	£	s.	d.
Witness my hand William Delafield, overseer of the fortifications of this garrison	32	18	1
2 July 1646	15	16	8
16 October 1646 To William Delafield which he paid towards the dismantling of the garrison of Aylesbury and other charges			

Table 8 Contributions from the Parish of Haddenham, Buckinghamshire, to the Garrison of Aylesbury (BA, D159/35)

A copy of the names of the receivers and collectors of any monies, horses, arms, ammunition, household stuff, and free quarters; and also an account of such warrants orders and commands as have been issued into our liberties by several persons in the service of the state							
Money lent by divers men of our parish according to a warrant sent from his excellently the Earl of Essex at Thame in the county of Oxon:							
	£	s.	d.		£	s.	d.
Thomas Rose	4	0	0	Richard Slater	5	0	0
Edward Rose	5	0	0	Thomas Greenwood	6	0	0
Leonard Fitch	4	0	0	Richard Rayner	2	0	0
James Franklin	3	0	0	Thomas Chapman	6	0	0
& spent in gross by ticket	4	0	0	Richard Brayngwin	5	0	0
John Barnard	5	0	0	Thomas Clark	5	0	0
George Franklin	4	0	0				
The names of the treasurers, receivers and collectors of those sums of money above written: John Lockey, John Fenton, William Skinner, Thomas Hammond, Charles Fleetwood, Richard Gardiner, John Harrison, Richard Bond and Thomas Jackson.							
Money horses, arms, and other things upon the first Propositions, and the 5th and 20th parts by sundry warrants and paid to the garrison at Aylesbury:							
Thomas Rose	15	0	0	Richard Greenwood	7	0	0
Edward Rose	20	0	0	Richard Slater	9	0	0
Leonard Fitch	5	0	0	George Hollyman	5	0	0
Thomas Very	2	0	0	William Mores	3	0	0
James Franklin	5	0	0	Thomas Chapman	44	0	0
John Barnard	2	0	0	William Nichols	2	10	0
Thomas and John Rose	5	0	0	Thomas Simms	8	0	0
George Franklin	4	10	0	Thomas Clark	6	0	0
Richard Braynwgin	10	0	0	A grey mare listed by Colonel Tyrrell	12	0	0
And his grey gelding listed by Colonel Thomas Tyrrell	20	0	0	And 2 horses more aforesaid to pay to have them again	16	0	0
John Marriot	15	0	0	John Cox	10	0	0
And a mare, Parliament's soldiers' prize	5	15	0	Henry Hill and Henry his son	7	0	0
The names of the treasurers, receivers and collectors of the last sums of money above written: Tho Sanders, knight late of Dinton; Thomas Westall, late of Kimble Magna; Joseph Seaton of Aylesbury; John Hodges, clerk to Thomas Scott, esquire, Richard Baldwin and Scott Baldwin, treasurers for the county; Thomas Tyrrell, sometime collector at Aylesbury; John Randolph, late of Crendon; Arthur Goodwin collector, late of Upper Winchendon and Richard Dalby, late of Normarson. And we also written will testify and make it appear, if it be demanded.							
Our monthly contribution that we paid for town only to Aylesbury, which is paid in money and returns	8	17	7				
Our monthly contribution was paid to Thomas Barnes as may appear by quittances for the first 5 months	74	14	4				
Our contribution has been ever since to Aylesbury is £8 17s. 7d. which has been paid in money and returns for the town only we received but little poundage Paid for the other 27 days £8 9s. 2d. besides returns for the farm and parish as it appears under the hand of Henry Goss bearing date 18 May 1646, which said Goss is Colonel Bulstrode's man, also for fees for the other 27 days 28s.	8	9	2				
What labourers and teams we sent to Aylesbury to work and carry turfs and hay by sundry warrants: 1642 120 labourers 1643 24 teams to carry hay and 100 labourers; 1644: 2 teams to carry turfs 4 days, 20 teams to carry hay and 200 labourers; 1645: sent to Eythrope under warrant from Captain Phipps 12 labourers, 2 sawyers and 2 carpenters, and received nor paid some	21	10	4				

By warrants we sent 9 beds to Aylesbury for soldiers to lie on, worth in price	11	0	0
By request of the Committee at Aylesbury we the inhabitants of Haddenham did set forth 14 voluntary men with a month's pay and armes which charge was	30	0	0
Given to 9 volunteers that went forth with Mr Richard Ingoldsby then captain about 20s. a man	20	0	0
Taken from us by the Governor and Committee of Aylesbury all the trained armes we were charged with, all and divers other armes for the full value of	100	0	0
Armes for the full value of eaten up in grass when his Excellency the Earl of Essex laid in Thame by the state horses to the full value of	1	0	0
Richard Barnard the younger of Haddenham had 1 close of grass eaten up by the soldiers horses of Captain Phipps and Major Shelborne when they did not quarter in the town worth	7	0	0
By warrant under the hands of Thomas Bridges, lieutenant to Major Evens dated 30 June 30 1644 to bring to Dinton 2 quarters of oats or beans and 1 load of hay daily for his time being there and paid upon the same warrant 7 quarters and 2 bushels of oats and beans price	45	0	0
Quartered free quarter for June 1645 Captain Aldridge's troop near 60 men 60 horses 10 days and 10 nights at 1s. 6d. day and night	60	0	0
Quartered free quarter in September 1644 Captain Shelborne's troop near 80 men and 80 horses 10 days and 10 nights at 1s. 6d. day and night	12	0	0
Quartered free quarter in May 1644 Captain Phipps his troop near, 40 men and 40 horses 4 days and 4 nights at 1s. 6d. day and night	4	2	0
Day and night by warrant from the said Captain Phipps we carried to Ethrope to his quarters there so much provision of victuals which cost	4	2	0
So much provision of victuals which cost sent to Aylesbury upon warrant 5 dragoon horses which cost	12	0	0
By warrant under the hands of John Heale high constable dated 28 August 1643 paid to Henry Phillips of Aylesbury for raising great horses for the Earl of Manchester's regiment	14	0	0
Paid to Captain Phipps upon warrant to provide within our liberties 2 dragoon horses, bridles and saddles	8	0	0

Table 9 Composite of Abstracted Military Accounts of Captain Richard Grenville, 1642–1645 (TNA, SP28/149/2, ff. 144r.–158v.)

The account of Richard Grenville, esquire of divers sums of money which came unto his hands, as sheriff, deputy lieutenant, 1 of the committees of the said county			
	£	s.	d.
About 18 January 1642 I paid unto William Austen of Thame £1, and unto Edward Pearce of Wotton £1 for training and exercising the horse of the county. And about 24 May 1642 I paid to one Mr Cottesford, a Londoner who came down to discipline the foot, 40s. And about 17 June 1642 paid to Mr Cottesford 40s., to William Ansten 20s. In all paid	7	0	0
About the latter end of August, or beginning of September 1642, by the direction of Colonel Bulstrode and other deputy lieutenants then at Aylesbury, I paid unto Mr Pym of Brill £3 11s., which he had laid out upon a foot company of Reading men, who came as far as Brill, to have joined with the companies then raising in our county, and to have marched along with then to the army, if there had been occasion to use them, but they were sent back again	3	11	0
Laid out at several times in October and November 1642 upon messengers and scouts upon several occasions happening by reason of these troubles, and for sending one scout to Kineton the night after the battle was fought	2	3	0
About the latter encl of October I paid unto Thomas Frere (by the hands of Joseph Sexton) £40 to be by him disposed of about the magazine) for which he is to account	40	0	0
About 25 October 1642 paid by direction of the deputy lieutenants unto Captain Francis Ingoldsby £20, unto Captain George Fleetwood £20, unto Captain Thomas Bulstrode £20, unto Captain Edmund West £20, unto Captain Thomas Lane £20, and unto Captain Christopher Egleton £20, for which I have acquittances. In all paid to the captains abovenamed	120	0	0
About the middle of November 1642 paid unto Colonel Henry Bulstrode £20 toward the pay of his company, he being then in London	20	0	0
About 21 November 1642 paid to John Chandler, 1 of Captain Francis Ingoldsby's officers, at the desire of Colonel Bulstrode and Mr Tyrrell	2	0	0

About 14 November 1642 being commanded by his Excellency the Lord General to take the horses which were of Captain Ingoldsby's troop (he having given them over) and to deliver them at Moorfields for dragoon horses, I paid upon the receipt of them at the Bell, Whitehorse, etc, in Holborne, where they had stood for 7 or 8 days and nights, the sum of £13 1s. 4d., and from there carried them to Moorfields, and delivered them to Commissary Richardson, as appears by his acquittances for them. There were in number 64 horses, naggs and mares	13	1	4
About the same time, I paid to divers of Captain Ingoldsby's soldiers towards their pay due to them, they being to go back into the country, upon his leaving the troop, £5 0s. 8d.	5	0	8
About the time that Captain Shelbourne and Captain Abercrombie were taken prisoners, there was brought to Aylesbury some moneys which they had collected in the county (of weekly assessment of horse money as I take it) which money was put into the hands of Sergeant Major Theed, and was afterward taken by Lieutenant Colonel Floyd for the pay of the garrison to be repaid out of the £3,000 ordered for the garrison in the beginning of March 1644 out of the Court of Wards	253	0	0
This £20 was paid to me, to the intent that I should therewith have bought swords for my troop, and accordingly I bespoke swords of a cutler by Charing Cross and left with him 22s. in earnest. But afterwards being provided of swords by warrant from his Excellency, I paid this £20 to Thomas Tyrrell, who then received the monies (and was as treasurer for Aylesbury) as appears by his acquittance of 16 October 1642	20	0	0
By warrant from his Excellency the Earl of Essex dated about 15 May 1644, I was commanded to pay the 1 half of this money, viz. £126 10s. to Captain Abercrombie for the recruit of his troop, which money I paid accordingly and have his acquittances for it. The other moiety, viz. £126 10s I retained toward the recruit of my own troop, being directed so to do by the warrant abovementioned. And you shall find it accounted for in the account of my troop	126	10	0
The account of Captain Richard Grenville, captain of a troop of harquebusiers, of the monies due to him for his said troop. This troop was in the regiment of Colonel Arthur Goodwin			
Due to me as captain of the said troop of harquebusiers from the 30 July 1642 inclusive, the date of my commission, to 28 March 1645 inclusive on which day I delivered over the troop to Captain John James, being 972 days, at 39s. per day, which amounts to	1895	0	0
Due to me for mounting myself and providing myself with arms	140	0	0
Due to me which I paid to Carlo Fanthom, lieutenant of the said troop for his mounting money	60	0	0
Due to me which I paid to Cornet John James for the like	50	0	0
Due to me which I paid to Quartermaster Alexander Davison the like	30	0	0
Due to me which I paid for mounting money to officers not in commission, viz:			
to Symeon Pister corporal	14	0	0
to Roger Gregory corporal	14	0	0
to John Robinson corporal	14	0	0
to Thomas Symons trumpeter, besides his horse and trumpet	10	0	0
to Nicholas Pepperell trumpeter, besides his horse and trumpet	10	0	0
to Richard Thornberry, farrier	8	0	0
to Robert Wrixon saddler	8	0	0
60 troopers each at 2s. 6d. per day	210	0	0
Due also to me which I paid for 60 scarfs for my 60 troopers, at 10s. for each scarf	30	0	0
Out of the £349 6s. received (upon a warrant to the treasurer of the army, or his deputy, dated about 16 August 1642) for 28 days' pay for my officers and 60 troopers, according to the muster taken 11 August 1642 at Aylesbury: Due to me which I paid to Colonel Arthur Goodwin towards a month's pay for the troops in his regiment, my own troop excepted	1200	0	0
The account of Captain Richard Grenville, captain of a troop of harquebusiers, in tile regiment of Colonel Arthur Goodwin in the army of the late Lord General the Earl of Essex, of money received by him for his troop			
In or about August 1642 I received for mounting or advance money for myself and officers in commission	280	0	0
Received upon a warrant dated about 22 August 1642 directed to the treasurer of the army or his deputy, for mounting my corporals, trumpeters, farrier, and saddler, and for scarfs	104	0	0
Received upon a warrant dated about 16 August 1642, of the treasurer of the army or his deputy, for 28 days' pay for the troop	349	6	0
Received in September 1642 of the Lord Saye, then at Aylesbury £1500 of which he directed me to pay £1,200 to Colonel Goodwin for the rest of the regiment and to certain £300 towards a months' pay for my own troop	1500	0	0

Received about 9 October 1642 of the treasurer at Worcester £49 6s. which made the £300 above mentioned to be a full months' pay for my own troop	4	9	6
Due to me which I paid for chests, cords, and a porter to pack up the 60 swords, received for the troop in August or September 1642, and for carrying them to the Waggoners Inn for carrying down the said 60 swords to my troop	3	0	0
Due unto me which I paid as follows, for carriage of the 20 cases of pistols, received 30 August 1642, and of the 10 cases received 2 September 1642, and of the 60 suits of arms also received out of the magazine, to the Carriers Inn, and for loading them	5	0	0
For carrying the said arms to Aylesbury	1	17	0
For carriage of 30 cases of pistols, received 27 September 1642 from the magazine, and carrying them to the Carriers Inn	3	6	0
For carriage of those pistols to Aylesbury, and sending them from thence to Worcester to my troop	1	7	0
For carriage of 15 carbines, about 4 January 1643 from the magazine to Aylesbury	4	6	0
For carriage of 30 cases of pistols about 23 January 1643 from the magazine to Aylesbury, for which Colonel Goodwin procured a warrant for my lieutenant, about 2 January		10	6
Paid also (by the hands of the said Gregory) the 6 saddles bought at Aylesbury	6	0	0
Paid also to William North for a saddle which Thomas Ballam had		15	0
Paid also for a saddle bought from John Haddinott of Wickham, which Thomas Lashbrooke had	1	10	0
Paid about 9 April 1643 for carriage of 10 cases of pistols and 15 carbines, from the magazine to the Waggoners Inn	2	10	0
For carrying the said pistols and carbines to the troop at Aylesbury		6	0
Due to me, which I paid Mr Webb of Uxbridge for keeping and curing a lame troop horse, which was left with him for 13 or 14 weeks	2	10	0
Due to me, which I paid to Mr Hussey of Henley for keeping and curing a lame horse, which was left with him for about 5 weeks	1	9	4
Received after my exchange and release from Oxford, viz: about February 1645 of my lieutenant, John James, £18 18s. for my personal pay for 14 days, according to the Establishment of pay by the ordinance of Parliament of 26 March 1644. The said Lieutenant John James, having received during my absence and imprisonment 14 days' pay for the troop, viz: at 1 time in August 1644 £87 13s. 6d. for 7 days' pay, according to the muster of 1 August 1644, and at another time £78 4s. 10d. for 7 days' pay, according to the muster of 4 November 1644. The residue he paid out among the other officers and troopers, and I have heard many of them confess the receipt of it	18	18	0
In February 1643 received of Mr Thomas Tyrrell, treasurer of Aylesbury, by order from Colonel Goodwin, for saddles and other necessaries for my troop	20	0	0
Due to me which I paid for 11 great saddles in June 1643, and for a pass to carry these saddles to the troop to the waggoner for carrying of them to the troop	11	1	0
Due to me which I paid (by the hands of William North) for 3 bridles and saddles in June 1643	2	0	0
Due to me which I paid to William Banks in October 1643 for 2 saddles and bridles	1	18	0
Due to me which I paid in January 1644 to Banks for 4 saddles and 5 bridles for the troop	3	10	8
Due to me which I laid out [in March 1644] for 6 pairs of holsters	1	6	0
And in May 1644 for 6 pairs of holsters	2	15	0

Amongst the military officers mentioned in the above accounts, Captain Jeremiah Abercrombie, a Scots professional officer, commanded a company of dragoons in the Earl of Essex's forces at the relief of Gloucester in 1643.[43] Moreover, during the Royalist encirclement of Essex's horse at Lostwithiel, Abercrombie's command – consisting of a lieutenant, a cornet, a quartermaster, three sergeants, three corporals, three drummers, and 64 dragoons – was almost wiped out whilst fighting a bitter rearguard action.[44]

---

43 TNA, SP28/5, ff. 205v.–206r; SP28/7; ff. 320r., 452r.
44 Sir Edward Walker, *Historical Discourses upon Several Occasions* (London: W. B., 1705), p. 64.

Described as being captured with Abercrombie was Cornelius Shelbourne, captain of another dragoon company in Essex's army, which had fought at the First Battle of Newbury the previous year.[45] Upon his release in May 1644, Captain Abercrombie received a commission from the Earl of Essex as captain of a troop of cavalry, to be attached to the Lord General's own regiment, and was paid the sum of £126 10s. 'for the recruit of his troop'. He was killed in action on 9 March 1645, and his command was reduced at Luton on 11 April, alongside Sergeant Major Robert Hamilton's cavalry troop of the same regiment.[46]

Captain Francis Ingoldsby, of Lenborough, Buckinghamshire, commanded a troop of horse in Essex's army. He appears in various pay warrants between May 1643 and April 1644, although not in the published list of Essex's officers in its early months nor in the list of cavalry captains mustered during the campaign of summer 1644 in the Southwest.[47] Of Chalfont St Giles, Buckinghamshire, Captain George Fleetwood was second cousin to Colonel Charles Fleetwood. In 1642 or 1643, George raised a troop of dragoons in the county and briefly commanded a regiment of foot. In 1644, he was appointed to the Buckingham County Committee. Carlo Fanthom, a Croat, served as lieutenant in Captain Richard Grenville's troop of harquebusiers in Colonel Goodwin's regiment of horse from its formation on 30 July 1642 to summer 1643, whereupon he was promoted to captain of a troop in the same unit. On 6 February 1644, Fanthom claimed £27 6s. in pay owing to him as captain of a cavalry troop.[48]

---

45 TNA, SP28/149/2, ff. 147v., 162r.–v., 168v.
46 TNA, SP28/43, f. 658r.; SP28/29/2, f. 419r.
47 TNA, SP28/7, ff. 87r., 434r.; SP28/8, f. 98v.; SP28/9, ff. 106r., 213r.
48 TNA, SP28/9, f. 99v.; SP28/10, f. 139r.

Chapter 4

The Parliamentarian Garrisons of Nantwich and Halton

During the early months of 1643, the Parliamentarian forces in Cheshire commanded by Sir William Brereton established a strong foothold in the county. They largely out-manoeuvred and out-fought their enemy during a series of operations, beginning with a confused fight against Royalist troops under Sir Thomas Aston at Nantwich on 28 January. It was a sound beginning that enabled Brereton to establish Nantwich as his base of operations. Nantwich was the second town in Cheshire in terms of size and importance and a far better hub for communications than its only rival, Macclesfield. As Chester was in Royalist possession during this time, Nantwich was the only viable alternative as permanent headquarters.[1] Brereton's decision to safeguard the town led to the establishment of Parliamentarian control over most of the county, except for Chester, and the western hundreds of Broxton and Wirral. Along with the trained bands of five of the seven Cheshire hundreds, previously raised units and new recruits continued to add to the build-up of the Cheshire army of Parliament. The Nantwich chronicler Thomas Malbon reported that, on 30 January, 'Mr Mainwaring and other great forces armed, came in aid of the town to Sir William Brereton. And the next week following came unto him also at Nantwich Captain Duckenfield, Captain Hyde, Captain Marbury and many other captains, and commanders with a good number of both horse and foot'.[2]

By late spring, the Cheshire forces would number about 2,000 men. On 10 February 1643, Brereton was able to report to a London contact, Captain Francis Rowe:

---

1 Andrew Abram, *More Like Lions than Men: Sir William Brereton and the Cheshire Army of Parliament, 1642-46* (Solihull: Helion & Co., 2020), p. 20.
2 James Hall (ed.), *Memorials of the Civil War in Cheshire and the Adjacent Counties by Thomas Malbon, of Nantwich, Gent., and Providence Improved by Edward Burghall*, Record Society of Lancashire and Cheshire, 19 (London: Record Society of Lancashire and Cheshire, 1889), pp. 36–37.

We have near upon 5 troops of horse in this county, but because they are independent troops and not subjected to command it was and is my desire that there may be a major sent down, and honest and conscionable man. We are much disadvantaged for want of such an officer, who is able to order a regiment of horse and if you please to send me a commission to command them I shall be thereby enabled the better to serve you and shall expect no increase of pay … I am much weakened for by reason of the thronging in of foreign forces out of Shropshire and Wales, and Lancashire, the earl of Derby being now at Chester and making his strongest design for Chester, and the Manchester forces not attempting to divert him, we must be constrained to raise another regiment, and therefore we could much desire some more commanders, otherwise for want of more forces the country will be in danger to be overrun and our forces disabled … Take care I pray that there may be a major to order a regiment of horse with some officers of foot sent down, for we have a great need of them, a lieutenant-colonel and sergeant-major of foot and some lieutenants of foot … some old soldiers for sergeants would do wonderous well.[3]

Nantwich

Following the seizure of Nantwich on 28 January 1643, Sir William Brereton and the deputy lieutenants of Cheshire issued warrants, summoning men between the ages of 16 and 60 to attend musters at Tarporley and Frodsham on 21 February. The Royalist commissioners of array in Chester responded by ordering troops under Aston to intercept Brereton en route to Tarporley. Other than a brief exchange of musketry, and a mounted clash near Beeston and Tiverton, 'both sides retreated without any more harm doing, the 1 party to Chester, and the other to Nantwich where they continued that week until they had fortified all the town round-about with strong trenches, and mudwalls of clods of earth'.[4]

On 23 December 1642, an agreement had been reached at Bunbury between representatives of the Royalists and Parliamentarians that Cheshire would remain neutral. While the 'Bunbury Agreement' lasted only a matter of weeks – partly because Sir William Brereton and his fellow deputy lieutenants of Cheshire received instructions from Parliament on 9 January 1643 to take command of the militia and put the county on a war footing – one of the articles of the agreement was that 'fortifications shall be removed at Chester, Nantwich, Stockport, Knutsford and Northwich'.[5] In Chester's case, the City Assembly agreed in September 1642 to an additional levy of 100 marks to repair the gates and accelerate the work on repairing the walls after decades of neglect. By December 1642, the latter walls had been re-enforced, and new gates hung, although the outworks had yet to be constructed. Nevertheless, on 29 September, 'the said town of Nantwich, being firm for the Parliament, standing in opposition against the Commissions of Array, having but small

---

3   HMC, *Thirteenth Report, App. I*, pp. 94–95.
4   Hall (ed.), *Memorials*, p. 38.
5   *LJ*, V, pp. 535, 538.

provision of arms and ammunition, and a little aided by the common people near adjoining, and having to make some barricades at the street ends for their own safety'.[6]

Before 15 March 1643, Arthur, Lord Capel was appointed Royalist lieutenant general of North Wales and Shropshire, and, by 23 March, he had taken up his command in Shrewsbury.[7] However, the area had been drained of military resources by the King's army, and Capel's attempts to press recruits and money in Flintshire and Denbighshire were far from popular. For several weeks, Royalist patrols from Capel's forward headquarters at Whitchurch harassed Brereton's forces, which by the early summer were proving formidable. Royalist soldiers pilfered livestock and goods from several villages across the Cheshire border, while, on 17 May 1643, with 'a great company of cavaliers both of Whitchurch and Shropshire, and other places to the number of 1,500 or more', Lord Capel made a perfunctory attack on Nantwich.[8] A few days later, Capel was ordered by Prince Rupert to assist the Royalist defenders of Warrington, but, as Capel marched, he was unaware that the garrison had recently surrendered.

Forewarned, Brereton side-stepped him and, 'with the horse and all the foot in Nantwich', destroyed Capel's base at Whitchurch and another recently begun at Market Drayton. During the early morning of 30 May, the Cheshire forces assaulted Whitchurch, of which Malbon reported, 'The Nantwich foot soldiers firing very fiercely upon them, and they in the town did the like, maintaining their works and town very bravely'.[9] The defenders, commanded by Sergeant Major Michael Woodhouse, were overcome, and the town was seized with a substantial amount of military supplies and additional plunder. A week later, Brereton's soldiers returned to Nantwich, although (according to Malbon) seizing 'no man's goods but only the cavaliers'.[10] On 12 June 1643, Parliament appointed Sir Thomas Myddelton as sergeant major general and commander-in-chief of the six North Wales counties – largely a paper command – but, although he brought barely a handful of troops, perhaps more importantly he had seven great artillery pieces, four cases of drakes, and 40 waggons of arms and ammunition.[11]

The English regiments brought back from Ireland between October 1643 and February 1644 following Charles I's cessation of hostilities presented the Parliamentarian cause in northwest England and Welsh borders with a major challenge. This was felt none more so than in Cheshire, as it threatened both the future existence of Brereton's army and its reduction of the Royalist stronghold of Chester. Modern assessments have concentrated largely on the acquaintance and psychological impact of the arrival of the army from Ireland to the King's cause, and, although such soldiers were generally admired on account of their fighting ability and familiarity with

---

6   Hall (ed.), *Memorials*, pp. 24–25.
7   *Speciall Passages*, 18–25 April 1643. TT, E116[41].
8   Hall (ed.), *Memorials*, p. 55; *Mercurius Aulicus*, 20 May 1643. TT, E246[26].
9   Hall (ed.), *Memorials*, pp. 56–60.
10 HMC, *Twelfth Report, App. IX* (London: HMSO, 1891), pp. 39–40; Hall (ed.), *Memorials*, p. 60.
11 *LJ*, VI, pp. 80, 90–92, 102.

harsh conditions, according to Lowe, they 'introduced licence and cruelty into the fighting in the northwest which had hitherto been conducted with essential chivalry on both sides'.[12] Thus, adding to a more general fear of 'bloody Irish rebels' in their midst, they provided Parliament an enormous propaganda opportunity. In late November 1643, the consignment of troops being mustered in Dublin for transportation to northwest England (earlier smaller bodies had been sent to the southwest) was hurried across the Irish Sea and landed at Mostyn on the Flintshire coast.

Consisting of around 3,000 infantry, the majority of these 'Irishmen' were English soldiers who had enlisted for service in Ireland. Mark Stoyle estimated that, of the approximately 9,000 men who were brought over to England and North Wales in 1643–1644, about 2,000 were native Irish.[13] Nevertheless, the notion of an 'army of papists' arriving on their doorstep alarmed Parliamentarian commanders, who had in recent months witnessed the collapse Royalist opposition in the northwest. Brereton and others helped circulate the rumour that the enemy were Irish Catholics. On 29 November, the main body of somewhat ragged troops from Ireland reached Chester, shortly in advance of Lord Byron's arrival from Oxford. They were quickly joined by a party from Hawarden Castle, and then, on 6 December, the second contingent, numbering 1,200 infantry and 140 cavalry, disembarked in Flintshire. Byron would take overall charge as commander-in-chief of Royalist forces in Lancashire and Cheshire.

Sir William Brereton's options quickly became limited, and, although the Parliamentarian retreat from North Wales was executed with some promptness, Malbon reported:

> Colonel Brereton and the rest of the Parliament's forces remaining in Wales, where they prospered well (having many gentlemen and others resorting unto them), but having intelligence that great forces were come from Ireland and landed in Wales to the number of 2,500, they all marched back again to Holt, and on Friday 24 November sent their ordnance back to Nantwich. And upon Saturday they all marched, some to Nantwich, others some to Northwich, and Lancashire men into Lancashire with all their carriage without fight or battle with the enemy, leaving Holt Castle unrelieved.[14]

Brereton, with a small body of cavalry, left a substantial garrison in Nantwich and rode to Manchester to raise more forces. However, some of the Cheshire Parliamentarian units continued to hold strong points in the north and east of the county, including Knutsford, Northwich, and Halton, whilst the bulk of the foot retreated to Stockport and Manchester. Warnings were issued to the constables of various townships by military officers and local officials in December 1643 against 'aiding any papist' and 'the violence and cruelty of the papists and the rest of their adherents of the array, who have used

---

12 John Lowe, 'The Campaign of the Irish Royalist Army in Cheshire, November 1643-January 1644', *THSLC*, 3 (1959), p. 61.
13 Stoyle, *Soldiers and Strangers*, pp. 209–10.
14 Hall (ed.), *Memorials*, pp. 88–89.

all possible means for the gathering of great forces towards the affecting of their malicious designs'. They were further ordered to turn out soldiers billeted upon them 'for the speedy raising of men and arms to be in readiness in *extremis exigence* and urgent necessity within divers townships ... with God's blessing to resist the enemy who otherwise will be ready to make much intrusion, waste and spoil in the country', while the deputy lieutenants authorised the impressment of men, carts, and horses for the service of Parliament, 'as the enemy is now advanced into the bowels of this county, threatening the same hereof with fire and sword'.[15]

On 10 January 1644, the Royalist commander Lord Byron issued the first of two summonses to surrender to the town of Nantwich, which was well-fortified with earthworks.[16] His officers supposed that the garrison was inadequately provisioned and its morale low. As Sir Nicholas Byron had assured Rupert, 'Nantwich is in very much pain, and frets underhand, so that the settling of the business is the greatest work to be done in Cheshire, Shropshire, and North Wales; upon which my Lord Byron intends to march for Lancashire, this last blow having made a fair way for his design there'.[17] The summons was defiantly rebuffed, and, as one Parliamentarian account of the siege of Nantwich declared:

> the enemy were of great strength, and the siege was feared; the enemy's cruelty did much grieve the country, and accordingly as it was feared the enemy returned again to Nantwich, and laid close siege before it; and did attempt to scale the works three several times, and shot almost 100 fiery hot bullets, with a kind of fire balls to burn the town. But blessed be God, there was none of them that did any considerable hurt; the greatest harm the town sustained by those balls, was by one which light upon a stack of wood, and fired part of it, which was quenched without doing any further mischief. Captain Booth, the governor of Nantwich, a young man of about 21 years of age, but of a valiant spirit, behaved himself bravely; his soldiers consisting of about 1,200 in number, who withstood the enemy bravely, and did good execution upon them, and slew Lieutenant Colonel Broughton, and 4 captains more; amongst which, Captain Sandford is one, and kept the town in despite of them Captain Booth still encouraging the soldiers, and promising unto them that he would lose his life in their defence before he would yield up the town to such traitorous Irish Rebels.[18]

Although the above account places Colonel George Booth of Dunham Massey as governor of Nantwich during the siege of 1643–1644, there is no certainty about this, however, and the prospect appears slim. The answer

---

15 Unlisted warrants, 4 December 1643, 13 December 1643, 20 December 1643.
16 *Magnalia Dei. A Relation of some of the many Remarkable Passage in Cheshire before the Siege of Namptwich, during the continuance of it: and at the happy raising of it by the victorious gentlemen Sir Tho. Fairfax and Sir William Brereton* (London: Robert Bostock, 1644). TT, E31[13].
17 Warburton, *Memoirs*, II, pp. 355–56.
18 *The Kings letter intercepted coming from Oxford with a ioyful and true relation of th[e] great victory obtained by Sir Thomas Fairfax, Sir William Brereton, and Sir William Fairfax, against the Irish at the raising of the siege at Nantwich on Friday last January 26, 1643* (London: Andrew Coe, 1644).

Welsh Row, Nantwich. (Photo by Paul Wright)

sent to Byron's summons to surrender on 10 January 1644 professes to come from 'George Booth', meaning either the 78-year-old baronet and deputy lieutenant or his grandson, Colonel George Booth. R. N. Dore suggested that 'In some ways the older man would have been more suitable, as he would have had much administrative and diplomatic work to do as well as military'.[19] Booth senior was active throughout the war as a leading Parliamentarian in Cheshire. Malbon listed a Colonel Booth among the officers who came to raise the siege of Nantwich, in addition to his uncle, Colonel John Booth, who commanded a regiment of Lancashire foot.[20] Either way, following Thomas Croxton's promotion to sergeant major in Sir William Brereton's regiment and appointment as deputy lieutenant for Cheshire in May 1644, he became governor of Nantwich, a post he held until 1647.[21]

Following the rejection of Byron's demands, the Royalist bombardment of Nantwich continued. But, anticipating a sudden attack, the defenders continued to man their posts, whilst the townswomen rushed to put out

---

19 R. N. Dore (ed.), *The Letter Books of Sir William Brereton*, Record Society of Lancashire and Cheshire, 123, 128 (Liverpool: Record Society of Lancashire and Cheshire, 1984, 1990), II, p. 64.
20 Hall (ed.), *Memorials*, p. 117.
21 *CJ*, III, p. 484; John S. Morrill, *Cheshire 1630-1660: County Government and Society during the 'English Revolution'* (Oxford: Oxford University Press, 1974), pp. 81–83, 235–36.

fires caused by the barrage. On 16 January, Byron accused Nantwich's town corporation of misleading the inhabitants, although, as events would prove, they were immune to such propaganda. The Royalist assault, when it came, was fierce and targeted against five different points, while artillery directed their close-range fire at the town, although such attacks were repulsed with heavy casualties. Among the dead was Captain Sandford, whose 'big letter' had intimidated the defenders of Hawarden before their capitulation and was repeated at Nantwich with threats to the garrison with dire punishments if they refused to surrender. Further bombardments failed to break the resolve of the garrison and civilian population, and Byron consequently settled upon starving them into submission. It was probably his best policy to persist – his troops were fully committed, and the situation was becoming desperate for the defenders.

In response to Sir William Brereton's appeal for reinforcements, the Committee of Both Kingdoms ordered the Yorkshire commander Sir Thomas Fairfax, who was wintering in Lincolnshire, to raise the siege of Nantwich. When he reached Manchester, he found some reluctance among the Lancashire Committee, although the Lancashire and Cheshire foot, albeit ill-clad, were keen to march. On 21 January 1644, Fairfax left Manchester, making slow progress in difficult conditions through Northwich towards Nantwich. Sir Thomas, assisted by Brereton and some of the Lancashire commanders, had at his disposal a composite force of 1,800 cavalry, 500 dragoons, and 'near 3,000 foot'. On 24 January, mounted Parliamentarian patrols encountered a Royalist blocking force at Delamere Forest, before concentrating at Tilston Heath, about eight miles from Nantwich. That night saw a rapid thaw that caused the River Weaver to flood. Byron ordered his infantry and artillery to shift to the west bank of the Weaver around Acton, where the ground was drier, but the bridge at Barbridge was then swept away by the floodwater while Byron himself with 1,800 horse remained on the opposite bank. He was forced to make a march of six miles by way of another crossing at Shrewbridge to support his foot regiments at Acton, although this enterprise did not get underway until 8:00 a.m. the following morning.

The course and outcome of the resulting battle, fought on 25 January 1644, was well-documented by contemporaries and continues to be debated by historians. Even so, this is beyond the scope of the current book, other than to say that, around 4:00 p.m., the Royalist centre collapsed, just as 700–800 musketeers of the Nantwich garrison sallied out of the western suburbs, pushing aside Sir Fulk Hunke's infantry regiment, which had been positioned to prevent it, before overrunning Byron's artillery in Acton churchyard. The Parliamentarian victory was complete, with some 1,500 prisoners taken, about a third of whom took the Covenant accepted service in the Parliamentarian army. On 13 February, a day of prayer was held for Nantwich's deliverance. It had been a decisive defeat for Byron's forces, and, although reinforcements arrived from Ireland in February, he never completely reconstituted his army. At least 600 prisoners enlisted in Brereton's army, and, given their quality, Brereton and other Parliamentarian commanders were keen to recruit them. Fairfax, a man not known for wasting words, described them as:

men of great experience who had run through all sorts or services, and were not new to the policies of war … They were men acquainted with the greatest hardship, habituated to cold and want, and whatever suffering a winter siege could require … They were put in heart by their former successes, and that they would make them the more daring and desperate, and they were valiant before, being used to nothing but conquests.[22]

Furthermore, Brereton made use of soldiers who had served in Ireland and North Wales in the former firelock companies of Captains Sandford and Langley.[23] Sandford played a leading role in the capture of Hawarden Castle and, with a small number of men, took Beeston Castle in a surprise operation. He was killed leading Byron's unsuccessful attack on Nantwich on 17 January 1644.[24]

Some of the Royalist firelocks were later absorbed into Sir William Brereton's dragoons. Brereton later talked about the Cheshire dragoons, 'which were soldiers in Ireland', as 'very serviceable' and 'well-accommodated'. He also informed Lord Leven on 22 May 1645, 'I can bring no more foot than 1 regiment and some choice dragoons – firelocks which were soldiers in Ireland lately mounted'.[25] Though the fighting and relief of Nantwich had been ferocious on both sides, the importance of the sortie by its garrison to the overall outcome was clear. The intervention of these troops at such a critical point in the battle was not lost on Brereton, who, in October 1645 when prosecuting the siege of Chester, urged the Committee of Both Kingdoms that Sir William Vaughan's forces advancing to the relief of the city should be engaged at a distance so that the besieging troops were not attacked in the rear. He wrote, 'We learnt this by experience upon our enemy, the Irish army at Nantwich battle. For our soldiers (when the battle was in hot dispute, the success being very doubtful) issued out of the town and put a period to the debate, fell upon the rear, routed that part of the enemy and made way for a glorious victory'.[26] Brereton would repeat these sentiments a month later when he led a taskforce to Whitchurch in response to intelligence reports of Royalist troops under Vaughan and Sir Jacob Astley approaching from the Welsh borders.

Following Sir William Brereton's seizure of Nantwich on 28 January 1643, a substantial garrison was established in the town. Within weeks, mud walls (made of rammed earth) or ramparts and a series of trenches were constructed around the town, with defended gates, whilst contemporary sources, such as Parliamentarian sequestration accounts for the town entitled 'Grounds lying in public in Nantwich 1644', provide evidence of three guard houses and a gatehouse at the end of Wall Lane and Welsh Row, both being

---

22 Bodl. Lib., Ms Fairfax 36, f. 47r.
23 Andrew Abram, '"Sufficiently Different' to the Rest of the Army": The Cheshire Parliamentarian Dragoons in the First Civil War', *JSAHR*, 98 (2020), pp. 220–38.
24 Hall (ed.), *Memorials*, pp. 91–109.
25 HMC, *Fourteenth Report, App. IV* (London: HMSO, 1894), pp. 62, 124, 131, 143; BL, Ms Add. 11331, f. 142v.
26 BL, Ms Add. 11332, f. 35v.

defended gateways into the town.[27] It is likely that the town's defensive structures were strengthened following the relief of the town and garrison by Parliamentarian troops in January 1644 because John Roseworm, a Dutch or German professional soldier and military engineer, accompanied Brereton and Sir Thomas Fairfax. Roseworm, who had served on the Continent and in Ireland, was employed by the citizens of Manchester to fortify the town and was a leading figure during the siege in September 1642. He was commissioned lieutenant colonel of Colonel Ralph Assheton senior's infantry regiment in January 1643, but he relinquished this to become captain of an infantry company in the Manchester garrison. Roseworm was also appointed Master of the Ordnance at the siege of Liverpool in August 1644.[28]

One entry in a receipts book belonging to the treasurer of the Cheshire army of Parliament records, 'received 18 January 1645 of James Croxton to pay the workmen for work done on the gates and drawbridge in Nantwich £3 11s. 8d.'[29] Brereton ordered further work on the Nantwich town fortifications upon the advance of the King's Oxford Army through the Midlands preceding the Battle of Naseby. On 13 May 1645, Sir William ordered the Parliamentarian Committee at Nantwich to 'finish and strengthen the works' and to supply a month's victuals for the garrison:

> The Committee of Both Kingdoms expect your garrisons should be well provided. Your own care and judgment will I hope prompt you sufficiently thereunto and the rather because what is not brought into your garrison is but left to sustain and nourish the enemy. I desire every one of the commissioners would take a part and set themselves in earnest to work, after you have all considered and resolved in what way to prosecute his work. *Quod facis fac cito* ['What you do, do quickly']. I desire Mr Peartree (and every of you who has any acquaintance and opportunity) would send out some intelligencers, who may give timely notice of the enemy's approaches. Set all your people in town on work to finish and strengthen your works. Make proclamation that every inhabitant in the town make speedy provision for 1 month beforehand.[30]

Two documents – the first being 'A particular note of work done at the mud walls', compiled on 15 July 1645, and the second, dated 7 November 1645 – probably relate to the efforts carried out at Nantwich. These list monies owed to various men for up to 21 days' work, including 6s. 'to John Street for pulling down the old barn at Pillory Street'.[31]

From the Excise, first levied by Parliamentary ordinance in July 1643, Sir William Brereton was authorised to collect the tax on salt. In December 1643, Parliament ordered the receipts from the salt excise to be employed for the payment of the Cheshire forces.[32] Entries in Treasurer Croxton's

---

27 TNA, SP28/152/10, unf.; Hall (ed.), *Memorials*, pp. 36–37.
28 George Ormerod (ed.), *Tracts Relating to Military Proceedings in Lancashire during the Great Civil War* (Manchester: Chetham Society, 1844), pp. 215–44.
29 TNA, SP28/144, f. 1r.
30 BL, Ms Add. 11331, f. 88r.
31 TNA, SP28/224, ff. 13r., 46r.
32 *CJ*, III, p. 331.

accounts contain incomplete records of the collection of the tax at Nantwich in late 1643, while, in October the following year, Brereton ordered all the proceeds to be paid to the townsmen who 'have been ready in the absence of the trained bands to watch for the safety and defence of the said town … and have never received any pay for their service'.[33] Like other garrison troops during the British Civil Wars, those at Nantwich suffered from inadequate pay, which often caused discontent. On 13 September 1643, the Sequestration Committee of Nantwich hundred ordered the widow Elizabeth Minshull to 'send in your rent presently to pay soldier with, or else the soldiers will come for it themselves'.

Likewise, an acquittance dated 15 May 1644 is for other rents belonging to the same woman, but by then under sequestration, for the use of Sergeant Major John Marbury's company of Colonel George Booth's regiment, which was probably quartered in the town of Nantwich at that time.[34] On 10 April 1645, the 'deputy lieutenants and committees of Nantwich' drew Brereton's attention to bodies of 'wandering discontented soldiers, both of our own country and foreigners. These, under pretext of want of pay, wander up and down the country, rob and spoil it and will obey no orders of yours nor command of any officer, quarter where they will and remove when they will'.[35] Such gentlemen appear to have possessed little if any sympathy for the plight of the soldiery. Several complaints from local people highlight the nature of these violations, although there is little sense of violence being used by soldiers and there was never a Clubman movement in the county.[36] In some instances, officers either turned a blind eye or even joined in.

Arrears of pay among the Cheshire forces reached near epidemic proportions in 1645–1646. On 18 December 1645, the horse was some four months in want of pay, while

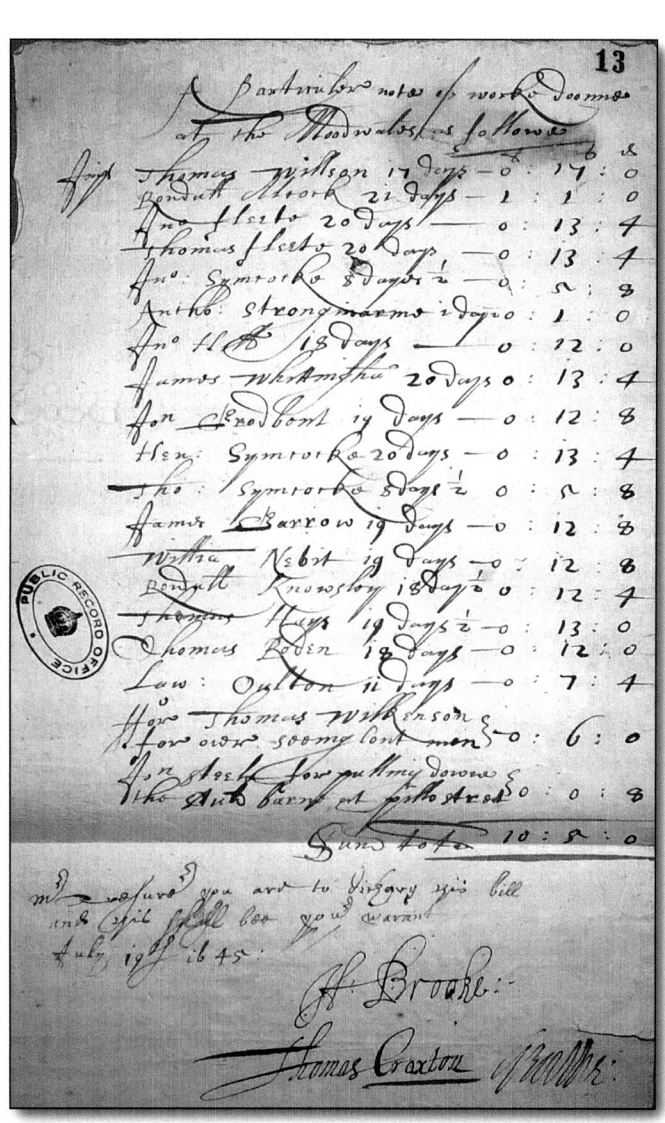

List of work done at the mud walls of Nantwich, 19 July 1645. (TNA, SP28/224, f. 13r.)

---

33   TNA, SP28/152/3, ff. 1r.–2v.; SP28/225/1, unf.
34   BL, Ms Harley 2128, ff. 72r., 103v.
35   CRO, DDX/428, ff. 88r.–v.
36   BL, Mss Harley 2128, f. 150v.; 2126, f. 16r., 1943, f. 48v.

elements of the foot suffered considerably.[37] In late June 1646, troops revolted in Chester, while sequestrators and tax collectors were assaulted, the disturbances only being subdued by hurried loans on the part of the deputy lieutenants and the promise of £2,000 from London.[38] More severe was the mutiny by some of the Nantwich garrison on 14 July 1646. According to the somewhat partizan Malbon:

> Mutiny was made in Nantwich by some of the rude and unseemly sort of the town soldiery to the number of 300 or thereabouts, without either command or aid of their captains or head officer, being all in arms and forcing many honest townsmen to join with them, did by violence draw some of the committee of sequestrations for Nantwich hundred (being in peaceable manner executing their office for the state) forth of the office where all their books and records were, and fetched some of them (and one of the collectors) forth of several houses, wherein they were at dinner, and put them all in the common prison in Nantwich amongst cavaliers, common thieves and horse stealers (which were then there) having been the common prison from the first making the town a garrison … Neither would they allow them to have either meat or drink, or quarter in any other house or place, although it desired both by the high sheriff [Colonel Henry Brooke], and many of the deputy lieutenants and justices of the peace being then in town … neither would they suffer them to go further for doing of their needs during the whole space of 54 hours (laying nothing to their charge) but alleged that their wages were presently paid. Although they knew that the same committee never paid them, nor no other soldiers any, neither had they any warrant to pay them any, for they received their pay always from the treasurer, by warrant of the deputy lieutenants. But as some of them said, they would beat Jack for Jill, yet they would not deliver them further until Colonel Lothian and some other gentlemen had undertaken for their pay.[39]

Even though the town's governor, Sergeant Major Thomas Croxton, was attacked and wounded when he tried to intervene, and the justices and collectors forced to flee, it is significant that the soldiers put their faith in James Lothian (and a few others), who had led the Cheshire foot from the early days of the war. Still acting independently of their officers, the soldiers sent representatives to the county committee, although they backed their demands with veiled threats of further disorder. They had shown themselves capable in somewhat complex operations in defiance of their officers and had argued their case some eight months before the election of agitators in the New Model Army. Disorder on the part of the Cheshire soldiers finally abated in mid-1647, although not before the provision of £12,000 from Parliament and the disbanding of the Nantwich garrison (which was four months in arrears) in addition to a further mutiny in Chester during which the governor and other officials had been arrested.[40]

---

37 BL, Ms Add. 11333, ff. 30r.–v.
38 *Kingdomes Weekly*, 28 July–4 August 1646. TT, E306[22].
39 Hall (ed.), *Memorials*, pp. 208–10.
40 Bodl. Lib., Ms Tanner 58, ff. 323r., 326r., 429r.

THE PARLIAMENTARIAN GARRISONS OF NANTWICH AND HALTON

Some Cheshire parish accounts and Quarter Sessions petitions included claims for providing free quarter and other services to troops. In August 1643, when elements of Colonel Brooke's regiment were billeted at Frodsham, Robert Ragin was paid 8d. by the Bucklow Sequestration Committee for housing two soldiers (probably of the Halton garrison) of Lieutenant Colonel Richard Brooke's company for a day and a night, while Thomas Modshall had 1s. 4d. for accommodating two men under Captain John Brooke for two days and two nights.[41] Less forthcoming are details for towns, such as Northwich, Nantwich, and Tarvin, which housed full-time Parliamentarian garrisons. On 24 July 1645, Richard Hickok, a townsman of Nantwich, was given £1 5s. 'for the discharge of tickets for the quartering of soldiers, he being a poor man and not being able to forebear the cost himself'.[42] Similarly, the widow Margaret Pratchett petitioned that, during the time of the garrison of Nantwich, she 'did quarter divers wounded and maimed soldiers in her house, who did not only spoil much of her bedding to her great loss and hindrance, but also were much in arrears and unpaid for their quarters to the sum of £46 9s. 6d.'[43]

The chief magazine (for the storage of powder, ammunition, and other military stores) of the Parliamentarian forces in Cheshire was located at the army's headquarters in Nantwich. However, a subsidiary depot was established at Runcorn, where a tidal dock on the south bank of the Mersey supplied the forces in the northern and eastern part of the county. Its main function was to provide a secure storage point for ammunition brought upriver from Liverpool and thence transported by waggon to Brereton's headquarters. Magazines were controlled by commissary officers and their assistants, who directed the procurement and distribution of supplies. Commissaries for the Cheshire forces included Commissary General William Hinde; assistant commissary Robert Lunt; William Becket and Henry Rogers, commissaries in Nantwich; and Ralph Metcalfe, commissary at Beeston Hall in early 1645. Edward Podmore acted as wagon master.[44] William Becket acted as commissary in Nantwich in 1644–1645, while Commissaries Henry Rogers and Roberts are recorded supplying victuals to the garrisons of Nantwich and Tarvin, respectively.[45]

Following the first arrival in North Wales of Royalist troops from Ireland, on 20 December 1643, the deputy lieutenants issued warrants for the provisioning of the Cheshire army to each township in the hundreds of Nantwich, Eddisbury, Bucklow, Northwich, and Macclesfield, stating:

> Forasmuch as the enemy is now advanced into the bowels of this county, threatening the same hereof with fire and sword which cannot be prevented by a general and universal joining together in arms into the above, and for continuing with cannot be effective and held together, but by a speedy and large supply of

---

41 BL, Ms Harley 2137, f. 75v.
42 BL, Ms Harley 2166, f. 132v.
43 CRO, QJF 82/4, f. 145r.
44 BL, Mss Harley 2137, f. 153r.; 2126, ff. 129v.–130r.; 1943, f. 7r.; TNA, E121/5/7/351, f. 5v.
45 BL, Mss Harley 2166, f. 130r.; 1943, ff. 7r.–8v.; 2137, ff. 105v., 152v.

victuals. These are to command you immediately upon receipt hereof to repair to all your houses in your said parish, and demand and gather from every householder according to his ability, provisions of bread, butter, beef, bacon, cheese, veals, muttons and other partial provisions … to require all commissaries are to convey the same to the constables at Sandbach with all possible speed and arrive here by this power to the said commissaries, to press and take carthorses and divers of the said persons for the said service, wherein you are to be hiding and dissenting unto them and hereof fail not [under] pain of imprisonment … you are likewise to bring in all the able men within your parish with their best arms and every man a week's provisions for himself.[46]

During the winter of 1643–1644, the Nantwich tailors Peter, John, and William Burstow and Thomas Greenall made 344 infantry coats and 55 troopers' coats and delivered them to Commissary Hinde on 22 February 1644. They were paid 1s. 2d. per soldier's coat and 1s. 8d. per trooper's coat for their construction and carriage.[47] Outer clothing, such as coats and breeches, were usually made by tailors in their own workshops, although the Cheshire Parliamentarian soldiers may also have been supplied from a magazine or factory, perhaps in Nantwich. Captain John Bramhall, a dragoon officer under Brereton and possibly a mercer before the war, manufactured garments with his mother in the town, charging his soldiers various sums for various items. For instance, on 20 May 1643, Bramhall disbursed £1 4s. 3d. 'for cloth to make my drummer a suit of clothes' and a further 3s. to a tailor for making it up. He also paid the sum of 11s. 1d. to Thomas Mottershaw for made-up uniforms and 5s. 4d. to Henry Meeke for trimming a suit, with a further 9d. for buttons.[48]

On 1 December 1644, 74 pairs of shoes were purchased at Nantwich by Lieutenant Thomas Hunt for Captain Sadler's company.[49] On 5 June 1644, the army's Cheshire treasurer, Richard Worrall, expended 3s. for shoes for William Hickman, a soldier under Lieutenant Colonel Venables' command, while, 10 days later, a pair of boots costing 8s. and stockings to the value of 1s. 6d. were purchased for the gunner John Fox.[50] On 29 September 1645, the Nantwich sequestrators paid John Tench, shoemaker, £3 3s. 6d. 'for boots and shoes for the soldiers'. Moreover, the accounts of the officials of the upper division of Wirral hundred reveal that, in November 1645, they disbursed for the garrison at Hooton £1 10s. for three pairs of cavalry boots, as well as 5s. 6d. for leather for making shoes.[51] In terms of ammunition, in 1644, cannon shot and mortar rounds were received by the Nantwich garrison from nearby Hough furnace. Similarly, during the siege of Chester in October 1645, the sum of £16 2s. was disbursed to Richard Hopkins of the Mereheath foundry in Staffordshire for 23cwt of bullet at £14 per ton, with an additional £4 'for

---

46 Unlisted warrant, 20 December 1643.
47 TNA, SP28/49/1, f. 100v.
48 BL, Ms Harley 2128, ff. 23v., 26v., 28v., 31r.
49 TNA, SP28/225/4, f. 723r.
50 TNA, SP28/152/9, f. 9r.
51 BL, Mss Harley 1999, ff. 17r., 69r.; 2166, fol. 132v.

the workmen that made them, and for making the mould they were cast in'. A further 30cwt was provided from the same source on 14 November at a cost of £26.[52] During the previous summer, Sir Thomas Myddelton had brought 40 chests of arms and ammunition to Nantwich upon his commission as commander of the counties of North Wales.[53]

This garrison of Nantwich consisted of companies drawn from three regiments of Cheshire foot (Sir William Brereton's, Colonel George Booth's, and Colonel Henry Brooke's). The soldiers were mostly recruited from volunteers and trained bandsmen from the town, although such units also served throughout the Parliamentarian area of operations in Cheshire and the Welsh borders from 1643 to 1646 as required. According to an estimate of the Cheshire Parliamentarian forces made on 30 April 1645, Nantwich contained 830 common soldiers in eight infantry companies.[54] Moreover, given that each foot company habitually contained approximately 10 commissioned and non-commissioned officers during the British Civil Wars, the overall total could have been more than 900 infantry. There were also gunners, pioneers, and engineers within the garrison. The following foot companies formed the main garrison of Nantwich.

Sergeant Major Thomas Croxton's Company (Sir William Brereton's Regiment)

This was drawn from the Northwich hundred trained bands and was quartered semi-permanently at Nantwich. Even so, the company's officers and soldiers were highly experienced and dependable and participated in numerous operations, including the relief of Wem in 1643 and the Battle of Montgomery in 1644. Thomas Croxton of Ravenscroft, near Northwich, was captain of the Northwich hundred trained bands before the war and was serving under Brereton by February 1643.[55] He was promoted to sergeant major and appointed as deputy lieutenant for Cheshire on 7 May 1644. Croxton also acted as the governor of Nantwich until the beginning of 1647.[56] Amongst the army officers and deputy lieutenants, he was deeply loyal to his commander-in-chief. Reflecting his key importance to the Parliamentarian war effort in the county, Croxton became a colonel in late 1645, while, in 1651, he raised a regiment of Cheshire foot that fought at the Battle of Worcester. His arrears of pay as 'captain and major of foot in the county of Chester' amounted to £1,648 12s. 6d., of which he received £1,103 10s. 10½d. on 5 December 1651 and a further £558 9s. 3d. on 6 August 1652.[57] The following officers, non-commissioned officers, and private sentinels were present on 10 November 1645 and 4 March 1646:

---

52 TNA, SP28/35/5, ff. 751r., 754r.
53 Hall (ed.), *Memorials*, pp. 71–72.
54 BL, Ms Add. 11331, ff. 44r.–45v.
55 BL, Ms Harley 2119, ff. 211v.–213r.
56 *CJ*, III, p. 484; Morrill, *Cheshire*, pp. 81–3, 235–36.
57 TNA, E121/3/1, f. 287v.

Lieutenant Samuel Ratcliffe
Ensign Pearson
Sergeant Bostock
Sergeant Worsley
Sergeant Widdows
Corporal Smallwood
Corporal Higginson
Corporal Perrin
Corporal Cramager
Drummer Edward Griffith
Drummer Edward Walmsley
Clerk William Culcheth
Surgeon Humphrey Pearson.[58]

Captain John Sadler's Company (Brereton's Regiment)

Sadler was a Nantwich yeoman who distinguished himself by defending Acton Church during the siege of the town in 1644. His company consisted of Nantwich volunteers. In February 1645, together with part of Colonel Mainwaring's regiment, Captain Sadler's soldiers engaged in siege operations at Holt and Farndon and later played an important role in the surrender of the castle, of which he became governor.[59] Although his company was nominally part of Brereton's regiment in October 1645, following the seizure of Chester the following spring, Sadler appears to have transferred to Mytton's command in North Wales, where he was promoted to sergeant major. The total outlay to 'Captain Sadler for himself, his officers and soldiers' from central sources amounted to £80 19s. 8d.[60] On 18 October 1645, the company mustered 60 common soldiers along with:

Lieutenant Thomas Hunt
Ensign John Roberts
Sergeant Lancelot Lewis
Corporal Edward Bath
Corporal John Brown.[61]

Captain Thomas Hulse's Company (Brereton's Regiment)

Hulse was a Nantwich man, and his company may have been recruited from the town. In 1645, his company was quartered at Cholmondeley House, and, following the capture of the Parliamentarian governor, Captain Anthony

---

58 TNA, SP28/152/7, f. 8r.; SP28/122/3, ff. 432r.–443r.
59 Hall (ed.), *Memorials*, pp. 98–99; CRO, DDX/428, f. 107v.
60 TNA, SP28/128/13, f. 17v.; SP28/224, unf.
61 TNA, E121/1/5/7, f. 394v.; E121/5/7/351, ff. 34r., 43r., 51v.–52r.; BL, Ms Add. 11333, f. 3v.

Brereton, in that October, Hulse was appointed in his stead. Upon the fall of Beeston Castle to Brereton's army a month later, Captain Hulse was also made commander-in-chief there. The company reported 60 soldiers on 30 April 1645 and 80 soldiers (with Captain Brereton's men) on 18 October 1645.[62]

Lieutenant Colonel William Massey's Company (Colonel George Booth's Regiment)

Drawn also from the Nantwich hundred trained bands, this operated virtually as a 'frontline' unit from its base in the garrison. The total funds disbursed to its officers and soldiers from London sources was £4,197 5s. 10d.[63] Muster rolls show that Massey's company had 160 common soldiers fit for duty on 30 April 1645, 140 on 18 October 1645, 136 on 30 November 1645, 98 on 15 January 1646, and 80 on 28 June 1646. Of Moss House, Audlem, William Massey had been commissioned captain of foot by 10 April 1643 and promoted to lieutenant colonel before 25 September 1643. He took command of Colonel George Booth's regiment following his resignation around April 1645 and was promoted to colonel. Massey was a valuable and highly competent field officer, particularly during the siege of Chester, where his company operated on the Welsh side of the city. In January 1646, he commanded a force of Cheshire and Montgomery foot besieging Harwarden Castle. Between 1646 and 1649, William served on the county committee and was governor of the city during the 1647 army mutinies.[64] On 28 June 1645, Massey's company contained the following:

>   Captain Lieutenant George Massey
>   Ensign Thomas Rutter
>   Sergeant Roger Warburton
>   Sergeant Richard Wilson
>   Corporal Ralph Maddon
>   Corporal Peter Sutton
>   Corporal Thomas Hawsley
>   Drummer Ralph Burton
>   Drummer Thomas Worrall.[65]

Captain Lieutenant Browne can be identified among pay warrants dated 11 June and 8 November 1645 as leading a company of foot from Nantwich hundred, which was probably Massey's.[66] Lieutenant Clark is referred to in a warrant of 27 May 1645 with the command, while Thomas Massey was

---

62 BL, Mss Add. 11331, f. 45r.; 11332, f. 3v.
63 TNA, SP28/128/13, ff. 17r., 25v.; SP28/208, unf.
64 BL, Mss Add. 11332, f. 31r.; 11333, ff. 30r., 101v.–102r., 118r.
65 TNA, SP28/124/1, ff. 10r., 88r.
66 TNA, SP28/224/1, ff. 47v.–50r.

serving as company clerk on 2 August 1645 and was promoted to ensign in the trained bands before 28 June 1647.[67]

Captain George Malbon's Company (Booth's Regiment)

The unit was originally raised from Nantwich townsmen by Captain Richard Clutton. George Malbon was the eldest son of Thomas Malbon of Bradley, near Nantwich, the Cheshire lawyer and annalist, and brother of Captain Thomas (below). Both companies under command of the Malbon brothers participated in the Parliamentarian assaults on Cholmondeley House and Oswestry during the summer of 1644 and served reliability at the Chester Leaguer. A lieutenant, one ensign, five corporals, and 86 soldiers under Captain George Malbon received pay on 31 October 1644, although, in the army list of April 1645, his company is given as a combined figure of 200 with that of his brother.

Lieutenant John Acton was named as lieutenant to the company in pay warrants of 24 and 27 December 1644. On 21 March 1645, the following were also rewarded for their service:

Corporal William Fairclough
Corporal Roger Davies
Corporal Thomas Marchant
Corporal Richard Pemberton
Corporal Thomas Birch.[68]

Captain Thomas Malbon's Company (Booth's Regiment)

The unit was originally formed in early 1643 under the command of Captain Edward Minshall. He died and was buried at Nantwich on 14 July 1643. Captain Malbon junior (brother of George above) subsequently led the company, and his men were raised and quartered in town.

Captain John Delves' Company (Colonel Henry Brooke's Regiment)

An illegitimate son of Sir Thomas Delves of Doddington, John was a leading citizen of Nantwich both before and after the civil wars. His volunteer company was probably raised during mid-1644 as part of the Nantwich garrison. The unit numbered 99 common soldiers for duty on 4 September 1644, 98 on 14

---

67   TNA, SP28/30/7, ff. 698r., 758v.; SP28/124/1, f. 80v.; BL, Ms Harley 2128, f. 91r.
68   TNA, SP28/21/294, f. 295r.; SP28/225/3, f. 503r.

September 1644, 100 on 26 September 1644, 98 on 29 November 1644, and 80 on 30 April 1645.[69]

Captain Francis Bramhall's Company (Brooke's Regiment)

A Nantwich resident, Bramhall and his volunteer company were quartered in the town from 1643 onwards. Eighty common soldiers were mustered on 30 April 1645.[70]

Lieutenant Thomas Brooke, a younger brother to Colonel Henry Brooke of Norton, was mortally wounded at the Battle of Nantwich on 25 January 1644 and buried in the town three days later. On 3 October 1646, his widow, Jane, was granted £20 due to her late husband 'for provision by him brought into Norton House for the use of the soldiers there when the same was a garrison'.[71] Given the family connection and reference to provisioning the garrison of Norton, it is likely that Lieutenant Brooke served in his brother's regiment of foot (perhaps in the colonel's own or one of the Nantwich town companies of Captains Delves and Bramhall, or as a supernumerary officer).

On 20 February 1643, Sir William Brereton ordered Beeston Castle to be garrisoned with between 200 and 300 men under Captain Thomas Steele and 'caused the breaches to be made up with mud walls, the well of the outer ward to be cleansed, and a few rooms erected'.[72] Having placed garrisons in both Nantwich and Beeston, Brereton was now in a position to consolidate his grip on central and eastern Cheshire. On 25 February, he led a combined force of horse and foot, numbering 500 men, to Knutsford and the market town of Northwich, which were garrisoned for Parliament. These garrisons had recently been formed at Northwich with volunteers from the hundreds of Northwich, Bucklow, and Eddisbury. Captain (later Lieutenant Colonel) Gilbert Gerard received a commission to raise a company on 14 February 1643 and was appointed governor of Northwich on 1 March, whilst defensive earthworks were constructed about both towns.[73] Eleven miles to the northwest, Norton House, the home of Colonel Henry Brooke, had come under siege from Royalist forces under Earl Rivers. The Brookes were the only major Parliamentarian supporters in upper-Bucklow hundred by early 1643, being direct neighbours of Rivers and Sir Thomas Aston, both of whom raised forces for Charles I during the early months of the war.

---

69   TNA, SP28/225/3, ff. 491v.–492r., 499v.; SP28/225/4, f. 703r.; BL, Ms Add. 11331, f. 44v.
70   BL, Mss Harley 1999, f. 328v.; 2126, f. 35v.; Ms Add. 11331, f. 44v.
71   TNA, SP28/225/3, f. 519r. In the will of his mother, Katherine Brooke, dated 21 April 1651, Thomas is referred to as 'my late son', while Jane was bequeathed a silver watch, and their son Richard and daughter Katherine were left £30 and £20, respectively (TNA, PROB 11/220/237).
72   *Kingdomes Weekly*, 21–28 February 1643. TT, E85[15].
73   TNA, SP28/152/4, unf.; SP28/208, ff. 33v.–34r.

Halton Castle

With his estates located at Rocksavage, near Runcorn, John, Earl Rivers recruited his regiment of foot from the locality in 1642, which later joined the Oxford Army. Furthermore, he maintained a gun battery that protected the crossing of the River Weaver at Frodsham, a Royalist newsbook reporting on 17 September 1642, 'The Earl Rivers has 5 pieces of ordnance, 10 barrels of powder, and 60 bullets landed at Frodsham'.[74] In addition to garrisoning his own home, he placed troops in Halton Castle and reportedly threatened his neighbours, the Brooke family of Norton, who were the first to declare for Parliament in the area. Depositions given before the Sequestration Committee of Bucklow hundred in 1645 by Colonel Henry Brooke, and his relatives and tenants, reveal that Rivers also attempted to raise the local militia. According to Richard Jennings of Norton:

> in July or August 1642 John, Earl Rivers did recruit the Commission of Array in several places of the county, and did raise divers of the trained bands of this county, and so this person did credibly hear, did forth set forth his warrants for collecting of moneys, and did also as this person had heard, send several of the assorted plans to the people to inform and threaten others.

Brooke himself testified that Royalist soldiers had plundered his tenants 'and many of the county round about'. Moreover, the deputy lieutenant and brother-in-law of Brooke, Thomas Marbury, stated, 'The said did fortify Halton Castle and Rocksavage House, and there kept two garrisons against the Parliament, which garrisons did much did much against the Parliament's party. Therefore, of the said Earl did imprison those well-affected to the Parliament and did take their horses and cattle to a very great value'.[75]

Halton Castle, located atop a steep promontory dominating Runcorn Gap and the Mersey, was garrisoned for the King in November 1642 by a company of Rivers' regiment under the command of Captain Walter Primrose. Due to the proximity of Halton to Warrington (and being barely a mile from the Parliamentarian garrison of Norton), it was vital that the stronghold was seized. Shortly after the surrender of Warrington on 27 May, the blockade of Halton commenced, the Royalist newsbook *Mercurius Aulicus* reporting on 25 June, 'They have now procured several pieces of ordinance from Warrington, threatening to batter the castle walls; but the captain hangs out his flag of defiance, resolving to lose his life rather than the castle [of Halton]'.[76] The Parliamentarian siege lasted roughly six weeks. A guard post, placed opposite the castle's gatehouse, was reported by a Royalist source, and trenches and gun embrasures are likely to have been constructed by the besiegers, perhaps at the 'mount', positioned to the southeast. Details of the

---

74 *The Latest remarkable truths (not before printed) from Chester, Worcester, Devon, Somerset, Yorke and Lancaster counties* (London: Thomas Vnderhill, 1642). TT, E240[23].
75 CRO, DCH/X/15/14.
76 *Mercurius Aulicus*, 25 June 1643. TT, E246[9].

Halton Castle. (Photo by Paul Wright)

siege and its subsequent surrender are provided by contemporary accounts, one of which recounted:

> This day it was advertised, that on Monday last Captain Walter Primrose (whom the earl Rivers appointed to keep Halton Castle in Cheshire for His Majesty) apprehending an opportunity that the rebels who had besieged the castle were gone to their old trade of plundering: the captain issued 32 of his soldiers out of the castle, fell upon the house where the rebels kept their sentries, killed one of them, the other fled; took from them 20 good muskets, their provisions of match, powder, and bullet, besides good store of victual, which they out of zeal had robbed from His Majesty's good subjects. The rebels finding that castle was relieved, which they for a month before had strongly besieged, and being enraged to see anything which concerned His Majesty undestroyed, they with fresh forces approached and faced the fort, but were so entertained by this valiant captain, that they all fled, leaving some of their friends dead on the place. On Tuesday evening they appeared again before the castle, but received better welcome than before, for the soldiers forth of the castle killed 10 of them presently, and made the rest fly; which their commanders perceiving, comforted themselves with some new plunder, which is their chief errand. They have now procured several pieces of ordinance from Warrington, threatening to batter the castle walls; but the captain hangs out his flag of defiance, resolving to lose his life rather than the castle.

The garrison surrendered on 20 July 1643. Seven days later, it was reported, 'the forces which took Warrington, have ever besieged Halton Castle near thereunto in Cheshire, and they had gotten it long since, if one of their commanders had not treacherously supplied the castle with gunpowder (which made them hold out) whom they have apprehended and imprisoned in Warrington'.[77]

Articles of the Surrender of Halton Castle, 20 July 1643[78]

Articles agreed upon betwixt Captain [later Colonel] Henry Brooke, esquire, on the one part, and Captain Primrose of Halton for the delivery of Halton Castle, the twentieth day of July 1643, as follows:

That the castle with all the ordnance, arms, goods, ammunition, provision and all things therein contained shall be forthwith delivered unto the custody of Captain Henry Brooke, esquire, according to the conditions before mentioned, and ensuring the same time will the delivery of the castle there to be no hostile attempt by the same Captain Primrose or his soldiers.

That none of the soldiers in the same castle shall use any treachery in the delivery of the said castle, neither to the ordnances, arms, ammunition, nor any other part of the goods therein.

Henry Brooke
Walter Primrose
Witnesses thereof:
Thomas Marbury
Richard Crosley
Peter Pickering

Firstly: Captain Primrose and all his soldiers shall have all their swords, firelocks and colours of all the besieged, and all other of Captain Brooke his party.

2: That the said captain shall have the honour of all his own arms and the benefit of all his goods whatsoever in the same castle.

3: That the same Captain Primrose shall have liberty after exchanging of his sufficient of hostages, which is twelve fewer after the delivery of the said castle, to inhabit at Frodsham Castle, and that Captain Henry Brooke shall protect and use his utmost orders to procure his protection for the parliament or anywise defend, as shall be thought requisite for his quiet residing there, and free liberty in the said county, he not taking up arms against the parliament or any of their party.

4: That all the soldiers now in garrison in the said castle shall have liberty and safety to pass, and dwell at peace [in] their own habitations without any disturbance.

5: That any household now within the castle shall choose desire shall be preferred to be housed [by] Captain Henry Brooke for his quiet living at his or their own houses without taking up of arms against the parliament.

6: That all the household goods in the aforesaid castle belonging to the Earl Rivers shall be by this in Captain Brooke's safety, preserved without loss or harm

---

77 *Speciall Passages*, 21–27 June 1643. TT, E89[14].
78 TNA, House of Lords, Journal Office, HL/PO/JO/10/1/224.

until that said earl shall make a fair composition for this, and that earl's estate in wellbeing shall now be safer passed away by the said Captain Primrose.

    Henry Brooke
    Walter Primrose
    Witnesses thereof:
    Thomas Marbury
    Richard Crosley
    Peter Pickering

The taking of Halton Castle by Parliamentarian forces was immediately capitalised upon by the storming of Rocksavage, Captain (later Lieutenant Colonel) Richard Brooke claiming its goods as a prize.[79] Such gains were crucial to the Parliamentarian war effort in both a local and wider strategic context. An end was brought to the activities in Cheshire of Earl Rivers and his troops, whilst Halton Castle in particular (which was straightaway garrisoned for Parliament) was part of a broader network of defences on the Mersey at Hale Ford and Warrington. Moreover, it enabled fortified positions to be established at Frodsham Bridge and ditch and a ford at Dutton and for the safeguarding of Runcorn dock (an important link in the supply chain between the port of Liverpool and the army in Cheshire). During Prince Rupert's advance through Cheshire in May 1644, (by then) Colonel Brooke placed the bulk of his regiment (and possibly his cavalry troop) in the Halton and Norton garrisons, while locally raised dragoons patrolled what was considered by the Parliamentarians as a 'safe area'.[80]

Since his appearance on the Welsh borders in spring 1644, Rupert had received appeals from the Earl of Derby to come to the rescue of Lathom House, the only Royalist stronghold remaining in Lancashire.[81] Prince Rupert's force left Shrewsbury on 16 May. It rendezvoused with troops from Chester and North Wales commanded by Lord Byron at Market Drayton, bringing the combined army to about 2,500 horse and 5,000–6,000 foot. On 19 May, they crossed into Cheshire near Audlem and, for the next week, marched through the county. The Parliamentarian response to Rupert's march through Cheshire, it would seem, was ineffectual, considering that the forces of the entire area, if combined, would have been near the strength of the Royalists. It seems that the Mersey and its locale were considered the best line of defence. Malbon mentioned that, on 20 May, about 1,000 Parliamentarian troops marched from Nantwich but failed to encounter the Royalists. He added, 'but the Prince's army was returned again to Audlem, so that they were not met withal'.[82]

Given the reputation of the Nantwich garrison, whose role in the Royalist defeat of 25 January 1644 had been crucial, Rupert's commanders seem to have avoided a fight with them and withdrew. Three days later, however, a

---

79 TNA, HL/PO/JO/10/1/224; BL, Mss Harley 2128, ff. 144r.–v., 201r.; 2137, f. 200v.
80 Unlisted warrants, 18 June 1644, 1 July 1644, 6 July 1644, 10 July 1644, 13 July 1644, 14 July 1644, 18 July 1644, 19 July 1644; BL, Ms Harley 2128, f. 166r.
81 Warburton, *Memoirs*, II, p. 304.
82 Hall (ed.), *Memorials*, pp. 129–30.

Parliamentarian outpost at Dodleston, a moated manor house four miles southwest of Chester, skirmished with Royalist troops. Rupert's line of march was governed to some extent, however, by his need to avoid further Parliamentarian strongholds, such as Northwich and Macclesfield, as well as the garrisons of Halton and Norton. Based on the misreading of a summary of a letter from Lord Goring to Rupert by William Beamont, tradition has it that Halton Castle fell to the Royalists as the Prince advanced through the county in May 1644 and was reclaimed by the Parliamentarians in early July.[83] Written at Leigh on 5 June, the dispatch notes, 'Colonel Fenwick's quarters at Alton beaten up this night by those of Warrington, beseeches Prince Rupert to send some musketeers, or to remove their quarters'.[84] In her biography of Goring, Florence Memegalos affirmed that:

> During the first few weeks of June, [he] was not quartered with the prince, but rather had based at Leigh, between Manchester and Liverpool, where his men were involved in several skirmishes with local parliamentarian troops. After the quarters of one of his colonels was overrun, George asked Rupert for some musketeers or the removal of their quarters to a safer location.[85]

'Alton' is Westhoughton, near Wigan, and the officer in question was Colonel John Fenwick, who commanded a regiment in Langdale's horse and was killed at Marston Moor.[86]

The Aston warrants show that Halton Castle and nearby Norton Hall were part of a wider strategic network of defences centred on the Mersey at Hale Ford and Warrington, as well as defensive positions at Frodsham Bridge and a series of outposts up the Weaver valley as far as Acton Bridge. Prior to Rupert's advance, Colonel Brooke had maintained the bulk of his regiment and cavalry troop at Halton and Norton, while dragoons patrolled what was considered by the Parliamentarians as a secure area. Warrants were specifically issued by Lieutenant Colonel Brooke from Halton on 18 May, 30 May, and 18 June 1644.[87] Thus, the notion that Halton Castle changed hands in mid-1644 cannot be sustained. In addition to this, the crossing into Lancashire at Warrington Bridge was barred to Prince Rupert by the town's Parliamentarian garrison. The next major crossing of the Mersey was at Stockport, roughly 20 miles to the east. When Rupert's force reached the town on 25 May, it encountered a 3,000-strong force, consisting of Duckenfield's and Mainwaring's Cheshire regiments and some trained band units, blocking its passage. According to *Mercurius Aulicus*:

---

83 William Beamont, *A History of the Castle of Halton and the Priory or Abbey of Norton* (Warrington: Percival Pearse, 1873), pp. 117–18.
84 Bodl. Lib., Ms Clarendon 28, f. 134r.; Ms Firth C7, ff. 289r., 302v.
85 Florence S. Memegalos, *George Goring (1608-1657): Caroline Courtier and Royalist General* (London: Routledge, 2007), p. 170.
86 Sir Henry Slingsby, *The Diary of Sir Henry Slingsby* (London: Longman, Rees, Orme, Brown, Green, and Longman, 1836), p. 114.
87 Unlisted warrants, 18 May 1644, 30 May 1644, 3 June 1644, 18 June 1644, 1 July 1644, 6 June 1644, 10 July 1644.

the cunning rebels withdrew themselves, and lined the hedges through which he was to pass with their musketeers. Which being perceived by the prince, he commanded Colonel Washington with some dragoons to scour those hedges; he performed the service with such speed and courage, that the rebels in great affright fled towards the town; whom the prince followed so close upon the heels, that he entered pell mell with them, and so took the town, together with all their cannon, most of their arms and ammunition, and 800 prisoners.[88]

Colonels Duckenfield and Mainwaring, with the remainder of their men, withdrew to Manchester, which left Lancashire open to invasion by Prince Rupert.

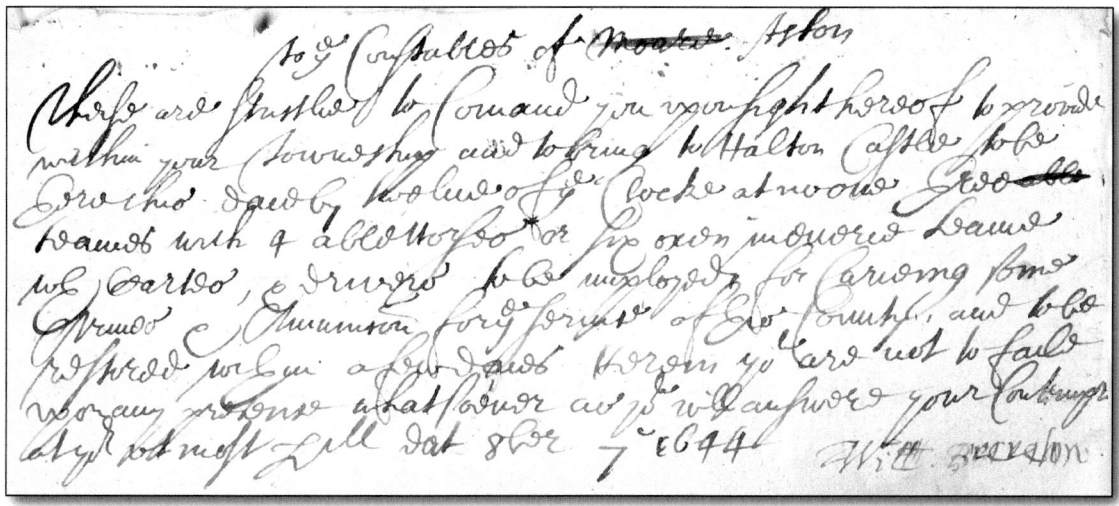

Warrant signed by Sir William Brereton to the constables of Aston to bring teams and carts to Halton Castle for the transportation of ammunition, 7 July 1644 (Unlisted warrant, Aston Collection)

The Parliamentarian garrison of Halton comprised Lieutenant Colonel Richard Brooke's company of foot. The third son of Sir Richard Brooke of Norton, Richard served as captain and lieutenant colonel in his brother's regiment, governor of Halton Castle, and sequestrator for Bucklow hundred. By his own admission, he was one of the earliest officers to declare for Parliament in northwest Cheshire, others having not done so because of Earl Rivers' presence in the area. The Brookes were particularly ill-disposed towards Thomas Savage, their Royalist neighbour, who had not only held sway in and recruited men from upper-Bucklow in 1642 and early 1643 but also attacked Norton and plundered their estates and tenants. Later in the war, Richard Brooke poured scorn on his previous enemy, stating, 'it was wonderful to all who knew his lordship's former voluptuous life, how he became so unexpectedly active and industrious', also claiming that Rivers' regiment was 'miserably routed and broken at Edgehill' (although the latter was an exaggeration).[89] Brooke had raised his company by February 1643, and, from an early stage, he engaged in local military operations. During mid-1643, as captain, he led the storming of Rocksavage House, the Cheshire home of Earl Rivers.

---

88   *Mercurius Aulicus*, 8 June 1644. TT, E244[30].
89   CRO, DCH/X/15/14, f. 1.

The contents of the property and its estates were inventoried by sequestration officials and exploited to provide money, provisions, and other resources for the company. How damaged the fabric of the structure was is uncertain, but, at a later date, Brooke's ensign, Thomas Davenport, was reimbursed by the sequestrators of Bucklow hundred the sum of £30 13s. 4d. 'for the repair of Rocksavage House', while a further £35 9s. was allowed towards his pay. In early 1645, 'arrears of meadowing and demising in Rocksavage the last year' were disbursed by the Bucklow sequestration agents – it was recorded that 'Lieutenant Johnson and his party in the meadowing and demesne land had all or most of the cattle plundered by the army'. Moreover, Brooke's soldiers received £84 13s. 4d. in pay out of the Rocksavage rents, whilst, in arrears for 1645–1646, several officers of Colonel Brooke's regiment obtained recompense from the same source, including Henry and Richard Brooke, who received £42 and £21 16s. each.[90] The Parliamentarian garrison at Halton was partly maintained via standing orders issued by the Sequestration Committee of Bucklow hundred to pay fixed sums to it. Hence, on 25 March 1644, £9 per week was allocated to the garrison.[91]

By mid-1644, Captain Richard Brooke had been promoted to lieutenant colonel. On 21 August, his soldiers fought with the Cheshire foot at Tarvin.[92] The accounts of James Croxton, county treasurer, record 34 payments to the company between February and July 1645, with a further disbursement of £248 4s. 2d. in pay to the lieutenant colonel 'and to his officers and soldiers'.[93] Moreover, on 10 January 1646, Sir William Brereton and Colonel Henry Brooke issued a warrant to Croxton for the urgent payment:

> unto Lieutenant Colonel Brooke for his officers and soldiers as follows: the lieutenant £2 16s.; the ensign £2; the clerk and 1 sergeant 28s. apiece; the drummer and 3 corporals 24s. a man; the soldiers 18s. 8d. a man out of the first monies that can be spared for that purpose, you receiving a muster roll examined by Captain Whitworth, and in acquittance from the receiver.[94]

On 30 April 1645, 60 common soldiers were listed as present, although a clearer picture of the composition of the company is provided by a muster list, dated 15 January 1646:[95]

Table 10

Lieutenant John Witter	Corporal Thomas Ditchfield
Ensign Thomas Davenport	Corporal Thomas Garratt
Humphrey Clayton, clerk	Corporal Stephen Woodfall
Sergeant John Reade	Drummer Edward Friar
Forty (named) common soldiers, although Andrew Tomlison was listed as killed on 11 January 1646, whilst 3 men – Thomas Gooding, Thomas Silcock, and Richard Brinston recently wounded.	

---

90 BL, Mss Harley 2128, ff. 98r., 144r.–v., 201r.; 2137, f. 200v.
91 TNA, SP28/225, unf.
92 Hall (ed.), *Memorials*, p. 142.
93 TNA, SP28/208, unf.; SP28/128/13, f. 18r.
94 TNA, SP28/36/5, f. 520r.
95 BL, Ms Add. 11331, f. 45r.; TNA, SP28/123/4, ff. 562v.–564r.

During the period 1643–1646, seven of the eight Cheshire hundreds operated sequestration committees, who were responsible to the army's commander-in-chief and deputy lieutenants for raising and receiving money, provisions, weapons, ammunition, manpower, horses, and victuals from the constables of their allotted townships. In upper-Bucklow, these townships were Aston, Runcorn, Weston, Sutton, Acton Grange, Halton, Norton, Lymm, Mere, Dutton, Bartington, and Netherleigh. A series of warrants issued by Lieutenant Colonel Brooke, and other military officers and officials, to such constables illustrates how the military garrison at Halton was supplied. However, although such documents offer a range of important information about methods of procurement and organisation at a local level, they present particular challenges, in that, due to their form and function, they can present a skewed picture of events and, in Aston's case, make it appear that the Brookes and the civil authorities were constantly at odds with the constables for non-payment of estate rents and a reluctance to cooperate. Thus, the warrants shed light upon some of the profound difficulties encountered by army officers and officials in funding, supplying, and mustering their soldiers and some of the methods employed by them in attempting to rectify the situation. A selection of warrants is given below:

Captain Richard Brooke to the constables of Aston, ordering them to provide teams to transport cheese from Aston Hall to Halton Castle. [after 20 July 1643]

Captain Richard Brooke to the constables of Aston to find 10 able men to guard Frodsham Bridge. 6 October 1643

Captain Richard Brooke to the constables of Aston to provide teams to transport 5 carts of firewood from Rocksavage to Halton Castle. 16 February 1644

Colonel Henry Brooke to the constables of Aston to provide 6 weeks' pay at 13s. a week for his troop under the command of Captain-Lieutenant Robert Wynn. 20 February 1644

Sergeant Major John Daniell to the constables of Aston, Sutton and Acton Grange, and others who have contributed towards the maintenance of the garrisons of Norton or Halton to render their accounts. 5 April 1644

Lieutenant Hugh Burroughs, Captain William Daniell and Ensign Thomas Davenport to the constables of Aston, censuring them for resisting previous warrants. 10 July 1644

Colonel Henry Brooke to the constables of Weston, Runcorn, Sutton, Halton, Norton, Aston and Acton Grange, ordering them to appear at Halton Castle to conclude how to put the country in a defensive posture. 11 July 1644

Lieutenant Colonel Richard Brooke to the constables of Aston to summon payment of all rents and profits due to Sir Thomas Aston. 14 June 1644

Lieutenant Colonel Richard Brooke to the constables of Aston to provide a horse team to transport hay from Rocksavage meadows to Halton Castle. 19 July 1644

Lieutenant Burroughs, Captain Daniell and Ensign Davenport to the constables of Aston instructing them to pay rents at Halton. 9 August 1644

Lieutenant Colonel Richard Brooke to the constables of Aston to provide as many teams as possible for transportation between Runcorn and Halton Castle. 5 September 1644

Sir William Brereton to the constables of Aston to provide 2 teams at Halton Castle for transporting arms and ammunition. 7 September 1644.[96]

---

96   Unlisted warrants, after 20 July 1643, 6 October 1643, 16 February 1644, 20 February 1644, 5 April 1644, 10 July 1644, 11 July 1644, 19 July 1644, 9 August 1644, 5 September 1644, 7 September 1644.

Chapter 5

The Parliamentarian Garrisons of Norton, Northwich, Tarvin, Hooton, and Puddington

Norton

In February 1643, the Parliamentarian garrison at Norton House in northwest Cheshire, the home of the Brooke family, was besieged by Royalist forces under Earl Rivers. According to contemporary accounts, it was defended by 80 men, including members of the family and estate tenants. They were supplied with a good stock of ammunition and provisions, although the site's chief strength was the recently constructed defensive works that augmented the pre-existing system of gatehouses, moats, fishponds, and an inner courtyard containing ancillary buildings of the former Augustinian abbey, which had been retained with much of the estates upon its purchase by the Brookes in 1545. The sale included 'the site and house of the late monastery of Norton, with the higher and lower court, the infirmary orchard, the great garden, the smith's orchard … a water mill, a windmill, a fishery called the Old Fish yard upon Mersey and numerous closes'.[1] Besides, the Inquisition Post Mortem of Sir Richard Brooke of Norton, dated 2 July 1634, details the following:

> Norton House:
> Containing: Hall, chamber at the end of the hall, the inner chamber and the closet above the nursery, the maids chambers, the Leighs Chamber, Cousins Chamber, Brooke's Chamber, the High turret Chamber, the middle turret, the Green Chamber, the low most turret, the two ground chambers, the two out huts butting out that end of the house, the lower gallery and the entry with the chambers at the side thereof for servants, the closet over the porch with the passages through the hall as they were then accustomed, the kitchen, and the dry and wet larders, the brew-house, bake-house, boulting-house with their passage, the dairy-house,

---

[1] TNA, C66/780.

the dairy vault and little store-house, the kiln, the malt lofts, the hack-house, the stable and slaughter-house at the end thereof, and the vast room at the end thereof, the nearer barn, the cow-house, the outbuildings for swine and pullen, the garden-house, the new building at the east end of the cow house, the lower garner with free egress and regress for horse coach or carriage through the gates, and as to all the residue of the demesne lands of the said manor of Norton, and the dove house and water corn mill at Norton, a windmill together with the tithes of Lady Katherine Brooke …[2]

Much of the complex appears in the engraving of the Tudor house by the Buck brothers in 1727 and was confirmed (with the moat and ponds) by archaeological excavation during the 1970s.[3] It is possible that the defensive capacity of the place was improved by the military engineer John Roseworm. He accompanied Brereton and Fairfax at Nantwich in January 1644, before advising Colonel Robert Duckenfield about fortifying Stockport (whose medieval town walls were in disrepair and the castle probably dismantled) a few months later. Duckenfield had also employed John Whitworth, Brereton's captain of pioneers.[4]

Like Norton, other former monastic sites were garrisoned during the British Civil Wars. In 1644, a Royalist garrison under the governorship of Colonel John Barnold was placed at the former Cistercian monastery of Abbey Cwmhir in Powys. According to a Parliamentarian report of its storming on 8 December by forces commanded by Sir Thomas Myddelton, the site was:

> a very strong house, and built with stone of a great thickness, and the walls and outworks all very strong, the house having been in former times an abbey of the Papists, which is situated upon the borders of Montgomeryshire, within 12 miles of Montgomery, or thereabouts; and the country, by reason of the cruelties, plunder, and unchristian usage of the cruel and merciless enemy towards them … suffered exceedingly, and were almost utterly undone; which, notwithstanding the great strength of the enemy, our General being troubled to hear of the cruelties against the poor people by the enemy, put on a brave resolution, trusting in the Lord, and went against them and marched thither.

The writer added, 'Since which our General having thrown down the enemy's works, and made the garrison unserviceable for the future, we made entrance and marched away from thence to Flintshire, where our General took great care for the securing of those parts and placed a garrison there'.[5]

On 28 February 1643, during the days preceding the main assault of Norton by an estimated 1,500 Royalist soldiers, Rivers threatened Lady Katherine Brooke – the dowager mother of Colonel Henry – to put everyone

---

2   CRO, CR63/1/226/n (102).
3   Fraser Brown and Christine Howard-Davis, *Norton Priory: Monastery to Museum, Excavations 1970–87* (Lancaster: Oxford Archaeology, 2008).
4   9 TNA, SP28/128/10, f. 7v.
5   *Perfect Occurrences*, 20–27 December 1644. TT, E49[18].

THE PARLIAMENTARIAN GARRISONS OF NORTON, NORTHWICH, TARVIN, HOOTON, AND PUDDINGTON

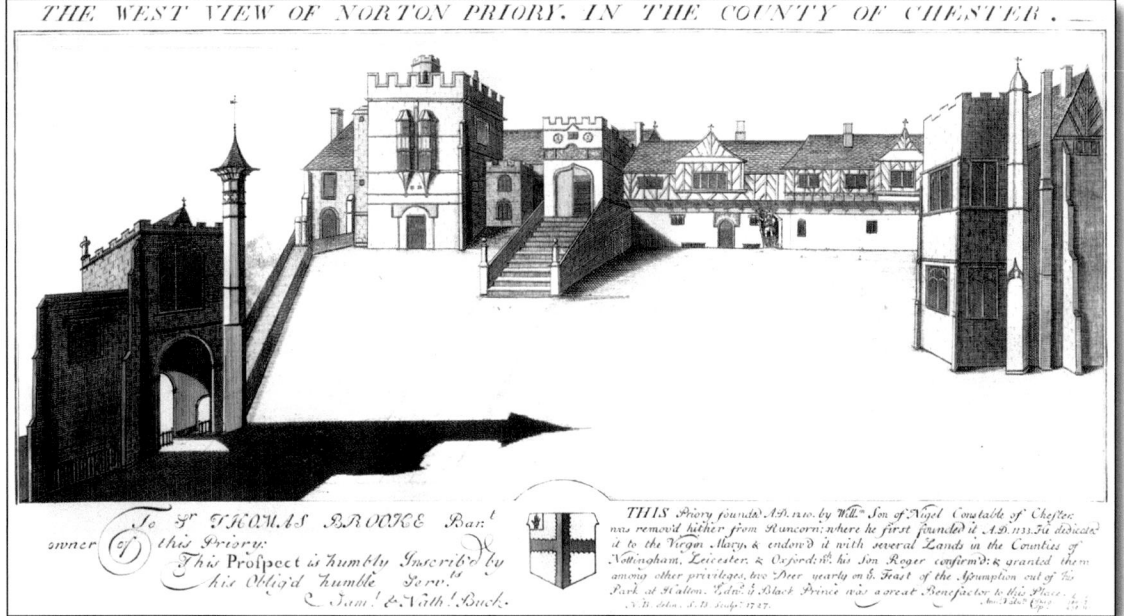

Norton Abbey, showing the Tudor manor house on the remains of the medieval undercroft, by Samuel and Nathaniel Buck (1727).

to the sword if they refused to yield, while his soldiers pilfered livestock from the estate.[6] As Lancaster reported, Norton held, although afterwards the Royalists 'plundered Mr Brooke's tenants, and returned home with same and hatred of all the country'.[7] Two of the defenders later petitioned the Cheshire County Committee for recompense in connection to wounds received. The case of unnamed maimed soldier, probably Robert Stevenson, was referred to by Lieutenant Colonel Richard Brooke in 1651 to his brother-in-law, 'I wrote to you formerly concerning this poor lame man, wounded you know in Norton House, where you were present and know that it was upon a sally to trouble you'. Similarly, in 1655, Samuel Pickering claimed to be 'in a very desperate service at and for the garrison at Norton in the county was shot in the arm, whereby he was since made utterly useless thereof, besides the great pain he many times suffers by occasion thereof'.[8]

The robust defence of Norton House gave the Parliamentarian war effort in Cheshire a significant boost as the Royalist garrison of Halton withdrew into the castle. It also enabled the Parliamentarian forces in the area to recruit, train, and equip military forces, including Colonel Brooke's troop of horse and regiment of foot, in the locality, whilst building up their power and isolating any remaining enemy outposts. Henry Brooke was an early deputy lieutenant in Cheshire and actively promoted the Parliamentary war aims in the county during the winter of 1642–1643, some months before Sir William Brereton arrived from London with his military forces. With Brereton's

---

6 Hall (ed.), *Memorials*, pp. 38–39.
7 John Lewis (ed.), *The Siege of Chester: Nathaniel Lancaster's Narrative* (Nottingham: Raider Books, 1987), p. 9.
8 CRO, QJF 78/4, f. 34r.; QJF 82/4, f. 154r.

support, Henry Brooke was placed on the original county committee for assessment and sequestration. He raised a cavalry troop and infantry regiment and, on 28 March 1644, petitioned Parliament for funds for the completion of his military commands. On 7 May 1644, Brooke was granted £1,000 towards the completion of military commands, whilst his power increased in September 1644 when he was appointed high sheriff of Cheshire by Parliamentary ordinance.[9] A Presbyterian officer, he was constantly with Brereton, endorsing his letters and instructions whilst serving with ability and loyalty.

Surviving warrants issued by Brooke, his officers, and local officials to the constables of the townships assigned to its upkeep offer an insight into how the garrison at Norton was paid, supplied, and maintained. Thus, on 2 September 1643, Colonel Henry Brooke ordered the constables of Aston to collect arrears for the dragoons' pay, which were in arrears:

> I formerly sent out several levies to them for collecting of monies for the dragoons and as you are, as appears, behind with your payment. These are henceforth to charge and command you that you are besides with and withal 4 weeks' pay more at 6s. 6d. per week, which you to are supply at Norton before 7 September to my clerk.

Captain John Brooke – a younger brother of Colonel Henry, whose company was quartered at Norton and the Frodsham area in 1643–1644 and at Bridge Trafford in 1645–1646 – issued the following warrant to the same constables on 18 December 1643:

> Forasmuch as your township has yet made no presentations of which arms they have provided. These are therefore strictly to charge and command you the constables to bring before me upon Thursday, being the 18th of this month [sic][10] to Norton Hall by 8 of the clock a true certificate of the names of those who hold whole or half ploughs within your said township, and you are charged by that time to gather moneys for the buying of ammunition according to 3lb of powder, 12 yards of match, 60 bullets for every musket, the which money is to be paid at Norton as aforementioned and at the same time, upon which receipt you shall be provided after the rates of 1s. 6d. powder the pound, match 8d. the pound, now for the better gathering of this money you are to understand that every whole plough, and every two half ploughs are to find a man, musket, sword and bandolier, and for you to gather proportionately. Hereof I charge you not to fail as you dare answer it at your utmost peril.

Moreover, on 2 March 1644, he instructed the Aston constables:

> By virtue of an original commission to me granted by the right honourable Lord Fairfax, general of these counties, for the speedy raising of my company to lie in

---

9 *CJ*, III, pp. 439, 484, 610; C. H. Firth and R. S. Rait (eds), *Acts and Ordinances of the Interregnum, 1642–1660* (London: HMSO, 1911), I, pp. 503–05.
10 The Thursday following would have been 24 December.

the garrison of Northwich, or in what other place shall be, by the general thought convenient. These are therefore strictly to command you, to warn all those who are to send men and arms under me according to my commission, that they repair to Norton Hall upon Tuesday next, being the 5th day of this present March by 12 of the clock and there to appear with their complete arms.

Two weeks later, Captain Brooke issued a further warrant to the constables, warning them that all listed soldiers under him were to report to Norton 'with their complete arms for training according to the discipline of war, and all others who are charged and not listed to be there also'. On 25 March, he further commanded the constables of Aston to 'collect and gather within your township by distress or otherwise, the sum of 10s. for the buying of drums and colours for my company, and the same to bring to Norton Hall on Thursday, being the 28th of this present March by 10 of the clock'.

On 1 July 1644, Brooke ordered the same officials thus:

By virtue of an official order to me from the Council of War at Nantwich for the speedy bringing in of my men to do such service as they shall be called unto, these are therefore strictly to charge you the constables, to command all those who are to find men and arms to repair to their rendezvous at Norton township tomorrow, being the 2nd day of July, by twelve of the clock at the furthest, and likewise those who have lately lost men and arms are to provide new men and arms, or to suffer sure punishment as shall be thought to ordain for great an offence, herein so neither you, nor they fail as you will answer the contrary.

Additionally, Captain Lieutenant Robert Wynn of Colonel Henry Brooke's troop of horse sent a warrant on 13 July to the constables of Aston to supply horses and deliver them to him at Norton House.[11]

Northwich

The salt town of Northwich was fortified by a system of earthworks and garrisoned in the name of Parliament in early 1643. During this time, the constables of Nether Whitley contributed 4s. 'for the making of mud walls at Northwich'.[12] The Northwich garrison was largely maintained by payments from the sequestration committees of the hundreds of Northwich and Bucklow, in addition to the constables of nearby townships. Between 1 October 1643 and mid-1644, numerous payments were received for Colonel John Leigh's regiment from the former, while the constables of Nether Whitley contributed 16s. for '2 bushels of oats brought to the Northwich garrison'.[13] Additionally, the Bucklow Committee complied with a standing order from the deputy lieutenants by granting some of the profits of the sequestered

---

11 Unlisted warrants, 2 September 1643, 18 December 1643, 2 March 1644, 16 March 1644, 1 July 1644, 13 July 1644.
12 BL, Ms Harley 2128, f. 43r.
13 BL, Ms Harley 2128, ff. 41v., 42r.

goods of Peter Leycester of Tabley to Lieutenant Colonel Gilbert Gerard and Captain John Holford for the use of the soldiers. Similarly, the sum of £9 15s. 3d. was disbursed out of the estate of Peter Venables of Marston to 'Captain Wright for the Northwich garrison', while, on 19 November 1644, 629lbs of cheese was supplied by the township of Netherleigh.[14]

A letter from Sir William Brereton to the Speaker, dated 8 November 1645, mentions that the large quantity of Royalist prisoners captured at Denbigh Green 'doth much add to our trouble and charge, having not only so many as all our prisons and garrisons are capable of, but we are forced to disburse them to several towns and parishes upon open quarters, as in Stockport, Grappenhall, Middlewich, Northwich and Congleton'.[15] This suggests that Northwich was no longer garrisoned by then. The tenure of its governor, Lieutenant Colonel Gerard, ceased on 2 February 1644, and his command was posted to Tarvin, although, according to marginal notes in Brereton's army list, Captain Richard Pigott's company of townsmen were still located in Northwich in April 1645.[16] Even so, the unit fulfilled various roles at the Chester Leaguer in October–November 1645 and was still mustered on 29 October 1646.[17]

The nature and extent of the earthworks at Northwich are an enigma, as nothing appears to remain today. Ormerod, in his *History of Cheshire*, described:

> At the entrance of the town from Chester, on the left-hand side of the road, is an ancient house … behind which is a curious garden, near to and about the height of the Castle Hill, consisting of 5 terraces, or platforms, one above the other. In these cannon balls have been found at various periods, and it has been thence conjectured that these terraces were a part of the fortifications, and a point of attack during the civil disturbances before alluded to.[18]

We are on safer ground, though, with evidence from a contemporary petition that mentions the garrison and town defences. On 31 August 1647, the Cheshire Committee wrote to the Committee for Compounding at Goldsmiths' Hall:

> We thought it our duty to inform you of the nature of the delinquency of Mr Robert Brownfield, of Hapsford, and late of Witton, near Northwich, a garrison held for the King and Parliament. In contempt of the Ordinance of 22 October 1643 against spies and intelligencers, Mr Brownfield did, about 26 May 1644, after his release as prisoner at Chester, where he ingratiated himself with Sir Francis Gamull, governor of that city, write a letter to the governor, which might have been attended with dangerous consequences both to the garrison of Northwich

---

14 BL, Ms Harley 2137, ff. 55v., 95v., 114r., 151r.–152v.
15 BL, Ms Add. 11332, f. 59r.
16 TNA, SP28/152/4, unf.; SP28/208, ff. 33v.–34r.
17 TNA, SP28/40/2, f. 190v.; E121/5/7/351, f. 22v.; BL, Ms Add. 11332, ff. 14r.–15r., 20v., 31v., 35r.
18 Thomas Helsby (ed.), George Ormerod, *The History of the County Palatine and City of Chester* (Revised and enlarged edition, London: Routledge, 1882), I, p. 311.

and the adjacent country, had it been effected according to the letter. In that letter he not only, according to promise, advertised Sir Francis of the moving, intents, and designs of our armies and of the Scots, but endeavored the ruin of the garrison at Northwich, directing when and by what means it might be surprised. By reason of his contempt of the Commons' order in not going up to tender himself a composition for his estate, he was by our warrant of the 18th inst. apprehended and committed to the custody of John Birch, keeper of the prison at Halton Castle, but was 2 days after released, notwithstanding our warrant. We crave your directions for our further proceedings herein, and wish that some course may be taken for punishing Birch.[19]

Similarly, in 1650, Katharine Stubbs of Northwich claimed compensation for damage inflicted upon her house in the town:

To Colonel Croxton with the rest of the justices at the sessions sitting at Middlewich. The humble petition of Katharine Stubbs formerly the wife of John Stubbs of Witton deceased, showed that whereas your petitioner having her habitation without the walls of Northwich in the time of the garrison, and being her house joined unto the outmost guard, upon the coming of Prince Rupert against the town as the officers and soldiers within the town suspected, the officers and gentlemen within the town caused 4 bayes of her building to be pulled down for fear of giving advantage to the enemy so that your poor petitioner sustained great losses there, after a greater and former loss, viz.: losing her dear husband in the service as is not unknown to many of the gentlemen. The humble petition of your petitioner is that you would be pleased to look upon my poor condition and be pleased to afford some small contribution towards my relief.[20]

The garrison of Northwich comprised the following military units:

Colonel John Leigh's Own Company

John Leigh esquire, of Norbury Booths, near Knutsford, raised a troop of horse, a company of dragoons, and a regiment of foot for the service of Parliament in Cheshire. In February 1643, he briefly became governor of Northwich, while, on 13 September 1643, he was appointed deputy lieutenant for Cheshire. The following May, he was placed on the county committee for sequestrations.[21] Leigh's infantry regiment and his own company were recruited in early 1643 from town volunteers and spent much of their service in the Northwich garrison. Leigh received various payments to the total of £49 7s. 6. for his soldiers from the Bucklow sequestrators between 4 April 1644 and 22 May 1645.[22] His company numbered 44 common soldiers on 25

---

19   *CSPD 1645–1647*, p. 569.
20   CRO, QJF 79/1, f. 20r.
21   *CJ*, III, p. 484; Morrill, *Cheshire*, p. 83.
22   TNA, SP28/40/2, ff. 57r., 92r.

November 1643, 44 between 17 December 1643 and 20 April 1644, 60 on 4 May 1644, and 100 on 30 April 1645.[23]

The following commissioned and non-commissioned officers were listed on 22 March 1643:

Captain-Lieutenant Newton
Ensign Cartwright
Sergeant Henley
Sergeant Taylor
Corporal Grimshaw
Corporal Roxtall
Corporal Davenport
Drummer William Newton
Clerk Humphrey Burgess.[24]

The following appear in undated pay warrants for the company:

Quartermaster Boden
Clerk Thomas Robinson
Surgeon William Ludlow
Corporal John Baxter.[25]

As part of the Cheshire contingent under Sir William Brereton at the final siege of Lichfield, on 5 June 1646, the company, under the command of Captain Lieutenant Hugh Birtles, comprised:

Ensign Cartwright
Sergeant Hindley
Sergeant Taylor
Corporal Davenport
Corporal Bradshaw
Drummer William Newton.[26]

Captain Richard Pigott's Company (Leigh's Regiment)

Captain Richard Pigott was 'of the town of Northwich' and might have been Master of Witton School in 1643 and Master of Shrewsbury in 1646.[27] In October 1643, the constables of Nether Whitley remunerated Pigott to the sum of £36, being an annual outlay from four of his sponsors. A similar system helped fund Gilbert Gerard of the same regiment.[28] A pay warrant, this time from central funds, exists for Captain Pigott's soldiers for 11

---

23   TNA, SP28/152/9, f. 15r.
24   TNA, SP28/35/2, f. 258v.
25   TNA, SP28/152/4, ff. 10v., 12r.–13r.; E121/5/7/35, f. 64v.
26   TNA, SP28/513/1, f. 87r.
27   Dore (ed.), *Letter Books*, I, p. 385, note 8.
28   BL, Mss Harley 2128, f. 42r.; 1999, f. 75v.

February 1645.²⁹ His large volunteer company of 120 common soldiers was formed from Northwich townsmen in early 1643 and habitually served in the town's garrison.

Tarvin

By January 1645, Sir William Brereton had begun to tighten the blockade of Chester by establishing a series of outposts to the south and east of the city. From his forward base, a force had been placed outside Beeston and another in Farndon at the Cheshire end of the Dee Bridge, to try to prevent raiding on the backs of the besiegers. New garrisons had also been established at Aldford, Oulton, Huxley, Tattenhall, Hawarden, Bridge Trafford, Barrow, and Upton, while, by early January, a strong base had been pushed forward to Christleton, barely a mile from the eastern suburb of Chester at Boughton. Although it is difficult to estimate the extent of the defensive works at Tarvin, during September 1644, Captain John Whitworth, who had been an officer of pioneers in Brereton's army, supervised their construction, for which he was remunerated the sum of £37 6s. 8d. He was similarly employed at the siege of Chester. During December 1645, Whitworth approved work carried out by Captain Hugh Holt's pioneers, who had dug trenches and built barricades below the Old Newgate on the eastern side of the city.³⁰

Malbon reported that, on 30 August 1644, 'all the forces at Nantwich, except Major Croxton's and the town companies marched forth to Middlewich, where they quartered that night. And the next day to Northwich and Great Budworth, and then to Tarvin, which they fortified with strong works, made it a market town and therein put a garrison'.³¹ Located four miles east of Chester, a garrison was established at Tarvin in summer 1644 along with others, including Christleton, Hooton, and Puddington, to blockade Chester on the English side, in addition to establishing a line of communications across Farndon Bridge and exerting military pressure on the Royalist garrison of Beeston. The Tarvin Committee was especially responsible for collecting assessments from Edisbury hundred and farther afield.³² In May 1645, Sir William Brereton told the Speaker of the House of Commons of his concerns that the approaching Royalists would 'being on their march for Chester there to recruit their army out of Wales, and assault Tarvin and Hooton, 2 of my principal garrisons situated to distress that city'.³³ Tarvin increasingly functioned as Sir William Brereton's operational headquarters for the Leaguer of Chester and, from November 1644, was administrated by the Tarvin Committee, composed of army officers and minor gentlemen from the hundred of Edisbury. As operational requirements demanded, Brereton and some of the leading deputy lieutenants of Cheshire, including

---

29 TNA, SP28/35/2, f. 266r.
30 TNA, SP28/128/13, f. 20r.; SP28/152/7, ff. 24v.–26v.; SP28/225/3, f. 582r.
31 Hall (ed.), *Memorials*, p. 145.
32 Morrill, *Cheshire*, pp. 87–88.
33 BL, Ms Add. 11331, ff. 158r.–v.

Colonels Robert Duckenfield and John Leigh, joined them there.[34] In 1644, Brereton also established special committees at Hooton and Puddington, whose responsibility was to organise the monthly assessment and collection of taxation and contributions in the surrounding locale. The need for a separate establishment to maintain these garrisons may have been the major administrative reason for the creation of these committees. Numerous warrants have survived showing how they allocated taxes directly for the upkeep of garrisons in the area under their control.[35]

On 17 September 1644, Commissary General Hinde issued the following warrant to the constables of Aston in Bucklow hundred to provide wheat for the army at Tarvin:

> By virtue of an order to me given by the honourable Sir William Brereton, commander-in-chief of the forces within this county for service for his Majesty and the parliament, for the constant supply of the army with provision. These are therefore strictly to charge and command you forthwith to provide within your township four Winchester bushels of the best wheat. And the same to bring into me or my deputy to Tarvin upon Monday next, being the twentieth day of this instant September, to be sent immediately after then. Hereof fail not as you tender the safety of your person and estates.[36]

On 2 May 1645, the sum of £120 was paid 'to the Treasurer at Tarvin to be disposed of by the Committee there for the buying of provisions for the garrison at Tarvin (which has been much exhausted by supplying the army with victuals and provisions) and for the army lying at Hoole'.[37] Moreover, on 26 October 1645, the Committee of Tarvin appealed to Brereton:

> We will not, God willing, be wanting in our power to provide what provision can be had in these parts. But we have all the time since the Leaguer been forced to take so much round about us at divers times, when present necessity required, that little or none is left upon the sequestered lands or in this garrison. Therefore, we desire you to command that what supply is possible may be had from Nantwich and those parts, as well as other places.[38]

The same day, the committee wrote to the sequestrators of Northwich hundred:

> You have ever been our storehouse and magazine upon all service. We fly unto you as our chief, if not our only, supply of the exigencies we are in at this present for victual and other necessaries, for the keeping of this our present and serviceable army together. If we be not forthwith supplied with bread and meal within 24 hours we shall be put to a greater mischief than we can express. For we

---

34 BL, Mss Add. 11331, ff. 75v.–86r., 115r.; 11332, ff. 28r.–30v.
35 TNA, SP28/208, *passim*; SP28/224, *passim*; SP28/225, *passim*.
36 Unlisted warrant, 17 September 1644.
37 BL, Ms Add. 11331, f. 52v.
38 BL, Ms Add. 11332, f. 14r.

shall not only lose the ground which we have gained upon the enemy, but have to disband our men and let at liberty to prey upon you and the whole county. For prevention whereof we entreat you forthwith to sent unto the Leaguer at Chester all the bread, cheese and other provisions that you either have in store, can borrow, buy or procure on such a design as we are now upon. And that you procure to be baked what more bread you can possibly, with all speed that may be, to be sent to us.[39]

The following day, Commissary William Hinde notified Brereton from the Chester suburbs:

I humbly entreat that your command may pass over the country for a greater supply of victuals than the gentlemen have already sent for. And especially with great quantities of bread and meal may come from Nantwich, Northwich, and Tarvin up to the army by tomorrow night or sooner if possible. Else it is not possible for the army to survive or keep together 24 hours. I have already sent to Warrington and to the forenamed places for all the bread that possibly may be had.[40]

In addition to a lack of victuals for the soldiers, the Parliamentarian garrison of Tarvin (like others in Cheshire) was considerably in arrears of pay, something that quickly resulted in discontent and mutinous conduct in the ranks. On 29 October 1645, Sir William Brereton wrote to the head constables of the hundreds of Macclesfield, Northwich, Bucklow, and Nantwich:

At my coming to the Leaguer I had no sooner dismounted at Tarvin, but I was met with complaints from [Lieutenant Colonel] Jones and [Adjutant] Lothian of a very hot mutiny amongst the soldiers for want of pay, alleging near 2 months' arrears. It pressed the commanders with great jealousies of strong distraction, yet in conclusion it was for the present appeased. Upon further looking into the occasion, it appears to be a want of bringing in the weekly pay upon the framing of the last model,[41] for the obtaining thereof there were undertakers in the said hundreds. I pray you gentlemen use your best endeavours for the bringing in of arrears in Nantwich hundred so that the soldiers may have some reasonable satisfaction to prevent the like. What monies I have is the most part of it upon security and specially ordered how to be disposed of, contrary to which is not safe.

Brereton added in a follow-up letter, 'the enemy has an army on foot to hinder our present design. We stand engaged both to fight them and to make good our Leaguers. If either swerve, it will be a mighty loss to the country, which I wish might be taken into a sensible consideration'.[42]

---

39 BL, Ms Add. 11332, f. 24v.
40 BL, Ms Add. 11332, f. 23r.
41 In mid-1645, there emerged among the Cheshire army a system of pay known as the 'new model' or 'Cheshire model'. Not to be confused with the New Model Army, this was an attempt by Jones, Lothian, and the deputy lieutenants to place the payment of the troops engaged at the Chester Leaguer on firmer ground after Brereton left for Westminster in June.
42 BL, Ms Add. 11332, ff. 27r.–28r.

The context for such logistical considerations was the concentration of Parliamentarian forces from Cheshire and the garrisons forming the Chester Leaguer in response to the possibility of a Royalist relief of Chester from the vicinity of the Welsh borders. On 24 October 1645, news had reached the commanders at the Leaguer from the Shropshire Committee that Sir William Vaughan, a soldier of experience of continental and Irish warfare, was at Ludlow with a force of 1,500 horse and foot, intent on the marching to the relief of the city. Other reports, however, put the number at 3,000 and alleged that Vaughan was to be joined by troops from North Wales and possibly from Ireland. But, although Byron had advised him that 'the enemy for the present being both weak and much discouraged since their loss upon the last assault, the Parliamentarians enjoyed a distinct numerical advantage and could be relatively confident of resisting any relief force'.[43] Brereton had arrived in Nantwich on 26 October as Vaughan's advance guard was nearing Chirk and his main body passing Oswestry.[44] He cautioned Jones and Lothian against premature contact and urged that they fight at a distance from Chester itself, 'since they in the city may by issuing out much annoy you by falling on your rear as the Nantwich [garrison] did by falling on the Irish army'.[45] On 27 October, Jones, commanding the Leaguer on the Welsh side of the Dee, assured Brereton:

> I find the horse under my command so gallantly resolved that were there no expectation of foot, yet I should give the enemy a meeting. However, I pray haste up all the forces you can that, the siege being secured, we may chase the enemy out of Wales and these parts. Were there 500 men commanded with spades, shovels and mattocks, I am confident that in four days to cast such a trench and outworks on this side of Chester from water to water that, if the enemy were master of the field, he should not relieve the city.

He also requested Sergeant Major James Lothian, in command on the English side, to send over Colonel Robert Duckenfield's veteran regiment and any other available foot, 'for it may be we shall fight this day'.[46] Jones' cavalry patrols had reported Vaughan first at Rhuabon and then at Ruthin, but, by 29 October, he reasoned that he was aiming to meet with Welsh troops somewhere in the Clwyd Valley. Allowing a day's pause to allow the Shropshire troops who had arrived exhausted from a forced march to rest, and to enable Lothian to coordinate the foot about to march from the Leaguer, the taskforce got under way. According to a list of 'those forces that marched under the command of Jones and Lothian', this consisted of roughly 1,350 cavalry (the figure for the reformadoes is not given) and 1,250 infantry. In response to promptings by the Committee of Both Kingdoms, the Cheshire army had been reinforced before Chester by around 2,000 horse and 1,350 foot from the counties of Yorkshire, Shropshire, Warwickshire, Derbyshire,

---

43 BL, Ms Add. 11332, ff. 13v.–14r., 21v.–22r., 81r.
44 Long (ed.), *Diary*, p. 276.
45 BL, Ms Add. 11332, f. 20r.
46 BL, Ms Add. 11332, ff. 22v., 25r.–v.

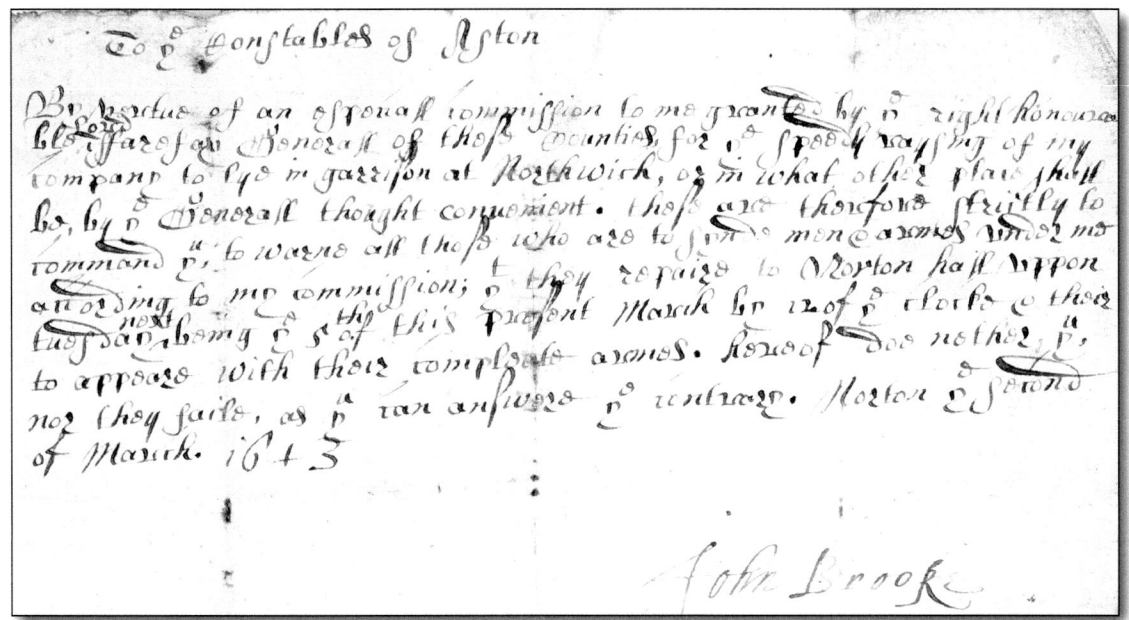

Warrant signed by Captain John Brooke to the constables of Aston to send men to Norton with complete arms, 2 March 1644. (Unlisted warrant, Aston Collection)

Staffordshire, and Lancashire.[47] The 200-strong reformado unit had come from London with Sir William Brereton. Lancaster gave 1,400 horse and 1,000 foot, while Symonds estimated the Parliamentarian infantry at '1,500 at least'.[48] Additionally, the Cheshire horse is described as participating in the forthcoming battle and probably rendezvoused with the taskforce at Ruthin, where, on 31 October, the Parliamentarians learned of Vaughan's presence near Strata Marcella (Whitchurch). The following day, the Parliamentarian forces inflicted a significant defeat upon Vaughan's troops at Denbigh, which put an end to attempts to relieve the Royalist garrison at Chester.[49]

In 1645, the garrison of Tarvin consisted of four Cheshire infantry companies – those commanded by Sir William Brereton (under its captain lieutenant, Lieutenant Colonel Robert Venables), Lieutenant Gilbert Gerard, Captain John Hardware, and Captain William Daniell. Venables, an officer of considerable ability and experience, acted as governor from 1 July 1645 until 8 January 1646, for which he received pay of £5 5s. 8d. per day.[50] He also served at the vanguard of the Cheshire foot, fighting with distinction at the siege of Nantwich, operations in Shropshire (including the defence of Wem), and the Battle of Montgomery in 1644. Moreover, Venables played a prominent role in directing the siege of Chester and was a signatory of the articles of surrender in February 1646. Brereton's own company was initially raised in Cheshire during the summer of 1642 and was completed in London before

---

47   BL, Ms Add. 11332, f. 32v.
48   Long (ed.), *Diary*, p. 258.
49   BL, Ms Add. 11332, ff. 76r.–v.; *A True Relation of a Great Victory obtained by the Parliament Forces in Cheshire, under Sir William Brereton, against the King's Forces, under the command of Sir William Vaughan, near Denbigh* (London: Edward Husband, 1645). TT, E308[14].
50   BL, Ms Harley 1999, ff. 58v.–63r.; TNA, SP28/224/1, f. 232v.

marching north in January the following year. In November 1645, Brereton informed the Committee of Accounts, 'As for my foot regiment I had my field officers and divers captains before the date of my commission. So had I also my own company consisting near of 9 score or 200 divers months before the date of my commission [20 September 1642], before which time as also before my coming down, they did perform good service'.[51]

Sir William Brereton's Own Company

This, like most of his infantry regiment, was recruited in London and from volunteers in Cheshire. It was at the forefront of the fighting in Cheshire, Staffordshire, Shropshire, and the Welsh borders during the spring and summer of 1643 and was among other Cheshire foot at Cholmondeley on 25 August 1643, when it was paid the sum of £506, being three months' pay in arrears.[52] Muster rolls dated to between 17 and 23 March 1646 record that Brereton's own company mustered the following:

> Lieutenant Colonel Robert Venables
> Lieutenant Lewis Griffith
> Ensign Brereton
> Sergeant Strothall
> Sergeant Hoden
> Sergeant Randle Hall
> Corporal Ratcliffe
> Corporal Henry Moore
> Corporal Bisson
> Drummer Richard Watson
> Drummer Thomas Younger
> Arnold Baxter and James Whitley}
> gentlemen of the company
> Clerk Thomas Chetham.[53]

Brereton's company numbered 120 common soldiers fit for duty on 8 June 1644, 150 on 30 April 1645, 140 on 18 October 1645, 90 on 30 October 1645, 89 between 17 and 23 March 1646, 130 on 15 August 1646, 85 on 4 November 1646, and 132 on 1 April 1647.[54] Before June 1647, Venables received a total of £3,641 19s. 10d. in pay 'for himself, and the officers and soldiers of the Macclesfield hundred trained and freehold bands' – formerly Sir William Brereton's company. His command is confirmed by a warrant of 30 December 1647, authorising a payment to Thomas Davies, who is stated to have 'served

---

51 BL, Ms Add. 11332, f. 43r.
52 BL, Ms Harley 1999, f. 61v.
53 TNA, SP28/124/1, ff. 25r.–30v.; E121/5/7/351, f. 46r.
54 TNA, SP28/196/1, f. 21v.; SP28/124/1, f. 29r.; SP28/123/3, ff. 463r., 495v.; SP28/123/4, f. 640r.; BL, Mss Add. 11331, f. 45v.; 11332, ff. 3v., 32r.

commendably in Cheshire as ensign to the freehold band, or company, of Macclesfield under the command of Lieutenant-Colonel Venables'.[55]

Lieutenant Colonel Gilbert Gerard's Company (Colonel John Leigh's Regiment)

Consisting of volunteers, this company was also recruited in the town. Several muster lists survive for the unit between 1643 and 1646. On 25 November 1643, three commissioned officers, three sergeants, three corporals, two drummers, one clerk, and 44 soldiers were present; the same strength was listed on 17 December 1643; the same with 60 soldiers on 4 May 1644; with 100 private sentinels on 30 April 1645; 123 soldiers on 21 October 1645; 123 soldiers on 7 February 1646; 109 soldiers on 27 March 1646; 130 soldiers on 23 May 1646; and 124 soldiers on 9 August 1646.[56] The distinct increase in the size of Gerard's company by the spring of 1645 is probably related to his promotion as lieutenant colonel as well as the disbandment and probable re-distribution of the regiment's major's company around that time. On 21 October 1645, the following junior and non-commissioned officers were present in Lieutenant Colonel Gerard's company:

> Lieutenant Edward Barker
> Ensign William Holt
> Sergeant Anthony Hitchins
> Sergeant George Spencer
> Sergeant Richard Southall
> Corporal Adam Hulmes
> Corporal Joshua Grimes
> Corporal Thomas Basnett
> Drummer John Catchpoll
> Drummer Henry Williamson
> Clerk Richard Starkey.[57]

Captain John Hardware's Company (Brereton's Regiment)

Hardware came from Bromborough in the Wirral. Raised in 1644 as a company in Brereton's infantry regiment, his command was part of the Tarvin garrison, and, on 8 March 1645, the sum £5 was made to Hardware 'towards paying the volunteers of my company'.[58] John's command was active at the Chester Leaguer – in late October 1645, it joined Leadbeater's company in

---

55 TNA, SP28/128/13, f. 16v.; SP28/125/3, f. 313r.; SP28/224, f. 276v.
56 TNA, SP28/152/4, f. 15v.; SP28/123/2, ff. 190v., 196r.; SP28/123/1, ff. 38r., 50r.; BL, Ms 11331, f. 44v.
57 TNA, SP28/123/2, f. 190v.
58 TNA, SP29/196/1, unf.

the siege lines opposite the city's Pikegate and the Bars in Foregate Street, on which occasion 40 common soldiers were present. On 18 January 1646, James Henley of Hardware's company was one of 16 Parliamentarian prisoners of war exchanged at Chester.[59] The command received the sum of £159 4s. from Treasurer Croxton later in the year.[60] On 12 November 1645, the following junior and non-commissioned officers were present:

> Lieutenant Christopher Ball
> Ensign Samuel Hardware
> Sergeant Richard Bakewell
> Corporal James Whitley
> Corporal Daniel Mather
> Corporal William Grimsdale
> Drummer Thomas Rathbone
> Clerk John Johnson.[61]

Hardware's company mustered 60 common soldiers on 30 April 1645, 80 on 18 October 1645, 40 on 31 October 1645, and 45 on 12 November 1645.[62]

Captain William Daniell's Company (Brooke's Regiment)

William was the third son of Peter Daniell of Over Tabley, near Knutsford, head of an established Cheshire gentry family. The loyalties of the Daniell family were divided during the civil wars. Two of William's brothers were officers in Earl Rivers' regiment – following the Royalist storming of Brentford on 12 November 1642, it was reported, 'we lost 16 men, whereof 1 was a son of Mr Daniell of Tabley … a fine young gentlemen, who was a lieutenant under my Lord Rivers, he and his captain were both slain'.[63] Captain Peter Daniell was wounded at Gloucester in August 1643 and later died in Oxford. Furthermore, three of William's sisters married Royalists, and the fourth, Mary, wed a captain in Brereton's army. William Daniell was a highly competent and industrious officer who held a commission in Brooke's regiment by early 1643. Although some of his junior officers were Frodsham men, his company was formed predominately from Bucklow hundred. During the early part of the fighting in Cheshire, Daniell's command operated in and around the local area. In August 1643, it was quartered in Frodsham, wherein the constables of the township disbursed £65 18s. in pay to Captain Daniell 'and to his clerk and soldiers under his command'.[64]

From June 1644, Daniell's company quartered at Tarvin (of which William might have been deputy governor). About this time, the constables of Lymm

---

59   BL, Ms Add. 11333, ff. 31v.–32r., 110r.
60   TNA, SP28/128/13, f. 18v.
61   TNA, SP28/122/3, f. 431r.
62   BL, Mss Add. 11331, f. 45v.; 11332, ff. 3v., 32v.; TNA, SP28/122/3, f. 431r.
63   Bodl. Lib., Ms Ashmole 830, f. 292r.
64   BL, Ms Harley 1999, f. 75v.

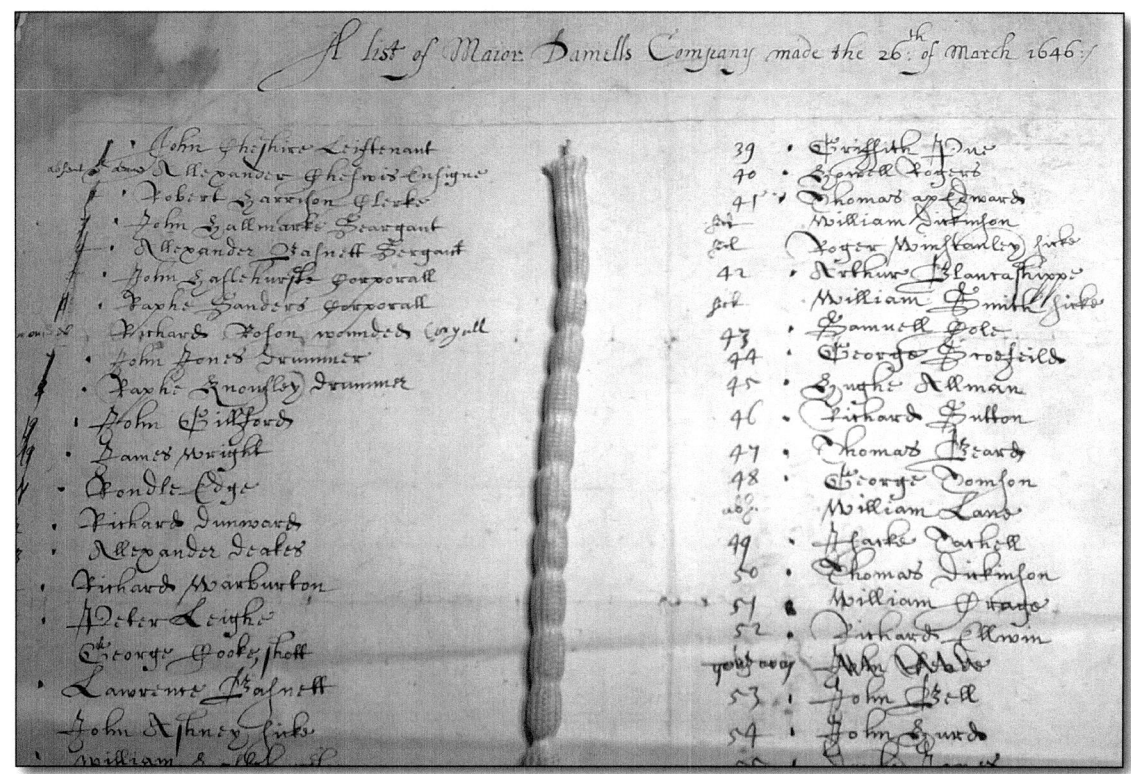

Muster roll of Sergeant Major William Daniell's Company, part of the Tarvin garrison. (TNA, SP28/123/1, unf.)

disbursed the sum of £44 4s. 4d. 'for maintaining fourteen foot soldiers under Major Daniell at Tarvin for 28 weeks at 3s. a week for every soldier'.[65] This entry could refer to John Daniell's command of Booth's regiment, given the not uncommon problem of assigning imprecise ranks by often overworked scribes, or those unfamiliar with particular officers and units, although it seems unlikely. For one thing, Colonel Booth's regiment (including the colonel's company led by John Daniell) was active elsewhere in Cheshire and Shropshire during this period, while the earlier entry recording the payment by the constables of Frodsham referred anachronistically to 'Major William Daniell' and his men. During the subsequent military operations in Cheshire occasioned by Rupert's march northwards during that summer, Daniell marched his men to the relative safety of the Halton garrison. In the first week of July, he joined other officers of Colonel Brooke's regiment in delivering warrants to the constables of Aston, demanding outstanding payment of rents from the estates of Sir Thomas Aston. Throughout 1645 and early 1646, Captain Daniell's company participated almost as a 'frontline unit' in the siege of Chester and military operations in North Wales. As such, William was particularly commended for his actions leading one of the two bodies of commanded musketeers at the Parliamentarian victory at Rowton Heath on 24 September 1645.

---

65   BL, Ms Harley 2128, f. 48v.

On 20 December 1645, Captain William Daniell attended a council of war that determined to intercept Royalist attempts to relieve the siege of Chester, his company duly participating in the march to Whitchurch. Six days later, it was ordered to march with Adjutant Lothian's command to strengthen the guards on the Dee at Lache, while, on 8 January 1646, Daniell's company was part of a joint force of Cheshire, Staffordshire, and Montgomeryshire foot commanded to march to Harwarden Castle. Soon afterwards, it assisted in the blocking up of Holt by Parliamentarian troops; there, on 14 January, Daniell was reminded by Sir William Brereton that 'We have had many shot for want of blinds and many by over-careless wandering. I shall entreat your care in causing blinds to be made, and use your advice to the soldiers not to hazard themselves indiscreetly and without cause'. Furthermore, during this period, he was entrusted with leading negotiations with the Royalist garrison in Chester for the exchange of prisoners of war.[66] A total of 89 private sentinels mustered under Captain William Daniell on 29 March 1646; 107 (including officers) on 5 May 1646; also one lieutenant, one ensign, three sergeants, two drummers, three corporals, and 92 soldiers were present on 30 May 1646, while, in December 1646, the company mustered 46 common soldiers.[67]

On 13 April 1646, Daniell's command was listed as the only volunteer company among 600 Cheshire foot in Chester (the others being five trained band units). Within a month, however, the company had joined the siege of Lichfield, where it was engaged in constructing and manning a breastwork with Lieutenant Colonel Gerard's company on the Beacon Hill side of the city. Whilst at Lichfield on 30 May 1646, Sergeant Major William Daniell's soldiers were paid with the rest of the Cheshire foot a month's arrears of £85 17s. 4d., being 18s. 6d. per man; later, on 5 June, the non-commissioned officers received payment 'according to the New Model' of £11 12s., their names being listed as:

Lieutenant Richard Heath
Ensign Joseph Witter
Sergeant Richard Smith
Sergeant Thomas Banner
Sergeant John Rodes
Corporal William Davenport
Corporal Thomas Garratt
Corporal Hugh Strang
Corporal William Cophall
Drummer Edward Hill
Drummer William Barratt
Clerk Hugh Davenport.[68]

---

66   BL, Ms Add. 11333, ff. 45v., 69r., 101v.–102r., 109v., 117v.
67   TNA, SP28/123/1, f. 98r.; SP28/38, f. 201v.; SP16/513/1, ff. 74r., 86v.
68   TNA, SP16/513/1, ff. 70r.–71r., 86v.–87r.; E121/5/7/351, ff. 64v.–65r.

THE PARLIAMENTARIAN GARRISONS OF NORTON, NORTHWICH, TARVIN, HOOTON, AND PUDDINGTON

Captain William Davies' Company (Brereton's Regiment)

Another volunteer company raised in Tarvin and the surrounding area, but not part of the garrison, was commanded by Captain William Davies as part of Brereton's regiment. Of Ashton-juxta-Tarvin, Davies was a member of the Tarvin Committee. He was commissioned as captain of a company of foot by Sir William Brereton on 9 September 1644, and he served in that capacity until 'the latter end of September 1645'. His commission, granted by Brereton as commander-in-chief, states:

> To Mr William Davies, captain by virtue of authority derived from the parliament, I do by constitute and appoint you to be captain of one company of foot soldiers consisting of 100 men to be raised by you within the several townships of Tarvin, Ashton, Alvanley and Hartford, and anywhere your talents within the county of Chester, to serve in my own regiment of foot for the service of protestant religion, the king, parliament and kingdoms, which the company being raised as aforesaid, you shall by virtue of this commission given you to receive into your care, charge and command as captain thereof receive the same diligently to lead and otherwise in arms for the said service of king and parliament, diligently attending the duty of the said place, hereby commanding all inferior officers and soldiers of the said company to obey you as their captain, and you yourself to obey and follow such orders and directions as from time to time you shall receive from myself and the superior officers of the army according to the discipline of war. Given under my hand and seal at arms, this ninth day of September 1644.

Moreover, Davies' testament of service, dated 10 July 1649 and endorsed by Lieutenant Colonel Robert Venables, says:

> These are to certify all whom it may concern, that Captain William Davies did raise a foot company according to his commission, which was ever ready on all occasions for the public service both at Eaton and other places, and from the date of his commission, being 9 September 1644 until the latter end of September 1645, performed duty in this garrison of Tarvin (where I was governor), and at all times when required for which service neither he nor they did receive any satisfaction that I know of. Witness my hand and seal, 10 July 1649.[69]

Hooton and Puddington

On 21 October 1644, Sir William Brereton notified Sir Samuel Luke, governor of Newport Pagnell, that he had 'marched to Wirral, a piece of land between the seas behind Chester, where we have been this fortnight, and where we

---

[69] BL, Ms Harley 1970, ff. 73v.–74r.

continue to assist the taking in of [Royalist-held] Liverpool … the inhabitants of this country are very importunate that we would garrison amongst them and we would willingly consent but there is no convenient place'. He added, 'provision and lodging not very plentiful'.⁷⁰ Two days later, Brereton reported to the Committee of Both Kingdoms from his outpost at Great Neston:

> we find the inhabitants very well-affected to the Parliament, except the gentry, most of whom have deserted the country and are in Chester and Wales. The inhabitants of this hundred would have us leave a garrison amongst them, but as there is no place more convenient, we are endeavouring to fortify Hooton House, 5 miles from Chester, whither the country comes in very freely to work. In the meantime, the rest of the army is to be stationed in the lower end of Wirral, next Liverpool, that they may assist Sir John Meldrum and the Lancashire forces against that town, now that the treaty [with the King] is broken off.

Furthermore, on 28 October, Brereton informed the same committee that he was remaining with his forces in Wirral between the besiegers of Liverpool and Chester to prevent the delivery of supplies to the garrison (presumably at Liverpool) and that 'our garrison at Tarvin is in good forwardness, and we proceed with all expedition in fortifying Hooton in the Wirral'.⁷¹

Hence, the key purpose of placing a garrison at Hooton was to observe any Royalist crossings over the Dee to the Wirral, although it was also responsible for directing the assessment and collection of taxes in Wirral hundred. Moreover, the garrison at Puddington commanded a ford across the Dee, which, along with outposts at Shotwick and Burton close by, provided a passage at low tide between North Wales and Chester to the west of the city. According to the early nineteenth-century Cheshire antiquarian George Ormerod, before its demolition in the 1780s, Hooton Hall or House was a very large and quadrangular timber-framed building dating from 1488, embattled and machicolated, and with a tower 'of extraordinary height'.⁷² Moreover, sequestrators' accounts relating to the period following the disbandment of Hooton's garrison in November 1646 include references to earthen ramparts, a defensive moat, and a chained drawbridge, in addition to sums paid to teams of men from Tranmere for work on its dismantling.⁷³ Both Hooton and Puddington suffered from a dearth of victuals, heightened by the difficulties encountered by the sequestrators' difficulty in gathering in monies from confiscated estates close to Chester, in addition to the isolated nature of the location of the garrisons themselves. One collector noted that tenants' rents were to be halved 'because the garrisons and forces in Wirral were not able to secure them from the enemy'.⁷⁴ In May 1645, the governor of both garrisons, Lieutenant Colonel Coote, issued warrants (through the Hooton Committee) to local bakers to supply bread for the soldiers, whilst,

---

70   Tibbutt (ed.), *Letter Books*, p. 862.
71   *CSPD 1644–1645*, pp. 67, 77–78.
72   Helsby (ed.), *History*, II, p. 415.
73   BL, Ms Harley 2018, ff. 27r., 57r., 82r., 105r.–106v., 118v., 171v., 176r.
74   BL, Ms Harley 2126, f. 160v.

on 30 October, Commissary Rogers was reimbursed £10 for bread 'for the use of the army'.[75]

Coote was the third son of Sir Charles Coote, head of a prominent Irish protestant family. He was an experienced officer who, like Lieutenant Colonel Michael Jones and others, refused to serve the King when the Cessation of Arms was signed and, in mid-1644, took up arms for Parliament in the army commanded by Sir William Brereton. When a military unit was desperate for provisions, the officers might intervene and requisition goods to avoid more serious trouble, even though they had no authority to do this. Whilst quartering in the Wirral in mid-1645, Captain William Shepley received hay and peas to the value of £4 10s. for his cavalry from the committee at Hooton. Anxious to obtain provisions for his men, this enterprising officer appropriated land at Burton for the cultivation of crops. Thus, local Parliamentarian officials complained when Shepley's troopers produced 50 measures of oats 'without order' at 12d. per measure and a further '46 measures of oats not paid for to the state'. In like fashion, in January 1645, the Hooton Committee disbursed 'to Captain John Glegg by order from Sir William Brereton towards raising a troop of horse, in barley 27 measures valued at £3 6s.'[76] Glegg, the son of William Glegg of Gayton in the Wirral, and a local officer, had raised his troop in late 1644.

Likewise, Captain John Rathbone commanded an infantry company from the Wirral in Brereton's regiment, which was quartered in various local garrisons. Described by Tony Dyson as 'easily the most prominent Parliamentarian officer in Wirral', and a man of 'combative, even reckless, qualities', Rathbone fell out with local officials in late 1644 and early 1645, having been accused of 'keeping diverse horses and beats' on its demesne and requisitioning goods before they could be inventoried and valued. He also grew a field of wheat at Burton.[77] Though John Morrill found it odd that Rathbone cultivated crops, it seems probable that he 'was concerned with feeding his men in the face of adverse conditions and an unhelpful bureaucracy'.[78] During spring 1645, Captain Rathbone's company had been stationed at Upton House, an important communications point north of Chester and an important link between the Leaguer and the Parliamentarian army's supply port of Liverpool (Rathbone had suitably received instructions to report on the arrival at the latter of a ship carrying rations, powder, and other items). The garrison had been established after the retirement of Prince Maurice from Chester the previous month. On 2 April, a Royalist night attack on the strongpoint was reported upon by the governor of Hooton:

> Three hours before this day morning the enemy came out of Chester towards Upton House, and thought to have surprised the garrison and cut our men to pieces. They came, every man with a match in his hat and a white cloth of

---

75 BL, Ms Harley 1999, ff. 62r.–68r.; TNA, SP28/224/1, f. 38r.
76 BL, Ms Harley 1999, ff. 17r., 69r.–71v.
77 BL, Ms Harley 1999, ff. 15v., 16r.–17r., 69r., 71v.; Tony Dyson, 'The Oaths at Woodchurch, 1643-1644: Tensions in Civil-War Wirral and Its Aftermath', *THSLC*, 164 (2015), pp. 15–16.
78 Morrill, *Cheshire*, p. 110.

distinction about his right arm to know themselves from our men. When they were about their intended butchery, our horse scouts decried them. After which they marched openly and demanded of our men to deliver up the house upon fair quarter. Our men answered they would have no quarter at their hands; so they fell upon and shot. Many of them were wounded; two of their men lay dead close by the door, and 16 more slain and taken off. Upton garrison is within a mile of Chester, newly garrisoned and maintained by Captain Rathbone, a Wirral man.[79]

The military operations in North Wales in the spring and winter of 1645 resulted in the procurement of significant quantities of victuals for the Cheshire army of Parliament. In April 1645, Lieutenant Colonel Michael Jones launched an incursion deep into Denbighshire in command of 500 horse and 400 foot, Jones later reporting, 'the county was driven by the assent of Sir Thomas Myddelton for the gaining of provisions for the army, which in a manner until that time was provided for by Cheshire, most of which cattle, the whole number of good cows not amounting to 400 nor the sheep 2,000, being not fit to be slain'.[80] The appropriated livestock was turned over to Commissary Hinde, although Sir William Brereton was anxious enough about reports of plundering that he wrote to the deputy lieutenant, William Marbury, on 11 April 1645:

> I was so sensible and so much troubled at the liberty many soldiers had taken to carry away cattle out of Wales that I appointed a guard at Puddington to seize and stay the cattle … I have written also to the Committee of Northwich and to Colonel Brooke to suffer none to pass without my order at Northwich, Frodsham or elsewhere over the river [Weaver] and to make stay of the same aforesaid.[81]

A total of 366 cattle were sold by the commissariat for 29s. each, whilst the 1,700 sheep were either butchered or went for cash. A significant proportion of the money received went on provisions for Tarvin and Hoole garrisons. On 1 May, it was ordered that:

> a great number of cattle taken from the enemy in Wales should be sold and moneys thereof arising bestowed in provisions for the army and garrisons belonging to this county, and whereas the said cattle are sold unto Commissary Hinde in pursuance of the same order, it is now ordered that £120 of the same due for the said cattle shall be paid unto the treasurer at Tarvin by Commissary Hinde within four days after the date hereof to buy provisions for that garrison (which hath been of late much exhausted) and for the forces at Hoole at the appointment of the Committee at Tarvin. The rest is to be paid unto Mr John Wettenhall, Mr Richard Leicester, and Mr [Richard] Egerton, to be by them disposed of in making provisions for the army and garrisons as occasion shall require.[82]

---

79   CRO, DDX/428, f. 60v.
80   BL, Ms Add. 11331, ff. 38r.–v.
81   CRO, DDX/428, f. 86r.
82   BL, Ms Add. 11331, f. 53v.

THE PARLIAMENTARIAN GARRISONS OF NORTON, NORTHWICH, TARVIN, HOOTON, AND PUDDINGTON

According to the 'Order for disposing of money from cattle taken in Wales', it was agreed the following day that £70 was to be distributed to Sir Thomas Myddelton's soldiers, whereas the outstanding sums went towards buying provisions:

> [£20] for the supply of the two ships now remaining in the river near Neston, those to the value of £30 for the garrisons of Hooton and Puddington in the Wirral, those to the value of £20 for the garrison at Upton Hall, and the rest for the supplying of the army at Eccleston and Dodleston … and of the garrison of Nantwich as there shall be occasion.[83]

Lieutenant Colonel Thomas (or Robert) Hunt, a Shropshire officer, succeeded Coote as governor of Hooton by January 1646.[84]

Lieutenant Colonel Coote claimed pay as troop commander in the Cheshire army from 20 October 1644 to 10 August 1645, at which date he took command of the Shropshire horse, being promoted to colonel on 8 November 1645 and serving with it until 31 July 1646.[85] In November 1645, the committee at Hooton disbursed 5s. to his men, while his cavalry troop was remunerated £23 out of the £100 received by Coote from Sir William Brereton for the Shropshire forces and the leaguer of Chester.[86] Coote's own company was bolstered by Irish soldiers who came over to him and Michael Jones from the siege of Liverpool in the autumn of 1644.[87] From late 1644 until the summer of 1645, Lieutenant Colonel Coote acted as governor of the garrisons of Hooton and Puddington, where special committees had been established by Brereton with the responsibility for the organisation and collection of contributions and taxations in Wirral hundred. These isolated garrisons were also pivotal to the maintenance of the fords over the Dee into Wales, and, to that end, Coote supplied Sir William with regular intelligence reports on the situation there. Although his troops regularly quartered at Hooton and Puddington, other commands (mostly 'country' companies) were brought up to operate from them when required. Whilst at Hooton on 21 April 1645, Chidley confided in Brereton that he had not replied to his commander's letters, as he was 'so sick and full of pain', although a week later he had recovered enough for Sir William to compel him (in a set of instructions issued by Brereton to troops appointed to guard the ford across the Dee) 'to assist with his soldiers the effectual observation of this order'.[88]

Towards the end of the month, Coote petitioned Brereton on behalf of his foot soldiers 'to give some competent satisfaction for our past service and what we cannot have at present – the remainder if our arrears – may be settled and assured to us, according to the power of the ordinance granted

---

83 BL, Ms Add. 11331, ff. 20v., 25r., 52r.
84 BL, Ms Add. 11333, ff. 113v.–114r. The signature in a letter of this date concerning the governorship is signed 'Robert Hunt'.
85 TNA, SP28/225/3, f. 770r.; SP28/196/1, ff. 506v., 510r.
86 BL, Ms Harley 1999, f. 71r.; Ms Add. 11332, f. 62v.
87 TNA, SP21/17, ff. 63v.–65r.
88 BL, Ms Add. 11331, ff. 7v., 26v.

to you, out of papists' and malignants' estates'.[89] Pay arrears were especially severe in early 1646, at a time of increasing reductions in income received by the local Parliamentarian committees. As in other garrisons in Cheshire and elsewhere, steps were taken to address this, especially as indiscipline on the part of the soldiers had become acute. Thus, in June 1646, the treasurer of Hooton, who was usually based in Bromborough, made a series of payments to soldiers of Captains Glegg and Rathbone at Hooton to 'quiet' them following disturbances made at sequestrators' meetings, whereas, the following month, similar disbursements were made by the committee to placate troops at Bromborough.[90] These unfortunate men suffered from lack of not only pay but victuals too. In May 1645, Coote issued various warrants (through the Hooton Committee) to local bakers to supply bread for them.[91] This was no inconsiderable task, because estimates of the number of Parliamentarian troops spread between Hooton and Puddington from muster lists and other documents show a figure of 600 foot and 100 horse during the period of their occupation.

Around this period, Lieutenant Colonel Coote, with the troop and company under his command, was seconded to the Shropshire Committee on a more permanent basis, although they continued to play an important role in the siege of Chester and military operations in the area. This seemingly necessitated the relinquishment of his governorship of the Wirral strongholds, because, on 19 July, the deputy lieutenants of Cheshire ordered:

> In regard Lieutenant Colonel Coote has earnestly moved this board to provide a governor for Hooton House in Wirral. It is therefore ordered that Captain Edward Glegg and Captain Birkenhead shall forthwith repair to the said garrison with their companies, and take the charge thereof, and of the provision there, and shall carefully keep and provide for the said garrison until order to the contrary.[92]

Both of these units were from Sir William Brereton's regiment of foot. Feasibly, the appointment of these officers to take command of the garrison in Coote's place reflected decreased military activity in the Wirral following the temporary lifting of the siege of Chester.

Edward Glegg was brother to John Glegg, one of Sir William Brereton's captains of horse. His company of the Trained Bands of Wirral hundred is referred to in Brereton's army list of 30 April 1645 as 'now disposed of', his soldiers having been recently combined with Captain Birkenhead's men. Twenty days previously, the deputy lieutenants at Nantwich had reported that most of his soldiers had deserted for lack of pay and that Glegg had laid down his commission.[93] The actions of Captain Glegg's soldiers were especially problematic because, at that time, the company was located at Tilston, an important garrison located six miles southwest of Beeston. Glegg,

---

89 BL, Ms Add. 11331, f. 29r.
90 BL, Ms Harley 2018, ff. 96r., 106r., 115r.
91 BL, Ms Harley 1999, ff. 62r.–68r.
92 BL, Ms Harley 2128, f. 174r.
93 CRO, DDX/428, f. 88r.

however, seems to have retained his commission, because he was with his soldiers at Hooton until at least October 1645. The total money disbursed to 'Captain Edward Glegg for himself, and his officers and soldiers' by Treasurer Croxton amounted to £683 19s. 4d.[94] While at Chester on 21 April 1646, Glegg's company had reported the following:

> Lieutenant Nathaniel Swettenham
> Ensign Robert Hall
> Sergeant Henry Waring
> Sergeant Edward Bennet
> Sergeant Alexander Barnet
> Clerk Thomas Bennet
> Corporal Lawrence Cooke
> Corporal Richard Jones
> Corporal John Merson
> Drummer Andrew Parrot
> Drummer Richard Beddow.[95]

Captain Henry Birkenhead was from Backford in the Wirral and, with his father, was a lawyer before the war. His foot company, raised from Wirral hundred, was quartered at the important Wirral garrison of Hooton in July 1645 and Hooton and Lache (southeast of Chester) in January 1646.[96] The total outlay from central funds to 'Captain Birkenhead for himself, and the officers and soldiers of the Trained and Freehold Band of Wirral Hundred' was £1,718 18s.[97] On 22 July 1646, the following commissioned and non-commissioned officers mustered were:

> Lieutenant John Astbrook
> Ensign William Rathbone
> Sergeant William Woolmer
> Sergeant Thomas Worford
> Corporal George Harrison
> Corporal Thomas Dudley
> Corporal John Harrison
> Drummer John Davy
> Drummer James Davy.[98]

Birkenhead's command fielded 160 common soldiers (with Glegg's) on 30 April 1645, 100 on 18 October 1645, 89 on 30 March 1646, 68 on 28 April 1646, 94 on 28 May 1646, 96 on 22 June 1646, 90 on 22 July 1646, and 78 on 9 December 1646.[99]

---

94 TNA, SP28/128/13, f. 18r.; SP28/224/1, unf.
95 TNA, SP28/123/2, ff. 242v.–244r.; SP16/513/1, ff. 71v., 88r.
96 BL, Ms Add. 11333, ff. 105r., 113r.–114v.
97 TNA, SP28/128/13, f. 18v.; SP28/224, unf.
98 TNA, SP28/123/2, f. 343v.
99 BL, Mss Add. 11331, f. 45r.; 11332, f. 3r.; TNA, SP28/123/1, ff. 179v., 181r.; SP28/123/2, ff. 343r., 352r.–v., 371r.

Captain Henry Greene's company of Brereton's regiment were Wirral countrymen 'who maintained the garrison at Hooton'. They mustered 120 common soldiers on 30 April and 100 on 18 October 1645. No muster rolls or pay warrants for the company have come to light. Greene was of Poulton Lancelyn in Bebington parish.[100] The volunteer companies of Captains William Coventry, Richard Coventry, and George Ball are listed in Brereton's regiment in April 1645, but they appear to have been disbanded by the end of the year. Little is known of their service, and the soldiers may have been billeted at Wirral garrisons such as Puddington and Hooton, although Ball's men were paid £1 18s. as 'trained soldiers' whilst quartering at Frodsham.[101] William Coventry of West Kirby was accused of taking the oath of loyalty to the King and of providing support to Royalist troops, but such charges were dismissed in October 1652 for lack of evidence against him. Captain George Ball was probably a son of William Ball of Irby and related to Lieutenant Christopher and Ensign Robert Ball under the command of Hardware and Edward Glegg, respectively. The problems encountered by many Wirral officers are illustrated by the case of Ball and Richard Coventry, who during 1643–1644 were compelled to take an oath of association at Woodchurch, when the area was under Royalist control. Upon Brereton's arrival in the Wirral in the autumn of 1644, they 'did immediately declare themselves for him; and have, ever since been trusted and employed in the Parliament's service, and discharged the same faithfully'.[102]

---

100 Green (ed.), *Calendar for Advance of Money*, III, p. 1210; Morrill, *Cheshire*, p. 215; Tony Dyson, 'Colonel Moore's Offensive against Wirral, November 1643', *THSLC*, 162 (2013), p. 43.
101 BL, Ms Harley 1999, f. 75r.
102 *CJ*, VII, pp. 61–62.

Chapter 6

The Parliamentarian Garrison of Warwick

Though a less formal arrangement existed during summer 1642 involving the county militia commissioners, effectively the deputy lieutenants, the Parliamentary committee for Warwickshire and Coventry was initially set up by the ordinance passed on 31 December 1642 for the Association of Warwickshire under the command of Lord Brooke.[1] The Association Ordnance gave wide powers that the Warwickshire Committee continued to exercise after the death of Robert Greville, 2nd Baron Brooke, on 4 March 1643 and the dissolution of the association. Brooke recruited soldiers in Warwickshire in August 1642 and brought up troops from London to the county to lift the Royalist siege of Warwick Castle. With events in the Midlands gathering momentum, Warwickshire was liable to be at the forefront of the national conflict, and Charles I appointed the Earl of Northampton as his chief representative in the county. He attempted to exert his influence over Warwickshire's commissioners of array. However, when Northampton arrived in Warwick on 25 June, he was faced by the hostility of its inhabitants, and thus immediate Royalist attempts to dominate the city and region backfired. The Royalist presence in Warwickshire was short-lived, and, on 11 August, the commissioners wrote to their colleagues at Worcester:

> Being desirous to give you a speedy account of our proceedings at Banbury and Warwick … we can do [no] less than acquaint you, that there are already certain forces upon the march from London towards these parts in opposition to his Majesty, his Royal authority and disturbance of the peace of this Kingdom, whereby we are all in danger to be embroiled in a civil war, if timely prevention be not had, and do therefore desire that for the mutual strength of us all and speedy resistance of such power, you will join with us in that correspondence as is requisite in this case, and to that purpose forthwith to raise and have in readiness all your forces as well trained bands as other to the end we may receive such speedy and necessary supply, as upon so great an exigency shall be requisite which

---

1   *LJ*, V, pp. 520–22; Firth and Rait (eds), *Acts and Ordinances*, I, pp. 53–58.

we doubt not, but with God's blessing will much redound to our common safety and the peace of this Kingdom.[2]

In her study of the civil wars in Warwickshire, Ann Hughes discovered no evidence of Parliamentarian impressment in the county and suggested that all those who served in the local forces were volunteers.[3] According to a newsbook, as an incentive for enlistment at the Militia Ordinance musters in Warwickshire, Brooke provided 'wine and strong drink' for all the trained bands and volunteers.[4]

Table 11 Charges for the Right Honourable the Lord Brooke at Stratford at the Settling the Militia at Stratford-upon-Avon, 30 June 1642 (WA, CR1886, ff. 29r.–33v.)

	£	s.	d.
Delivered to Mr Whateley 1 pottle of sack to the Lion		2	4
To the Unicorn 2 gallons of claret		5	4
Sent thither 1 gallon of lord's sack		4	8
More to the Lion, 1 pottle of sack		2	4
More 2 gallons of claret		5	4
More 1 quart of white wine			8
More 1 pint of sack			7
2 quart bottle broke			6
To the Lion for my Lord 1 gallon of claret and 1 pottle of sack		5	0
More to goodman Lobkins from Mr Brooke for Stratford men 6 quarts of claret		4	0
More sent into the Maidenhead 2 gallons of claret and 1 pottle of sack for the Henley men		7	8
More to the Lion for my Lord 1 gallon of claret wine		2	8
More for my Lord to the Lion 1 pottle of sack, 1 pottle of white wine and 1 pottle of claret		5	0
Paid for 34 men's dinners which sat at my Lord's table	3	8	0
Paid for 88 men's dinners more at 12d. a man	4	8	0
Paid for the baking of 5 pasties of venison	1	0	0
Paid for beef and bread my Lord's servants had to breakfast		3	0
Paid for stabling for horses and oats		11	0
Paid for 2 hogsheads of beer	2	10	0
Paid to the musicians		7	0
Paid to a cook for helping ours		2	6
To the poor given		4	0
Total	14	19	7

On 5 July 1642, Brooke also laid out the sum of £30 1s. 9d. for food and drink for the Warwickshire militia at Colehill and a further £30 14s.

---

2 WorcsA, BA1714/899, ff. 250v.–251r.
3 Ann Hughes, *Politics, Society and Civil War in Warwickshire, 1620-1660* (Revised edition, Cambridge: Cambridge University Press, 2002), p. 120.
4 *A True Relation of the Lord Brooke's Settling of the Militia in Warwickshire* (London: R. O. and G. D., 1642). TT, E669[50].

for victuals and other items at Coventry, including 5s. for bellringing that accompanied his removal of the county's magazine from Coventry to Warwick on 1 July.

According to *The Weekly Intelligencer*, on 14 November 1642, 'Today about 9 of the clock drums were beaten in Warwick for supplies to serve the Parliament, many offering themselves willingly, being able yeomen's sons in the Country, for the love they bare to the cause and to my Lord Brooke'.[5] In December, Brooke was appointed commander-in-chief of the Midland or associated counties of Warwickshire, Staffordshire, Leicestershire, and Derbyshire and began raising new regiments of horse, foot, and dragoons with commissioned officers largely recruited in London. One such officer was Captain Anthony Otway.[6] His surviving financial accounts record that he served as captain of foot under Lord Brooke in Warwickshire between 27 January to 6 April 1643; as captain of dragoons from 6 April to 3 June 1643; captain of horse in the regiment of Colonel William Purefoy between 3 June 1643 and 2 May 1645; captain in the same regiment but under Colonel William Colemore from May 1645 to August 1646; and under Sir Thomas Fairfax's command from 3 May to 20 June 1646. Captain Otway's company of dragoons was raised in part through the contributions of Warwickshire ministers, but they were converted into a troop of horse after two months' service.[7] By August 1642, Lord Brooke had recruited a troop of 60 harquebusiers and, on 12 August, received £30 to purchase scarfs for them.[8] He was also commissioned colonel and raised a foot regiment of 1,000 purple coats in London that joined Essex's army in time to serve at the Battle of Edgehill. On 9 August, the following warrant was issued by the Committee of Safety to Sir Gilbert Gerard, treasurer of the army, to disburse a month's pay to Lord Brooke's regiment as part of the Earl's army:

> These are to will and require you forthwith out of the treasure remaining in your hands to deliver to Robert, Lord Brooke for 1 month's entertainment due to him as colonel of a regiment of 1,200 foot £63; for his lieutenant colonel £42; for his major £33 10s.; for 7 captains £147; for 10 lieutenants £56; for 10 ensigns £44; for 21 sergeants £46 2s.; for 30 corporals £46 2s.; for a drum major £2 2s.; for 20 drummers £28; for a preacher £5 12s.; for a surgeon £5 12s.; for his 2 mates £5 12s.; for a quartermaster £7; for a provost marshal £7; for a waggon master ££4 4s. As likewise to deliver colours, partizans, halberds, and drums for his regiment £80; as likewise for the marshal's irons £7; surgeon's chest £15. As likewise levy money for 1,200 men £400; in all amounting to the sum of £1,044 16s.[9]

Brooke also placed a garrison into Warwick Castle, whilst, on 6 October, he received pay for 370 men and a further weeks' pay for the officers of a regiment

---

5 *The English intelligencer, shewing the true and most remarkeable passages that have hapned in this kingdome* (London: Francis Wright, 1642). TT, E127[26].
6 Andrew Abram, *Dragoons and Dragoon Operations in the British Civil Wars, 1638-1653* (Solihull: Helion & Co., 2023), *passim*.
7 TNA, SP28/136/33, unf.; SP28/332, unf.
8 TNA, SP28/1A, f. 102r.
9 TNA, SP28/126/1, f. 16r.

of dragoons. In this regard, Brooke was furnished with £100 towards buying saddles and the transportation horses to Worcester, and, on 10 December, he received £150 for more saddles.[10] It remains unclear, however, whether Brooke's regiment was an entirely new command or if he simply inherited parts of another formation.

The Parliamentarian garrison of Warwick was first established in the castle in summer 1642. It survived a brief siege in August by the Earl of Northampton's Royalist forces but was reduced over the winter of 1642–1643, before being reinforced under the authority of Brooke's association and later by the Warwickshire Committee, which, rather than sitting at Warwick, the county town, assembled at Coventry. A speech made by Lord Brooke at the appointment of his officers at Warwick Castle in February 1643 shows his skill at rallying men and his ability to connect their personal concern for the safety of their homes and families to the wider struggle. It also reveals the issues he thought would appeal to the men, whose towns and neighbours had been recently plundered by Royalist forces:

> We behold the flourishing and beauteous face of this Kingdom overspread with the leprosy of a civil war. In which, since we are forced for the safeguard of our lives, the preservation of our liberties the defence of God's true religion (invaded by the practices of Papists and malignants) to become actors, I doubt not but each of you will play your part with that noble resolution and Christian courage as the greatness and meritoriousness of the work does challenge.[11]

Characteristically, Brooke ended with a prayer:

> that God Almighty will arise and maintain his own cause, scattering and confounding the devices of his enemies, not suffering the ungodly to prevail over his poor innocent flock. Lord we are but a handful in consideration of thine and our enemies, therefore O Lord fight though our battles, go out as though didst in the time of King David before the hosts of the servants, and strengthen and give us hearts that we show ourselves men for the defence of thy true Religion, and our own and the Kingdom's safety.

Brooke's successor as commander-in-chief was Basil Feilding, 2nd Earl of Denbigh, although he was a dubious Parliamentarian who caused much discord among the military forces of the region. On 6 March 1643, Denbigh's treasurer disbursed the sum of £24 to the quartermaster of his own cavalry troop towards the payment 'due for their abode in the county of Warwickshire'. Correspondingly, Benjamin Mason, captain in Colonel John Fiennes' Parliamentarian regiment of horse, was paid £50 in London on 10 August 1644, 'to set forth his troop and to discharge his soldiers' quarters, [and] conveying arms and saddles to the regiment'. Hence, 10 days later, Mason

---

10 TNA, SP28/2A, ff. 326r., 328r.–329v., 339r.; SP28/143, ff. 28v., 59v.
11 *A Worthy Speech Made by the Right Honourable the Lord Brooke, at the election of his Captaines and Commanders at Warwick Castle, as also at the delivery of their last commissions* (London: John Underwood, 1643). TT, E90[27].

distributed the sum of £27 1s. 11d. to several innkeepers in Warwick for discharging the quarters of the colonel's and his own troops.[12] In May 1644, Colonel Richard Bagot, Royalist governor of Lichfield, reported to Prince Rupert the recent arrival of Lord Denbigh in Tamworth 'with 18 colours of horse and at most 1,500 foot'. He added that the Parliamentarian commander had sent to Leicester for further troops and had with him 40 wagons of arms and ammunition, eight cannon, and at least £30,000. Bagot consequently advised Rupert that the Prince's troops 'will have good sport in beating up his quarters, and if they quarter of this side [of] Stafford they shall have very little rest'.[13] Denbigh's failures and unpopularity with the Shropshire Committee, in addition to the enmity felt towards him by Sir William Brereton's infantry regiments who were at the forefront of its military operations, hastened his departure in autumn 1644.

The MP Bulstrode Whitelocke reported that, in April 1643, 'Warwick Castle held out against the King's forces, and Colonel Bridges the governor acquitted himself with much honour. The Earl of Denbigh was made Major General of Coventry, and some part adjacent'.[14] Nevertheless, according to Royalist reports, a substantial part of the Warwick garrison deserted in spring 1643 when Brooke left for Staffordshire, whilst, following his death at Lichfield, several commissioned officers were dismissed during the following months. Nonetheless, others – such as Sergeant Major Abraham Pont, who had probably been in Brooke's regiment of foot in the Earl of Essex's army in 1642 – continued under the Warwickshire Committee.[15] Meanwhile, the committee was left settling the debts incurred by Brooke's activities and was forced to disband most of the remaining foot for want of money and to stifle its efforts to raise its own cavalry units in Warwickshire. Such deductions in the county's forces are reflected not only in the accounts of the Warwick garrison but also in those of various army officers.[16] After March 1643, the Warwickshire Committee broke formal links with Staffordshire and began coordinating its own military forces. The following month, a cavalry regiment of 10 troops was raised under the command of Colonel Willoughby, whereas a small regiment of foot was quickly recruited from volunteers and trained bandsmen under Brooke's half-brother Godfrey Bosvile, MP, until he was replaced by Colonel William Colemore following the Self-Denying Ordinance of 1645. Subsequently, Bosvile's regiment was placed in the Warwick garrison.

In his *Antiquities of Warwickshire*, first published in 1656, Sir William Dugdale said of Warwick Castle:

> The castle is a fine building, beautiful both by situation and its decoration; it stands on a solid rock of free-stone, from whose bowels it may be said to be built, as likewise is the whole town; the terrass of the castle, like that of Windsor,

---

12   TNA, SP28/136/4, f. 9r.; SP28/139/19, unf.
13   WSL, Ms Salt 482.
14   Whitelocke, *Memorials*, p. 210.
15   TNA, SP28/136/25, ff. 20r.–22v.; SP28/139/3, unf.
16   TNA, SP28/248, unf.; E101/612/64.

> overlooks a beautiful country, and sees the Avon running at the foot of the precipice, at above 50 foot perpendicular height. The building is old, but several times repaired and beautified by its several owners, and it is now a very agreeable place both within and without: the apartments are very nicely contrived, and the communication of the remotest parts of the building, one with another, are so well preserved by galleries, and by the great hall, which is very magnificent, that one finds no irregularity in the whole place, notwithstanding its ancient plan, as it was a castle not a palace, and built for strength rather than pleasure.[17]

In comparison with other Parliamentarian garrisons in the county, such as Coventry and Kenilworth, details of the civil war fortifications at Warwick are less well-documented, although, like Windsor, the medieval structures associated with its castle were extensive. Nevertheless, the 'accounts of Captain Richard Bailles for the defences of Warwick Castle', dated late 1642 to early 1643, include various disbursements by the Warwickshire Committee, such as £42 10s. 3d. for materials and labour. Hence, £2 was disbursed to carpenters; 2s. 6d. for 5cwt of wood; 5s. for 1cwt of 'lead for the gate in the West Gate'; 10s. for oak timber for the gates; and 2s. 8d. for wood to be burnt for the melting of the lead.[18] The parish loss accounts surviving for the county illustrate the extent to which several inhabitants were obligated to contribute to the upkeep of Warwickshire's Parliamentarian military forces and garrisons through the weekly excise. These include in some cases relating to fortifications, labour services, and construction materials, although entries are commonly undated. In Warwick itself, the constables of Smith Street Ward in St Nicholas parish contributed various sums 'towards the making of the bulwarks' for a year and three months at the rate of 4d. a week. Likewise, £4 was paid by 'the inhabitants of the borough of Warwick by the discretion of the Committee of Coventry for and towards the making of fortifications of the borough aforesaid for 1 whole year and 3 quarters or thereabouts, 1s. 4d. the week and sometimes 2s. the week at the least'.[19] Correspondingly, the parish of Milverton claimed for sums laid out for labour and horse teams at Warwick and Kenilworth Castles:

> For work done with teams and divers day's works by labourers from the said [parish] of Milverton for making and repairing the bulwarks at Warwick and several carriages for Warwick Castle in the years 1643, 1644 and 1645 being charged by several warrants under the hands of Colonel Bridges, Captain Layfield and Sergeant Major Castle £8. The like work and carriages done from the said town at Kenilworth Castle in the said years 1644 and 1645 charged by under the hand of Captain John Needham, late governor there £2.[20]

Colonel John Bridges was officially appointed governor of Warwick Castle in May 1645, and, following his promotion to colonel, he also became

---

17 Sir William Dugdale, *The Antiquities of Warwickshire* (London: Thomas Warren, 1656), p. 665.
18 TNA, SP28/136/12, unf.
19 TNA, SP28/184/1, ff. 1v.–7v.
20 TNA, SP28/183/3/5, ff. 5r.–v.

THE PARLIAMENTARIAN GARRISON OF WARWICK

governor of Warwick town. From Alcester, and brother of the Parliamentarian officers William and Matthew, John Bridges had been a solicitor to Lord Brooke and captain in his regiment of foot in Essex's army since September 1642, before promotion to sergeant major by early 1643. Bridges also served as captain of a troop of harquebusiers from 5 January 1644 to 22 August 1646; sergeant major of foot and captain of a company of foot between 31 December 1644 and 17 March 1645; and colonel of a regiment of foot from 17 March 1645 and 22 August 1646.[21] In November 1642, Bridges undertook service under Colonel William Purefoy, commander of the Parliamentarian troops in Warwick Castle, but, as Purefoy was habitually in the field, Bridges was in a practical sense the commander of the garrison there. He successfully defended the castle and undertook several operations, including the conveyance of ammunition convoys to Gloucester, and contributed to the siege of Banbury in 1644.[22] During the latter part of the First Civil War, troops from Warwickshire participated widely in operations both close to home and farther afield. One Royalist source reported for 16 November 1644:

Richard Grenville, 2nd Baron Brooke (1607-43).

> A party of horse from Banbury (under the command of Captain John Moore) went into the town of Warwick, and discharged 20 carbines and pistols against Warwick Castle; at last they sallied out (after the challenge) but with so poor courage, that they suffered Captain Moore to bring away divers prisoners out of Warwick town, beside 120 yards of red cloth, wherewith the courageous captain intends to clothe his soldiers.[23]

Moreover, in April 1645, with a scratch force, Colonel John Bridges drove Royalist troops under the command of Prince Maurice out of Stratford-upon-Avon, before inflicting a heavy defeat upon them. For this, he was thanked by the Committee of Both Kingdoms. Bridges' published account is given below in full:

> Sir, be pleased to receive a relation of the victory whereof I have now sent an express to the Honourable Committee of both Kingdoms. Prince Maurice's regiment, the reformado troop, Colonel Knutsford's troop, Captain Wild's troop, and Captain Gunter's troop being sent by the Prince to intercept the convoy of powder and match which I sent with the party designed for Gloucester, and for

---

21   TNA, SP28/121, f. 25v.
22   *CSPD 1644*, pp. 55, 97, 472.
23   *Mercurius Aulicus*, 23 November 1644. TT, E246[26].

that end came to Quinton in Gloucestershire, but finding the party had passed by some hours before, and having intelligence that all our horse were marched from Warwick, resolved to take the advantage to plunder the country, and accordingly came to Stratford-upon-Avon, and demanded £800 or they would plunder the town; but upon the present payment of a £10, remitted the rest, and came toward Warwick, and in their march swept away all the beasts they met withal, of which I having notice (being desirous to save the country as well as I could) prevailed with Captain Andrews who was then accidentally in town with 80 of the Newport horse which were also to march to Gloucester, being also assisted by the Committee of Worcestershire with 30 or 40 of Captain Milward's and Captain Halford's troops, with these and about a dozen of our own horse that stayed behind our troop. Having drawn 4 companies out of the town and castle, I advanced towards the enemy, who by this was come within 2 miles of Warwick, having in Sherborne Field put themselves in 4 considerable bodies, and sent a small party away with their plundered beasts; we lined the hedges with our foot and faced them with our horse near 2 hours, in which time, in some loose skirmishes we having killed 1 and took 2 or 3 prisoners, the enemy drew off and being to march through a long lane I caused the foot to advance, and when the rearguard took the lane, I desired the horse to charge, which they did accordingly, but the enemy having a convenient place in the midst of the lane to draw up a reserve, made good their own retreat, and beat our men back in some disorder but Major Castle and myself hastening up with the foot, and having almost recovered the end of the lane perceiving them disordered, I galloped up, and by persuasions and threats, caused the horse to rally, and make a stand which the enemy perceiving forbore to pursue their advantage. Whereupon I desired Major Hawkesworth, who was also accidentally in town, and behaved himself very gallantly in the whole action that he would hold the enemy in play with the horse in the lane, that Major Castle and myself might in the interim bring up the foot on the other side of the hedge. But the enemy perceiving our intentions, marched so without any loss, and drew up a gain in the next field, and we did the like, and there faced each other 3 or 4 hours, sometimes skirmishing with small parties of horse, and the foot other whiles sending some musket balls amongst them, whereby the enemy received some small loss, as we did from their carbines, I having my horse also shot. At length I perceiving the enemy's resolution to march away, there being a short lane at the end of this great field through which they must necessarily march, and much troubled to think of the poor country's loss called the officers together and told them, this was the last opportunity which if lost the enemy would march clear away, and therefore desired Major Hawkesworth and Captain Andrews to be ready when the enemy's rearguard should come to take the lane to give them a resolute charge and conceiving that if they could put them to the rout, happily all the rest might thereby be disordered, and in case our horse should be put to the worse, I desired they would retire behind the foot, which I would cause to advance as fast as I could to countenance them, and did not doubt through God's blessing, but to hold up the enemy until they should have time to rally, and be ready to give, or receive another charge, which they assenting to, and I having imparted our resolves to the several divisions, caused the foot to advance which the enemy perceiving, and in a greater body than they expected, hasted to make a retreat through the lane, but in a very orderly manner. And Major Hawkesworth,

Captain Andrews, Captain Milward and some other horse officers according to the former conclusions took their time so right, and quitted themselves so bravely, as in their first charge they took Pitcher the captain of the reformadoes, who commanded the rearguard, and routed not only that party, but all the rest, killed about 10 in the place, and in the pursuit (whereof divers were officers and men of good quality) wounded very many, and divers mortally, took near 60 prisoners, of which many very considerable, 120 horses at least, 1 horse colours which was all I saw in the field, or could hear of, pursued them 4 or 5 miles, recovered all the plundered beasts, and one cart load of broad cloth, and utterly scattered the remainder of them. So as the Prince's surgeon that is sent hither to take care of their wounded men, tells us he hath not known such a rout, some flying to Camden, Evesham, and Worcester, which many without hats, others without horses, and few with swords, the praise of all which be given to God, who only gives all victories, I rest. This Victory was obtained Friday the 13 of April 1645.[24]

As governor, Colonel John Bridges was frequently at odds with the Warwick subcommittee of accounts, which accused him of plundering and abduction, in both Warwickshire and Oxfordshire, and embezzlement, including withholding his men's pay and misappropriating goods taken from the Royalist baggage train before the Battle of Edgehill.[25] Some of these claims might have been politically motivated, and the subcommittee members encouraged by their hostility to him as a social upstart, in that he lacked gentry status. Nevertheless, one person, Andrew Yarranton, who acted as scoutmaster to Colonel Bridges, later complained that, when he challenged Bridges over withheld pay, he was cashiered and added:

> That it was usual manner of Colonel Bridges, that when any officer or soldier under him, were he never so faithful or valiant, came to demand his pay, he would not only check him for it, but also give him such harsh and discouraging language that most men's spirits could not bear it, and by that means many of them went away from his service in discontent and left their pay in his hands.[26]

Lieutenant Charles Johnson was treasurer of the garrison of Warwick Castle between 16 December 1645 and 18 October 1646. His certificate of service records that he acted as:

> lieutenant in the garrison of Warwick Castle under the command of Captain Sandbach and Captain Matthew Bridges from 23 June 1643 to 22 August 1646, being 164 weeks and 5 days at 20s. per week amounts to £230 12s.; as treasurer of the said garrison from 26 September 1643 to 22 August 1646, being 151 weeks at 20s. per week amounts to £151; as clerk and storekeeper of the said garrison from

---

24 *A letter from Collonell Bridges governer of Warwick Castle to a freind of his in London, dated the 20 of Aprill 1645. Wherein is sett forth a great victory obtained by the said collonell against Prince Maurice his armie on the 17 of this instant Aprill* (London: R. B., 1645). TT, E278[27].
25 *CJ*, IV, p. 633.
26 TNA, SP28/253B, f. 110v.

22 August 1646 to 31 December 1647, being 71 weeks at 15s. per week amounting to £63 5s.[27]

The loss accounts of the Warwickshire parish of Packwood, located some 11 miles west of Kenilworth, rendered 'according to the directions of the Committee for Taking Accounts in the County of Warwick, delivered to the said Committee at Warwick 30 May 1646', list the assessments paid for the maintenance of the garrison of Warwick:

> Charged upon Packwood by order under the hands of the Committee for safety the sum of £11 6s. per month, being, £2 16s. 6d. weekly for 3 months beginning in July 1643, towards the maintenance of the garrison of Warwick Castle, under the command of Colonel Bridges governor there and charged since the end of those 3 months upon Packwood aforesaid by several orders under the hands of the said Committee the sum of £10 8s. per month, for the space of 31 months, towards the maintenance of the said garrison of Warwick Castle still under the command of the aforesaid Colonel Bridges, so charged upon Packwood since July 1643 until this present 30 May 1646 the sum of £356 6s. Whereof there is paid as may appear by this account following the sum of £270, the residue is taxed upon such as are solvent, and upon lands sequestered in the hands of the said Committee, whereof the Constable of Packwood for the time being has from time to time given returns at Warwick Castle to the receiver there. So paid in money and in returns the sum of £356 6s.[28]

The deployment of the Warwickshire forces to places outside their home county occurred during the buildup of the Parliamentarian campaign in Oxfordshire, which culminated in the defeat of Sir William Waller's forces at Cropredy Bridge on 29 June 1644. The Committee of Both Kingdoms wrote to Waller on 19 June earlier:

> We have certain intelligence that the King is come back near to Oxford with Horse and foot. We desire you to follow him, which way soever he takes, with as much speed as you can conveniently. If he should give you battle about Oxford, although we hope your army is able to fight with any strength the King can make in those parts where he now is, yet, because Oxford will be an advantage to him, and that the less hazard we run the better, we have appointed these forces underwritten to be in readiness to assist you upon your command: foot of Warwick, Colonel Bosvile's regiment, 240; of the Castle, Major Bridge's, 100; of Kenilworth Castle, Captain Needham's, 60; of Coventry, 200; of Northampton, 100; Sir Samuel Luke's, from Newport, 400; Sir Samuel Luke's, from Cambridge, 400. Total: 1,500 foot. Horse, from Colonel Purefoy, 250; Colonel Barker, 60; Major Bridges, 50; Northampton, 80; Sir Samuel Luke's, 80. Total, 520 horse.

A further letter, sent to the Warwickshire commander, Colonel William Purefoy, informed him:

---

27 TNA, SP28/136/14, f. 74v.; SP28/136/15, f. 39v.
28 TNA, SP28/184/4, ff. 1r.–v.

THE PARLIAMENTARIAN GARRISON OF WARWICK

> We have received certain advertisement of the King's return into Oxfordshire, and not knowing but he may give Sir Wm. Waller battle in those parts, for the further strengthening of Sir William we desire you forthwith to march with your regiment of horse to such place or rendezvous as he shall appoint, and there attend his further orders. It is our intention you shall abide there no longer than the King shall be in those parts.[29]

Similarly, in February 1645, Whitelocke reported:

> Letters from Major Bridges, governor of Warwick, informed that he sent 2 or 3 companies of his garrison by small parties into the country, as to gather contribution, but commanded the officers not to return without further orders from him. To these he got an addition of 80 foot and 70 horse. With these he marched all night, and the next morning by daybreak began to storm Stoke House, which the King's forces were then fortifying, and stood between 2 other of their garrisons. The house was strong, and stoutly defended for an hour and a half, and then Bridges entered to it by force, without the loss of 1 man, though they were without shelter, and bullets and stones flew thick about them. The King's garrison at Campden and Evesham drew out to relive their friends, but Bridges had done his work, took away his prisoners, and fired the house, being a fort only of papists. The prisoners were 5 papist captains, about 30 officers and gentlemen, all papists, besides the common soldiers.[30]

A schedule of the Warwickshire Parliamentarian forces listed in 1645, with muster dates, outlines the following:

Warwick Castle forces
Colonel Bridge's Company:
Sergeant Major Halford
Captain Matthew Bridges
Gunners, matrosses, etc.

Warwick Town forces
Lieutenant Colonel Castle
Sergeant Major John Halford
Captain Richard Halford

Colonel Bosvile's Regiment:
Colonel Bosvile's Company
Sergeant Major Castle's Company
Captain Halford's Company
Captain Slade's Company

Coventry forces
Colonel Willoughby's Company

---

29   *CSPD 1644*, pp. 253–54.
30   Whitelocke, *Memorials*, p. 388.

Lieutenant Colonel Phipps' Company
Sergeant Major Burgoyne's Company
Captain Matthew Randall's Company
Captain John Colmore's Compmany
Captain Robert Colmore's Company
Captain Gamaliel Purefoy's Company
Captain Samuel Ward's Company
Captain Brownell's Company

Kenilworth garrison
Captain Needham's Company
Sergeant Major Burgoyne's Company

Edgbaston garrison
Colonel Fox
Captain Tudman's Company

Tamworth garrison
Captain Willington's Company
Lieutenant Dickson

Maxstoke Castle
Captain Matthew Randall, governor

Troops of horse mustered
Captain Purefoy's Troop
Sergeant Major Hawkesworth's Troop
Captain Potter's Troop
Captain Wells' Troop
Colonel Bridges' Troop

Colonel William Colemore's Regiment:
Sergeant Major Hawkesworth's Troop
Captain Potter's Troop
Captain Wells' Troop
Captain Cotton's Troop
Captain Flower's Troop
Captain Otway's Troop
Captain Leyfield's Troop
Captain Hunt's Troop.[31]

---

31   TNA, SP28/34/1, ff. 64r.–v.

Colonel John Bridges' Troop of Horse

As governor of Warwick, Colonel John Bridges commanded an independent troop of horse, which was nominally attached to Colonel William Purefoy's regiment. This was raised in Warwickshire before May 1643 and formed part of the Warwick garrison. On 24 May 1644, the following commissioned officers were paid with the troop:

> Lieutenant Estop
> Cornet Christopher Wheeler
> Quartermaster Haselwood.

On 11 December 1644, the following received pay:

> Cornet Richard Round
> Quartermaster John White
> Corporal William Bilson
> Corporal Thomas Shelford
> Corporal Henry Wilson
> Trumpeter George Shaw.[32]

Similarly, a muster roll of Colonel Bridges' troop, dated 24 January 1646, lists the following:

> Captain-Lieutenant Christopher Wheeler
> Cornet Richard Round
> Quartermaster John White
>
> Corporal William Bilson
> Corporal Thomas Shelford
> Corporal John Rush
> Trumpeter Robert Bridges
>
> Corporal William Bilson's Squadron:
> 15 (named) troopers
>
> Corporal Thomas Shelford's Squadron:
> 16 (named) troopers
>
> Corporal John Rush's Squadron:
> 15 (named) troopers
> [46 troopers overall].[33]

In his accounts, Richard Round, 'lieutenant in Colonel Bridges' troop of horse', testified that he served 'as cornet to Colonel John Bridges from 6

---

32 TNA, SP28/121, unf.
33 TNA, SP28/123/3, ff. 465r.–468r.

September 1644 to 9 June 1646, being 91 weeks, which at the rate of £4 14s. 6d. a week, being whole pay as aforesaid comes to the sum of £429 10s.' He also acted as quartermaster under the command of Captain William Bridges and Colonel Purefoy from 14 April 1643 to 20 August 1644, being 72 weeks at the rate of £3 3s. per week, and thus his entire pay arrears came to £226 16s.[34] Similarly, Captain Lieutenant Christopher Wheeler served in the troop from 1 June 1645 to 9 June 1646, when he was killed 'in a charge before Worcester'. Wheeler was succeeded by Richard Round, previously the unit's cornet until the disbandment of the troop in August 1646.[35] Colonel John Bridges' troop contained an aggregate of seven commissioned and non-commissioned officers, 37 troopers, and 14 dragoons in January 1644; five officers and 29 troopers (plus two corporals and six men prisoners in Worcestershire) in December 1644; seven officers and 54 troopers in April 1645; and seven officers and 42–46 troopers between August 1645 and July 1646.

Overall, Warwickshire forces received good levels of pay, meaning that recruitment was buoyant. Thus, arrears were habitually lower than those in most Parliamentarian armies, especially among the cavalry. Nevertheless, on 3 April 1644, Colonel John Fox, governor of the outlying garrison at Edgbaston, complained to the Earl of Denbigh, 'Major General of the forces in the county of Warwick', of the want of money and necessaries for the subsistence of his soldiers, declaring, 'The garrison needs no enemy to destroy it, for, if money be not supplied, it will destroy itself'. Moreover, 12 days later, Fox described the discontentment among his men, saying, 'They run away apace and were this day upon training, ready to lay down all their arms and depart for want of supplies'.[36] At Warwick, the officers and soldiers of Captain Henry Flower's troop were in receipt of a third of their pay between April and August 1643, although, by late 1644, when funding from local sources was more regular, they had almost their full remuneration. Similarly, commissioned officers in Captain Creed's troop received as little as 40 percent of their half-pay before 1645.[37] The situation amongst the foot was somewhat different, in that they were more regularly paid. Among the Warwick garrison, Colonel John Bridges' and Captain John Halford's companies were only a few weeks in arrears between May 1643 and December 1644. Lieutenant Colonel James Castle's soldiers went six weeks in arrears between October 1643 and December 1644 and a further 13 weeks from December 1644 to its disbandment in June 1646.[38] One particular reason why wages were much regular and arrears were comparatively small was that the military organisation of Warwickshire was decentralised, meaning that the majority of the money for soldiers' pay went directly to their officers rather than the treasurer of the county committee.

---

34 TNA, SP28/136/40, f. 7v.
35 TNA, SP28/201, unf.
36 WA, CR2017/C9/76; CR 2017/C9/81.
37 TNA, SP28/11, f. 46r.; SP28/145, ff. 83r.–104v.
38 TNA, E101/612/64; SP28/182, ff. 182r.–183v.

THE PARLIAMENTARIAN GARRISON OF WARWICK

There is some evidence that the material condition of the Warwickshire soldiers drew the attention, and jealousy, of others. For instance, on 25 April 1645, Major General Edward Massie complained to the Committee of Safety, 'Our troops daily leave me and now they see the Warwick troops so well clothed, horsed, and armed, and so well paid, I fear I shall not keep one quarter part of those I have'.[39] Even so, in common with other civil war forces, wastage from the regiments in Warwick and other parts of the county remained problematic. Muster rolls show that, in January 1644, Colonel John Barker's regiment of foot and Colonel William Purefoy's cavalry regiment, the chief Parliamentarian military units in the county, were strong in numbers by civil war standards (prior to the New Model and Commonwealth Armies), with all ranks numbering 797 infantry soldiers and 428 cavalry and dragoons, respectively.[40] Lieutenant Colonel James Castle's company of foot in the Warwick garrison, however, struggled to retain men, even though they were as well paid as others. Between November 1643 and May 1644, the unit's strength dropped by half, from 64 private sentinels to 38, although, by January 1646, it had risen to 97.

Basil Fielding, Earl of Denbigh (c. 1608-75).

Similarly, Lieutenant Colonel Phipps' company of Willoughby's regiment saw a rapid deterioration in numbers in early 1644, although muster lists record that a solid core of veterans – comprising about 50 percent of the unit – remained within its ranks.[41] If, in most cases, regular pay to the county's troops provided a reason for solid recruitment and retention, another explanation for the greater shortfalls among the horse and foot belonging to the Warwick garrison must be that, in comparison with the regiments at Coventry and elsewhere, the cavalry frequently participated in military operations outside of Warwickshire, whilst the various infantry units served elsewhere, including the siege of Banbury. In September 1646, Abraham Pole petitioned the Warwickshire Committee that he:

> being in the Parliament's service under the command of Captain Matthew Bridges for almost 2 years and being on his duty firing his musket, the barrel broke and struck off the thumb of [his] left hand, who being by trade a comb-maker is altogether disabled to do anything thereat. And being lately disbanded, without your commiseration is likely to be undone.

Sergeant Thomas Arme claimed that he had:

---

39   Bodl. Lib., Ms Tanner 60/2, f. 127r.
40   WA, CR2017/C9, ff. 39r.–40v.
41   TNA, SP28/121A, ff. 115v., 154r.; SP28/123/2, f. 147r.

been in the Parliament's service in the garrison of Warwick Castle for the space of above 4 years. And being sent out upon a party, was shot in the face by the enemy, which shot deprived him of the sight of his left eye. And afterwards, being at the first siege before Banbury Castle, by reason of another shot in the face, your petitioner's other eye was much endangered, and he is at continual charge for the preservation of the sight thereof.

Moreover, George Harthill of Atherstone petitioned the dame committee in 1648 that he 'had 3 sons slain in the State's service, whereof 1 of them was named Nicolas Harthill, who was slain at Stourton fight under the command of Captain Thomas Hunt'.[42] This officer, as already stated, was a captain of dragoons and horse under Colonels Bridge and Willoughby.

Colonel William Purefoy's Regiment of Horse

The regiment was raised in March–April 1643 and mostly disbanded in August 1646. William Purefoy's commission, dated 6 March 1643, from 'Robert Earl of Essex, Captain-General of the Parliamentary Army', appointed him 'colonel of a regiment of horse and dragoons raised in the county Warwick for the defence of the King, Parliament, and Kingdom'.[43] The following muster list – undated but probably compiled in early 1644 – details the composition and strength of its troops, in addition to its company of dragoons:

Table 12 'Colonel Purefoy, his regiment of horse' (WA, CR2017/C9, f. 40r.)

Colonel Purefoy	Sergeant Major Pont	Captain Potter
Captain-Lieutenant	Lieutenant	Lieutenant
Cornet	Cornet	Cornet
Quartermaster-General	Quartermaster	Quartermaster
3 Corporals	3 Corporals	3 Corporals
1 Trumpet	1 Trumpeter	1 Trumpeter
1 Marshall		
67 troopers	45 troopers	55 troopers
Captain Hawkesworth	Captain Wells	Captain Otway
Lieutenant	Lieutenant	Lieutenant
Cornet	Cornet	Cornet
Quartermaster	Quartermaster	Quartermaster
3 Corporals	3 Corporals	3 Corporals
1 Trumpeter	1 Trumpeter	1 Trumpeter
46 troopers	54 troopers	42 troopers
Captain Thomas Hunt's dragoons		
Lieutenant		
Cornet		

---

42   TNA, SP28/248/1, f. 38r.; SP28/248/3, unf.
43   *CSPD 1641–1643*, p. 449.

2 Sergeants		
2 Corporals		
1 Drummer		
59 dragoons		
Minister		
Surgeon and his mate		
Regimental clerk		

The quartermaster of the regiment was John Hunt. His water-damaged financial accounts reveal that he 'received commission of his Excellency the Earl of Essex from the Lord Brooke as provost marshal for his army, raised or to be raised in the counties of Warwickshire and Staffordshire' on 20 January 1643, serving in this capacity until promotion to quartermaster on 30 May 1643.[44] Hunt's latter role is confirmed by an undated entry in the loss accounts of Exhall, Wixford, and Oversley in Arrow Parish, which records, 'Lost by a party of soldiers of the Warwickshire regiment of horse, in linens, and other things which they plundered. The party being commanded by Mr John Hunt, quartermaster to the said regiment £3'.[45]

Captain Thomas Hunt of Coventry – one the 'comparatively obscure men', described by the unfavourable *Mercurius Aulicus* as 'a broken mercer' – was commissioned by Colonel John Bridges to command 40 dragoons and foot in February 1643 and was a captain of horse in February 1644.[46] Hunt's dragoon company was part of Colonel William Purefoy's cavalry regiment. Hunt had previously been a lieutenant of dragoons in Lord Brooke's association army, and, throughout much of 1644, he was ostensibly the commander of two separate forces: dragoons serving at Tamworth and cavalry at Astley, where he was governor. From August 1644, the forces at Astley were effectively commanded by Hunt's brother Lieutenant Goodere Hunt, while the company of dragoons converted to a cavalry troop under his own direct control.[47] Various quantities of horses, saddles, and tack were supplied to Captain Hunt for himself and his dragoons by the inhabitants of Bailey Lane Ward, Bishop Street, Gosford Street, and Jordan Well Wards of Coventry, whilst (among other things) Thomas Woodard of Beauchamp in Alcester Parish claimed 9s. 'paid in free quarter to 6 red coats under the command of Captain Hunt for 36 meals'.[48]

Captain William Bridges' Troop

Of Alcester, brother of Matthew and John, commanders at Warwick Castle, William Bridges led a troop between March and August 1643. He gave up his command, possibly because as an official of the Greville family was required

---

44 TNA, SP28/136/30, unf.
45 TNA, SP28/183/25, f. 4v.
46 *Mercurius Aulicus*, 27 April 1644. TT, E246[16].
47 TNA, SP28/253B, unf.; HMC, *Eighth Report, App. I*, p. 596.
48 TNA, SP28/185, ff. 11r.–12v., 15r.; SP28/201/3, f. 1r.; SP28/201/5, ff. 1r., 15r.

on their estate in Warwick after Brooke's death. The troop became Colonel Purefoy's own, under the command of Captain Lieutenant John Cheshire, until that officer's death in June 1644. Sergeant Major George Purefoy took over the troop afterwards, while Purefoy was governor of Compton House, and the unit became part of the garrison there. In January 1644, the troop comprised eight commissioned and non-commissioned officers and 66 troopers, 27 of whom lacked arms. During this period, the captain, lieutenant, cornet, and quartermaster received a third of their pay.

The detailed accounts of Lieutenant Henry Smith record that this officer 'served as cornet to Captain William Bridges about two months before I could receive a lieutenant's command, of which I began about the end of March 1643, and received my commission about 10 May next after'. Smith received this from Colonel William Purefoy. In August 1643, command of Captain Bridges' troop passed to Purefoy as his own troop, wherein he continued cornet from 1 August 1643 until 4 May 1644. On 1 June, the unit was turned over to Sergeant Major George Purefoy of the Compton garrison, and Smith continued as cornet to it until 18 May 1645. Furthermore, Smith attested that:

> From 1 June 1644 to the last of December next following, being seven months, I received my full half pay from the major's own hands, it being £9 9s. a month due unto me as cornet of the said troop. Afterwards the said Sergeant Major George Purefoy upon 1 January 1645 assigned to me for my own pay and for my man's (by warrant under his hand) the town of Chipping Norton of the county of Oxford, the said town being assessed at £3 3s. per week. I received from the said town in part of 4 months' tax (it is to say, 1 January aforesaid to 30 April 1645) the sum of £44. Received the overall sum from Chipping Norton £78. On 18 May 1645 I received from Colonel Purefoy a commission for lieutenant of the aforesaid troop, the said Sergeant Major Purefoy (who was captain-lieutenant thereof before) being made an absolute captain.

Thus, Henry Smith received a commission as lieutenant from the Warwickshire Committee, 'of the troop of harquebusiers formerly under the immediate command of Colonel Purefoy'.[49]

As previously mentioned, Richard Round initially served as quartermaster in Captain William Bridges' troop. His commission is given below:

> William Purefoy, Esquire, colonel and one of the commanders-in-chief of all the forces raised or to be raised in the counties of Stafford or Warwick, with the city and county of Coventry, and city and county of Lichfield, and parts adjacent, to serve for the defence of King, Parliament and Kingdom.
>
> To Richard Round, quartermaster to Captain William Bridges.
>
> By virtue of the commission of his Excellency the Earl of Essex, according to the authority to him given by Ordinance of the Lords and Commons assembled in Parliament, I do constitute and appoint you to be quartermaster to Captain

---

49 TNA, SP28/136/44, ff. 1r.–6v.

William Bridges, captain of a troop of Horse in my own regiment raised or to be raised in the said counties or cities or parks adjacent for the defence of the King, Parliament and Kingdom, which office you shall by virtue of this commission receive into your charge, these are therefore to will and require you to make present repair to the said troop, and as quartermaster diligently to execute and perform the duty and office of your place commanding inferior officers and soldiers of the said troop to obey you as their quartermaster in the service abovementioned according to this commission given you. And upon likewise to obey and follow such orders and directions as from time to time you shall receive from myself and the superior officers of the armies according to the discipline of war. Given under my hand and seal this third day of June 1643. William Purefoy.[50]

Captain Anthony Otway's Troop of Horse

In January 1644, Captain Otway's troop mustered 10 commissioned and non-commissioned officers, 42 troopers, plus a chaplain, Nathaniel Macham. Otway claimed that his men were 30 weeks in arrears for their service between May 1643 and June 1646 and had, in any case, only received the sum of 12s. per week, rather than the usual 17s. His accounts list the following:

> The state of debt to Captain Anthony Otway his troop:
> For the pay of 45 troopers from 3 June 1643 to 2 May 1646 (being so many onetime or another) 152 weeks at 12s. per week for every trooper £4,076 14s.
> For 1 trumpeter 152 weeks at £1 1s. per week for 100 weeks £219 12s.
> For 3 corporals 152 weeks at £1 1s. per week for 100 weeks £476 16s.
> For the quartermaster two-thirds of his pay 152 weeks at £2 2s. a week £319 4s.
> For the cornet half pay 152 weeks at £2 7s. a week £359 11s.
> For the lieutenant half pay 152 weeks at £3 3s. a week £478 16s.
> For the captain's half pay 152 weeks at £6 16s. d. a week £1,037 8s.[51]

The damaged accounts of 'Captain Thomas Chiswell of Warwick' include payments from 11 January to 8 June 1645 to Cornet John Willington, Corporal Pratchett, Corporal Chiswell, Trumpeter Thomas Shine, Quartermaster Robert Abbot, and 44 troopers.[52] No other information seems to be known for either Captain Chiswell or his command.

Sergeant Major Joseph Hawkesworth's Troop

Originally secretary and estate manager to Lord Brooke, Hawkesworth was a valuable and determined commander. Colonel William Purefoy – as commander-in-chief in Warwickshire and Staffordshire – commissioned him captain of a troop of 80 harquebusiers in his regiment on 25 April 1643,

---

50 TNA, SP28/136/40, ff. 9r.–v.
51 TNA, SP28/136/33, f. 9v.
52 TNA, SP28/24, ff. 242r.–243r.

whilst the Warwickshire County Committee authorised his promotion to sergeant major in the same regiment on 15 November 1644. The civil war loss accounts for the parish of Baddesley Clinton include items claimed by Edward Ferrers, a Catholic recusant who attempted to remain neutral, though his home was plundered by local Parliamentarian troops twice in 1643. After the conflict, Ferrers submitted claims for compensation, amounting to £472 4s. These included the following:

> The 12 May 1643 Hopkins and Bovey attended with a troop of horse and men, being under the command of Captain Joseph Hawkesworth, came to the house of the said Edward and then and there, took out of the stable these horses following:
>
> One big gelding of a bright bay colour which cost the said Edward £10
> One grey coloured mare £5
> Then the said troops entering the house of the said Edward plundered it and carried away from thence these parcels and particulars following the same day:
>
> One rich plush saddle trimmed round about the skirts with a gold lace, and a gold fringe with the cloth cover belonging to it and other furniture £4
> One back part and breast plate of armour 6s. 8d.
> Two large fowling pieces £2 3s. 4d.
> Four pair of double bullet moulds and shot moulds, and shears to cut them 10s.
> One musket barrel 10s.[53]

There is also much evidence for the upkeep of Hawkesworth's command. Hughes proposed that his cavalry troop was 'probably the best paid and best led of the regiment'.[54] Hence, the loss accounts for the Warwickshire parish of Milverton record a payment of £16 to 'Captain Joseph Hawkesworth (since major) at the first raising of his troop about the months of May or June 1643 with his troop consisting of about 40 men and 40 horses 4 days and nights at the rate of 2s. per day for man and horse'.[55] The troop was particularly maintained by the parish of Tanworth-in-Arden. A selection of contributions made by its inhabitants is given below:

> Margaret Warner, widow, paid upon the weekly assessments for her lands in Tanworth for the use of Serjeant Major Joseph Hawkesworth unto the said Edward Emmes, late constable in 1643, and to the soldiers in his time for 10 months; and to Henry Bissell late constable in 1644, and to the soldiers in his time for 12 months; and to Thomas Anderton now constable for 4 months; which is in all 26 months' contribution after the rate of 31s. per month, and arose to the sum of £40 6s.
>
> John Greene paid upon the weekly assessments unto Edward Emmes, late constable of Tanworth; to Henry Bissell, late constable, and to Thomas Anderton

---

53 TNA, SP28/136/33, f. 11v.
54 Hughes, *Warwickshire*, p. 199.
55 TNA, SP28/183/3/5, f. 3r.

junior, now constable, and during their respective offices, unto the soldiers of Serjeant Major Joseph Hawkesworth for the use of the said Major for 30 months' contribution the sum of £12 10s.

Hugh Lea, churchwarden, informs that he has paid upon the weekly assessments, for the use of Serjeant Major Joseph Hawkesworth to Edward Emmes late constable, and during his office to the soldiers of the said Major for 10 months; and to Henry Bissell late constable, and to the said soldiers during his office, for 12 months; and to Thomas Anderton, now constable, and to the said soldiers for 8 months; all which is 30 months' contribution at 8d. per month, and is in all 20s.

John Hunt paid upon the weekly assessments during the office of Edward Emmes, late constable to Sergeant Major Hawkesworth's soldiers for 10 months' contribution at 3s. per month, the sum of £1.

William Chambers paid upon the weekly assessments during the office of Edward Emmes, late constable to Sergeant Major Hawkesworth's soldiers for 10 months' contribution at 3s. per month, the sum of £5 4s.

Samuel Roberts paid Thomas Anderton, now constable, on 18 of January 1645 for 4 months' contribution more for Sergeant Major Hawkesworth at 4s. per month, the sum of 16s.

John Norton informs upon the weekly assessments to the respective constables abovenamed: to Emmes for 10 months; to Bissell for 12 months; and to Anderton for 6 months' contribution; and to the soldiers of Serjeant Major Joseph Hawkesworth for his use, which contribution so paid as aforesaid is for 28 months, and was allowed forth of his rent by his said Landlord Chambers and arises to the sum of £6 8s.

Henry Hunt informs that he paid [as above] to Sergeant Major Hawkesworth's soldiers for the use of the said Major, upon the weekly assessments for 28 months' contribution after the rate of 3s. 4d. per month for his own land, the sum of £14 13s. 4d.

John Yoxhall paid [as above] for the use of their Sergeant Major for 28 months' contribution at 2s. 8d. per month, which rose to £3 14s. 8d. Thomas Anderton, constable, paid more since for 2 months' contribution for Hawkesworth 5s. 4d.

Edward Collet paid upon the weekly assessments in 1643, and since for the use of Hawkesworth 26 months' contribution at 5s. per month, arising to £6 10s.

Richard Waring paid upon the weekly assessments for the use of Hawkesworth unto the respective constables beforenamed, and to Corporal Christopher Flower and the soldiers of the said Sergeant Major for 24 months' contribution at 5s. 4d. per month, the sum of 6s. 8d.[56]

In late 1645, the Warwickshire Committee agreed to send a detachment of horse under Sergeant Major John Hawkesworth to assist Sir William Brereton's forces at the Leaguer of Chester and further military operations in the region. Hawkesworth and his men were especially commended for their conduct at Denbigh on 1 November 1645, and, on 20 December, 200 Warwickshire horse were included in the Parliamentarian force that marched

---

56 TNA, SP28/184/3, ff. 1v.–9v.

List of Parliamentarian forces in Warwickshire. (TNA, SP28/34/1, f. 64r.)

to Whitchurch to block a Royalist attempt to relieve the beleaguered city of Chester. However, the Warwickshire Committee at Coventry pleaded for their return, which was refused by the Cheshire commander. Soon afterwards, the usually positive relationship between Brereton and them was severely tested when the latter insisted that Colonel William Colmore should take over Hawkesworth's command, possibly as a step towards the recall of their troops entirely. On 16 November, the deputy lieutenants – who included Colonels William Purefoy, Thomas Willoughby, and Sergeant Major Gamaliel Purefoy – wrote to Sir William:

> You know the condition of our country, how it is encompassed within the enemy's garrisons, whereby our sufferings are extreme, in the favourablest times. But now they upon us, for the garrisons that are taken by General Poyntz's forces near Newark empty themselves into Banbury, whereby that garrison is become very populous and strong to the impoverishing of that part of the country, and mastering our strength. The garrisons on the other side of the country, as Dudley, Lichfield, and Ashby, serving their turn to be next after the taking of Chester, and General Poyntz's leisure from Belvoir (which is now begirt), do scourge the country for provisions to victual themselves. To which purpose Dudley plundered Birmingham on Thursday last of all manner of provision the town could afford them. Our request is that you will dismiss our regiment of horse, whose absence is the cause of much misery to this county, and every day like to more and more, the rather for that you are amply supplied of horse by General Poyntz, so many whereof we hope you will retain to hold on the service of that siege.[57]

The wisdom of this is questionable, because, when the regiment returned to Warwickshire, its troopers received their new commander with derision and were openly disrespectful and mutinous towards him. Of the whole episode, the editor of the published editions of the Brereton letter books remarked:

> The matter was in the course of being settled as the siege of Chester drew to its close, and the letter which Brereton sent to them about it, together with his advice to Hawkesworth as to how to conduct himself towards the Committee are outstanding examples of tact and moderation, which were such valuable assets to Brereton in his work as a war leader.[58]

Captain Benjamin Lovell's Troop

Lovell was rector of Preston Bagot from 1636 and Lapworth from 1643. He served as captain of a troop in Warwickshire from April to October 1643, when, on his own evidence, he was 'forced' by Colonel Purefoy to give up the troop to Sergeant Major Abraham Pont. Abraham Pont died in January 1645, and he was succeeded in command of the troop by Captain John Cotton. Pont's widow, Isabel, petitioned the Committee for taking the Accounts in August 1645 that 'her said husband served as captain and major of horse in Warwick and Coventry before the Lord Brooke's death, by whom he was entertained, until about October last, he was unfortunately slain upon service'. Additionally, Isabel testified that he:

> received not in all that time so much pay as would defray the charge of raising his troop. And when she was a suiter for her husband's arrears, which are great, the Committee for taking the Accounts of Warwickshire sent for her husband's clerk and took from him her husband's book of accounts and all papers belonging to his troop. By which means, she cannot learn what is due unto him and in the meantime, she is

---

57 BL, Mss Add. 11332, ff. 41r., 47r.; 11333, ff. 15v., 45v., 107r.
58 Dore (ed.), *Letter Books*, II, p. 20.

ready to famish. She does therefore humbly desire this Honourable Committee for taking the Accounts of the Kingdom that they will direct their order or warrant unto the said Committee of Warwickshire to send up her husband's book of accounts and other papers and writings unto you, that so his arrears justly appearing hereby, a course may be taken for her speedy satisfaction in part or in whole.[59]

Lieutenant Hannaway served in Captain Lovell's troop. According to a 'list of those soldiers or troopers which were assigned with their horses and arms to Sergeant Major Pont, 17 October 1643, being unto there enforced by Colonel Purefoy', the following commissioned and non-commissioned were also present:

> Lieutenant William Halford
> Cornet Thomas Baldwin
> Quartermaster French
> Corporal Barron
> Corporal Rush
> Corporal Such.[60]

Colonel Godfrey Bosvile's Regiment of Foot

This formed the mainstay of the garrison of Warwick. In June 1645, John Bridges succeeded Bosvile as colonel of the regiment when that officer stepped down because of the Self-Denying Ordinance.

Colonel Bosvile's Own Company

The company was commanded by Captain Lieutenant John Browne, until his death sometime before November 1644. Browne was replaced by Ensign Richard Walford, who became captain in June 1645. On 20 March 1644, Bosvile's company mustered the following commissioned and non-commissioned officers:

> Captain-Lieutenant John Browne
> Ensign Richard Walford
> Sergeant John Gee
> Sergeant Parker
> Sergeant Whitehead
> Corporal Edward Mynson
> Corporal George Codson
> Corporal Whitehead
> Drummer William Pumfrey
> Drummer John Pollard.[61]

---

59 TNA, SP16/510/82, f. 142v.; *CSPD 1645–1647*, p. 100.
60 TNA, SP28/136/35, unf.; SP28/136/32, ff. 1r.–8v.
61 TNA, SP28/122, unf.

The accounts of William Skinner state that he was commissioned by Lord Brooke on 31 January 1643 'to be provost marshal to my own regiment [Colonel Bosvile's]'. He served in that capacity until 22 August 1646. Furthermore, Skinner's pay for the entire period, being 46 months at the rate of £1 15s. per month, amounted to £322, of which the sum of £181 18s. 4d. remained in arrears.[62]

Below is 'A list of the officers and number of soldiers under the command of Sergeant Major John Bridges, Governor of Warwick Castle', dated early 1644:

> In the Governor's Company
> Richard Smith, Lieutenant
> John Bridges, Ensign
> William Sward, Sergeant
> Nicholas Broughton, Sergeant
> George Modley, Drummer
> 109 soldiers
>
> In Captain Halford's Company
> William Rollinson, Lieutenant
> John Hopkins, Ensign
> Luke Cooke, Sergeant
> Henry Woakes, Sergeant
> Henry Millard, Drummer
> 95 soldiers
>
> In Captain Bridges' Company
> Charles Johnson, Lieutenant
> William Bowkey, Ensign
> Nicholas Hawes, Sergeant
> Thomas Orme, Sergeant
> Edward Hopkins, Drummer
> 80 soldiers
>
> In his troop
> Fulke Estoppe, Lieutenant
> Christopher Wheeler, Cornet
> Andrew Armdon, Quartermaster
> George Shaw, Trumpeter
> 3 Corporals
> 37 troopers
> 14 dragoons.[63]

On 24 May 1644, the following commissioned and non-commissioned officers were present in Colonel Bridges' company:

---

62 TNA, SP28/136/41, ff. 236r.–238v.
63 WA, CR2017/C9, ff. 41r.–v.; TNA, SP28/136/15, f. 25r.

Captain Lieutenant Richard Smith
Lieutenant Charles Johnson, clerk and commissary
Ensign John Bridges
Sergeant Nicolas Broughton
Sergeant William Bird
Corporal Thomas Queeny
Corporal John Heron
Corporal Robert Jones
Corporal Lingham
Drummer George Medley
Drummer Thomas Goode
Lance-pasando Thomas Queeny
Lance-pasando Henry Butler
Thomas Hind, gunner
George Medley, matross
Barnaby Butler, matross
Edward Bradley, scout
John Hill, scout
58 private sentinels.[64]

Lieutenant Colonel James Gray's Company

An officer under Sir William Constable in the Earl of Essex's army from 30 July 1642 to 15 April 1644, Gray became lieutenant colonel to Bosvile's regiment of foot, serving until March 1645.[65] Little is known of his company in Warwickshire.

Lieutenant Colonel James Castle's Company

Castle was commissioned as a captain in the association army by Lord Brooke on 27 January 1643. He remained in Warwickshire after Brooke's demise, becoming sergeant major in June 1643 and succeeded Gray as lieutenant colonel under Colonel Bridges in March 1645. In September 1646, Castle was commissioned colonel of a regiment for Ireland to be raised in Warwickshire and Worcestershire.[66]

Below is a muster list of Lieutenant Colonel James Castle's company, dated 3 November 1643:

Lieutenant William George
Ensign Thomas Colborne
Sergeant Richard Barrow
Sergeant Richard Knight

---

64   TNA, SP28/121, unf.; SP28/136/15, ff. 25r., 31r.
65   TNA, SP28/2A, f. 81v.; SP28/265, f. 460v.
66   TNA, SP28/136, 2A, ff. 1r.–6r.

Corporal Thomas Aspinall
Corporal Samuel Wilkes
Corporal Michael Corbet
Drummer Henry Jones
Drummer John Jordan
Drummer Joseph Brockenhurst
73 private sentinels.

For January 1646:

Lieutenant Thomas Colborne
Ensign Richard Barrow
Quartermaster Clarke
Marshal William Skinner
Sergeant Richard Knight
Sergeant Robert Fox
Sergeant Nicholas Jackson
Corporal Thomas Bagot
Corporal Stephen Keane
Corporal William Bowen
Corporal John Heath
Drummer John Jordan
Drummer Joseph Brockenhurst
91 private sentinels.[67]

Table 13 'Disbursements to Colonel Godfrey Bosvile's regiment of foot the regiment 12 October 1643 the space of 5 weeks, ending 17 November 1643' (TNA, SP28/182, ff. 182r.–183v.)

	£	s.	d.
To Captain-Lieutenant Browne 1 week's pay for 55 common soldiers at 4s. 8d. by the week and for 2 sergeants at 8s. apiece, 3 corporals and 2 drummers at 6s. apiece by week	15	2	18
To Captain-Lieutenant Browne 1 week's pay for 55 common soldiers at 4s. 8d. by the week and for 2 sergeants at 8s. apiece, 3 corporals and 2 drummers at 6s. apiece by week	14	8	8
To the surgeon's mate		12	0
For a wooden horse		8	0
For bread and beer given to the soldiers upon a muster		7	0
To a physick for sick soldiers	1	10	0
For drumheads, cords, snares, and mending of drums	1	2	10
For 6 muskets, 3 bandoliers, 1 sword, and for mending arms	1	2	9
For 54 drumheads, cords, and snares	3	8	0
For bringing ammunition from Coventry to Warwick		14	0
For stocking of muskets, heading of pikes, and otherwise mending of arms at several times	2	15	0
To Lieutenant Colonel Gray for bringing and keeping recruits from London before they came to Warwickshire	2	0	0

---

67 TNA, SP28/123/2, unf.

Captain Henry Slade's Company

Slade was one of the officers who stayed in Warwickshire after Lord Brooke's death in 1643. He was a captain in Colonel Bosvile's Warwick-based regiment of foot until August 1646, although the unit was periodically at Coventry. According to the financial accounts of 'Captain Henry Slade of the Warwick garrison', dated 23 October 1643 to 21 August 1646, he disbursed £1 to Martin Kemp, clerk to the regiment, £3 4s. for three drums, and a further £4 18s. for 'drumheads, cords and mending drums'. A further £1 10s. was laid out for the burial of Lieutenant Robert Stephens. Slade's testimony records:

> Ensign Robert Stephens, his commission bears the date 27 January 1643, which continued until 1 September 1643, at which time he was made lieutenant, and so continued 60 weeks and then died by a shot he received in the service; his pay at £1 1s. the week during the time he was ensign comes to £31 10s. And during the time he was lieutenant, being 6 weeks, [his pay] comes to £8 8s.; his whole pay as ensign and lieutenant comes to the sum of £39 18s. 3d.[68]

---

[68] TNA, SP28/136/42, ff. 7r.–9v.; SP28/136/43, unf.; SP28/182, unf.

Chapter 7

The Parliamentarian Garrisons of Coventry and Kenilworth

Coventry

In July 1642, the city of Coventry was not yet considered a safe Parliamentarian refuge. When Lord Brooke, exercising the authority given to him to levy forces under the Militia Ordinance, held musters of the trained bands and volunteers of Warwickshire in late June, 800 recruits reportedly came from Coventry. Thus, Brooke's activities had the effect of forcing any Royalist influence from the county. On 15 August, the Warwickshire commissioners of array informed their 'very loving friends the lords and others the commission of array for the county of Worcester' that:

> great numbers of men from several parts of this county have since we sent to you gathered themselves together in a warlike manner, and are already entered in the city of Coventry (a place of great strength) there waiting their fittest opportunity by joining with others as we have cause to suspect, which powers, if timely resistance do not may prove dangerous consequence not only to these parts, but to the Kingdom in general.

Similarly, writing on behalf of Charles I from Stoneleigh Abbey on 21 August 1642, Sir Edward Nicholas informed the Worcestershire commissioners:

> His Majesty taking notice of the forwardness and good affection of the gentry of that county, as well as in raising a troop of horse for his service, as by being inclined to levy some foot also for his Majesty's service, has commanded me by these to send his Royal thanks, and to desire you in his name to send all possible diligence the gentlemen's troop to the Earl of Northampton and Lord Dunsmore to Warwick. And to let you know, it will be very acceptable to him, and much advantage of his service, if you will also send forthwith to send some foot to Warwick likewise, the sooner these forces shall be sent to Warwick the great advantage it will be to his service, which his Majesty knows you will by your expedition and diligence adventure.[1]

---

1   WorcsA, BA1714/899, ff. 260r., 274r.–v.

The continued and successful campaign waged by the local Parliamentarians for the popular support of the county meant that men from all over Warwickshire poured into Coventry in particular. It may have been stronger in the northern part of the county. It was claimed that 400 recruits arrived from Birmingham on 19 August 1642.[2] Yet, in June, for example, Captain Thomas Willoughby, a minor member of the gentry, was commissioned to raise men in the Sutton Coldfield and Tamworth areas, whereas Colonel John Barker mustered 207 common soldiers in Coventry in August. By contrast, in the garrison at Warwick, merely 22 men were in pay in August 1642, with 83 the following month.[3]

On 10 August, Parliament had ordered Brooke, with a force consisting of Colonel John Hampden's, Denzil Hollis', and Sir Hugh Cholmley's regiments of foot, along with 6 troops of horse under Lord Grey of Groby, Colonel Thomas Ballard, and Colonel Nathaniel Fiennes, and supported by 9 cannon, to advance from Buckinghamshire to Warwickshire. In attempting to hasten these forces, on 21 August, a letter from the city informed Brooke that 'the King lay now before Coventry, and he was playing upon the town with his ordnance … that had battered the gates open, and the town is in great distress'.[4] Coventry, however, could not resist the King indefinitely, because, the following day, it was reported in the Parliamentarian press that:

> the citizens, careful of the cost of accommodating all his troops, the mayor offered to admit Charles and 200 of his adherents only. Nevertheless, the Cavaliers would not suffer the people to speak of it until they might all come in with his Majesty. The King's army consist not above 1,500, and of them is horse, which the country would not yield to; so they hung out the bloody flag and stood upon their guard. The King's army had beaten down the gate, but there are 2,000 able fighting men within the walls which are resolved to stand it out to the last man, not doubting before that time to be relieved by the Parliament.[5]

Below is a much fuller account of events reported from Coventry on 20 August 1642:

> Upon Wednesday the 24 August, information was given to the honourable House of Commons, of all such eminent passages that hath happened since his Majesty came to Coventry: that on Saturday last about 9 of the clock in the morning, with an army consisting of about 1,700 or 1,800 horse, his Majesty came to Coventry, which were the only strength of all his forces that came with him out of Yorkshire. And the citizens of Coventry having intelligence of drawing near the said city with a great army, every man that bore arms in the city, together with about 500 of the trained bands of the county presently put themselves into a posture of defence,

---

2 *A continuation of certaine speciall and remarkable passages from both houses of Parliament*, 23–30 August 1642. TT, E114[36].
3 TNA, SP16/539/91–92; SP28/147, f. 363v.
4 *CJ*, II, pp. 720, 731; *LJ*, V, p. 313.
5 *The True Proceeding of the Severall Counties of Yorke, Coventry, Portsmouth, Cornwall* (London: Richard Best, 1642). TT, E114[6].

resolving to spend their lives for the King and Parliament, and in maintenance of the laws of the Kingdom, whereupon the mayor and divers of the aldermen and chief commanders in the city, met his Majesty at the gates thereof, and shewed their dutiful respect to his Majesty, proffering their service at his feet, expressing their earnest desire to accommodate his Majesty in the maintaining of his just rights and prerogative, offering his Majesty free enter course into the city with a complete guard for the safety of his Royal person. But he demanded entrance with his whole army, and caused the proclamation to be read, proclaiming them traitors that should oppose him therein. But the Cavaliers being impatient of any delay, thinking to have had present admittance made presently an attempt to enter the gate, but quickly were driven back, and the gate shut against them. At which his Majesty seethed to be very much moved, and after some consultation with his general and other commanders, they planted 6 pieces of ordnance against the gate, and plaid upon it all that day, the Cavaliers threatening to fire the town, or beat it down about their ears, if it were not presently rendered up. But the citizens hearing that some forces from the Parliament were repairing thither to aid and assist them were resolved to stand it out, although they had not above 3 pieces of ordnance in the town, and those were unmounted this day being far spent, his Majesty repaired to a knight's house near Dunsmore about 4 miles from Coventry, and on Sunday morning the Cavaliers began again to play upon the gates of the city, and drove open the south gate thereof, and began to march into the city, not doubting but to make a prey thereof, thinking it impossible to be withstood; yet we may see God's wonderful hand of providence towards us in stirring up the soldiers within the city with such courage, and true affection to the Parliament, that at the first entrance of the cavaliers into the gate they welcomed them with such a volley of shot, that 7 of them were slain, and many more of them hurt, whereupon they were forced to retreat, and the women and others that were unfit to fight, brought an abundance of household stuff, as tables, stools, and other lumber, and threw them in the street, which quickly made the way unpassable, so that the horsemen durst not sally any more into the town, but played upon it with cannon and sometimes came riding up to the walls thereof. The Lord Brooke, Colonel Holles, Colonel Hampden, Colonel Fiennes, and Colonel Goodwyn, with their regiments, both of horse and foot, having intelligence hereof (being at Banbury) marched towards Coventry with all speed, and the King's army fearing that they would fall on the backs of them, presently raised their forces from against Coventry, carrying their ordnance with them, and came to meet the Parliament's forces, which met on Monday last about 8 of the clock in the morning upon Dunsmore Heath, about 4 miles on this side Coventry.[6]

The Parliamentarian forces commanded by Lord Brooke reached Southam in Warwickshire on 22 August 1642. It was on the same day that the King 'again took to horse, and with his company rode to Nottingham, where

---

[6] *A famous victory obtained by the citisens of Coventry, and the Parliaments forces, under the command of the Lord Brooks, and colonell Hambden, against the Kings army, August 22* (London: R. Wood, 1642). Dr Williams' Library, F390A.

was great preparation for the setting up of the standard'.[7] On learning of Brooke's movements, the Earl of Northampton (who had been assisting the King at Coventry) mustered his men on Dunsmore Heath and march southwards with 800 cavalry and 300 foot to meet him. The battle fought at Southam on 24 August is beyond the remit of the present study; suffice to say, Northampton's army suffered a decisive defeat. Due to his inferiority in cavalry, however, Brooke did not order a pursuit, although the Earl of Northampton disengaged his besieging troops from Warwick, whilst other Royalist soldiers in Kenilworth Castle departed about the same time.[8] The Parliamentarian commander proceeded to Coventry, reaching the city the same evening; nonetheless, he had accomplished an almost unassailable supremacy of Parliamentarian authority in most of Warwickshire.

Although Coventry had undergone a severe economic crisis in the sixteenth century, it had to an extent recovered by the early 1600s. When Nehemiah Wharton arrived in the city with the Earl of Essex's forces on 24 August 1642, he was somewhat impressed by its physical condition and reported it to be 'a city with a wall co-equal, if not exceeding that of London for breadth and height. The compass of it is near 3 miles, all of freestone. It has 4 strong gates, strong battlements stored with towers, bulwarks, courts of guard and other necessaries'.[9] Under the authority of the governor, Colonel John Barker, the garrison and inhabitants of Coventry soon prepared themselves for additional Royalist attacks by increasing the effectiveness of the city's fortifications. In areas outside Bishop Gate, Well Street Gate, Spon Gate, New Gate, Hill Street Gate, and Gosford Gate, properties were demolished and levelled to provide a clear field of fire, whilst, except for the main gates, the others were blocked up. Furthermore, the council minute books for 1643 record that:

> The women went in companies to fill the quarries in the Great Park, that they might not harbour an enemy, being called together by a drum they marched together into the Park with mattocks and spades, being led by 1 Goodwife Adderley with a Hercules Club on her shoulder, and drew off from work by 1 Mary Herbert with a pistol in her hand that she shot off when they were dismissed.[10]

Nevertheless, a detailed picture of the expenses and type of work done on the fortifications at Coventry is provided by the financial accounts of Colonel Barker, which are provided below:

---

7   *A True and exact relation of the manner of His Maiesties setting up of his standard at Nottingham on Munday the 22 of August 1642* (London: F. Coles, 1642). TT, E115[4].
8   *The manner and good successe of the Lord Brookes forces in pursuing the cavaliers from Coventry. In a letter to an honourable person in London, August 24. 1642* (London: Humphrey Blunden, 1642). BL, 669, ff. 6r.–v.; *A true and perfect relation of the first and victorious skirmish between the army under the conduct of the Right Honourable the Lord Brooks, the Lord Grey, Collonel Hampden, Collonel Hollis, Collonel Chomley, and others members of the honorable Houses of Parliament* (London: Matthew Walbanck, 1642). TT, E114[25].
9   Peachey, *Letters of Nehemiah Wharton*, p. 12.
10 CA, BA/H/11, ff. 39v.–40.

Table 14 Disbursements for the Construction of the Fortifications at Coventry from August to November 1642 (TNA, SP28/136/19, ff. 4r.–15v.)

	£	s.	d.
Paid to several poor men for work at the fortifications		12	2
Paid to poor men for work and 2 drumheads		3	4
Paid to Mr Legge and Mr Owen which they laid out for the fortifications	2	15	3
Paid to John Lake, smith, for work at the gates	2	9	0
Paid to Colonel Barker which he disbursed at the fortifications	17	8	0
Paid for 5 spades for the fortifications		5	0
Paid for 11 bags of lime for the towers	1	5	8
Paid to Daniel Ayres for felling timber and getting underwood for cannon baskets		1	8
Paid to Thomas Barton for carrying underwood for making baskets at the tower		3	0
Paid to Mr Sargison, mason, for work at Bishops Gate when the walls fell down, and for other work at the fortifications	24	8	1
Paid to Mr Dawkins for carrying 57 loads of stone and timber for the fortifications	1	18	0
Paid to Thomas Underwood for making 9 cannon baskets	1	8	6
Paid for felling wood and levelling ground near the city and Ardwall House	1	5	11
Paid to Mr Sargison for work at the fortifications	10	19	9
Paid to 2 men for filling cannon baskets		1	4
Paid to countrymen for carrying tiles and timber for 1 day	1	5	0
Paid to the basket maker for 25 days at 2s. 6d. per day	3	0	0
Paid to Drake the carpenter for 9 days working at the ordnance		10	6
Paid for 92 spades for the fortifications		5	11
Paid for 49 shovels for the pioneers	2	18	2
Paid for mending the bridge at Gosford Gate [the primary eastern entrance to the city from the market towns of Rugby, Lutterworth, and Market Harborough]		1	6
Paid to William Briscoe, mason, for work about the walls	4	18	0
Paid to William Dawkins for carrying 34 loads of stone to the works	1	14	3
Paid to William Briscoe for making loopholes in the walls	3	10	0
Paid to 3 men for taking down tiles at Little Park Gate		5	0
Paid to Mr Cole for 6 men trenching for 1 day		8	8
Paid to Mr Cole for 8 men levelling ground		6	8
Paid to Nathaniel Danwell and William Briscoe for getting turf for 6 days		8	0
Paid to William Monk for trenching in the water at Spring Gate	3	0	0
Paid for 4 baskets for the gunners at the tower		3	4

In addition to the above, the ward of Bishop Street in Coventry provided sums for 'the countrymen that came in by warrant 3 towns to carry in tiles and timber [with] bread and beer by Colonel Barker's appointment'; '24 gallons of 3d. beer to the butchers when they were digging the trenches'; '12 gallons of 3d. beer from John Tailor and Thomas Linsey, constables'; 'beer delivered to the soldiers when they were turfing the town wall'; '5 loads of faggots delivered for the fortifications at 5s. 4d. the load'; 'delivery to Thomas Bennett of 7¼ quarter planks, 3 inches thick and 10 inches broad as many as came to 26s. 6d. at 4½d. the foot'; and 'timber for the fortifying of the city by the appointment of Colonel Barker and the Committee, and valued by their appointment at £18 15s.' In addition, the constables of Spon Street Ward claimed to have lost four packs of wool, and 'pack clothes hung upon the towers by the appointment of Colonel

Barker', to the value of £2.[11] The practice of hanging of bales of wool upon structures and earthen banks to reduce the ballistic impact of projectiles was followed at other locations during the civil wars, such as Royalist-held Reading and Chester.

Like other garrisons, including that at Windsor, Coventry received considerable supplies of ordnance, ammunition, weapons, and other items both from London and local sources during the first few months of its existence. Thus, in August 1642, Colonel John Barker paid the sum of £5 for a barrel of powder; £4 9s. for 3cwt, three quarters, and nine pounds of musket bullet; £185 2s. 3d. for 40 muskets, 40 pikes, two pairs of petronells, 10 ensigns, powder, and 14 dozen links of match; £3 5s. was disbursed for 'ribbon and other things for the public'; a further £28 8s. 7d. for ribbons; 9s. 6d. for torches, horsehair, and coals for the guard; 6s. for four drum cords; 10s. for boring wooden guns; 2s. 5d. for 90lbs of match; and 1s. 10d. for candles for the guard and scouring arms. Various quantities were also laid out to carriers for transporting military stores to the garrison. This included £1 7s. to John Wright for carrying powder and match; 14s. for six horse teams to carry ammunition from Warwick; £2 16s. to four carters for bringing ammunition from Warwick; £1 3s. 8d. more for the same; £5 18s. 4d. to a carrier for 500lbs of musket bullets; £10 3s. 6d. to several carriers for bringing ordnance from London; in addition to 16s. for transporting carbines and £1 15s. for carrying 40 muskets and 40 pikes. Moreover, in November 1642, the garrison received (amongst other items) 41cwt of cannon shot, 1cwt of match, and 13 packs of musket ammunition from the Ordnance Office stores in London; eight large powder horns for the cannoneers; and 12 budge barrels.

The military governor of Coventry, Colonel John Barker, was a draper and alderman of the city and spent much of summer 1642 in Coventry working to recruit local forces and adding to the fortifications. His commission, dated 27 June 1642, authorised him to raise a regiment of foot, comprising 1,150 men besides officers, whilst his financial accounts record that he served as governor of the city of Coventry from 27 June 1642 to 29 June 1645; as colonel of a regiment of foot and captain of a company in the same regiment from 27 June 1642 until 28 June 1645; and as captain of a troop of horse from 1 March 1643 to 13 May 1645, being 803 days at £1 4s. per day for his personal pay and 15s. per day for his six horses: £1,564 16s. As such, Barker's total arrears of pay amounted to £6,205, of which he received £907 8s. 4d.[12]

Colonel John Barker's Troop of Horse

The troop was raised in Coventry in late 1642 and formed part of its garrison. On 13 May 1645, the troop was briefly taken over by Barker's captain lieutenant, Captain Henry Flower, himself a Coventry man. Until this date, this troop was part of the personal command of Colonel John Barker, along with his foot regiment, and hence partially independent of the main

---

11   TNA, SP28/182/1, ff. 7r.–8r., 11r.
12   TNA, SP28/136/19, f. 25v.; SP16/539, f. 33r.; SP28/147, f. 432v.

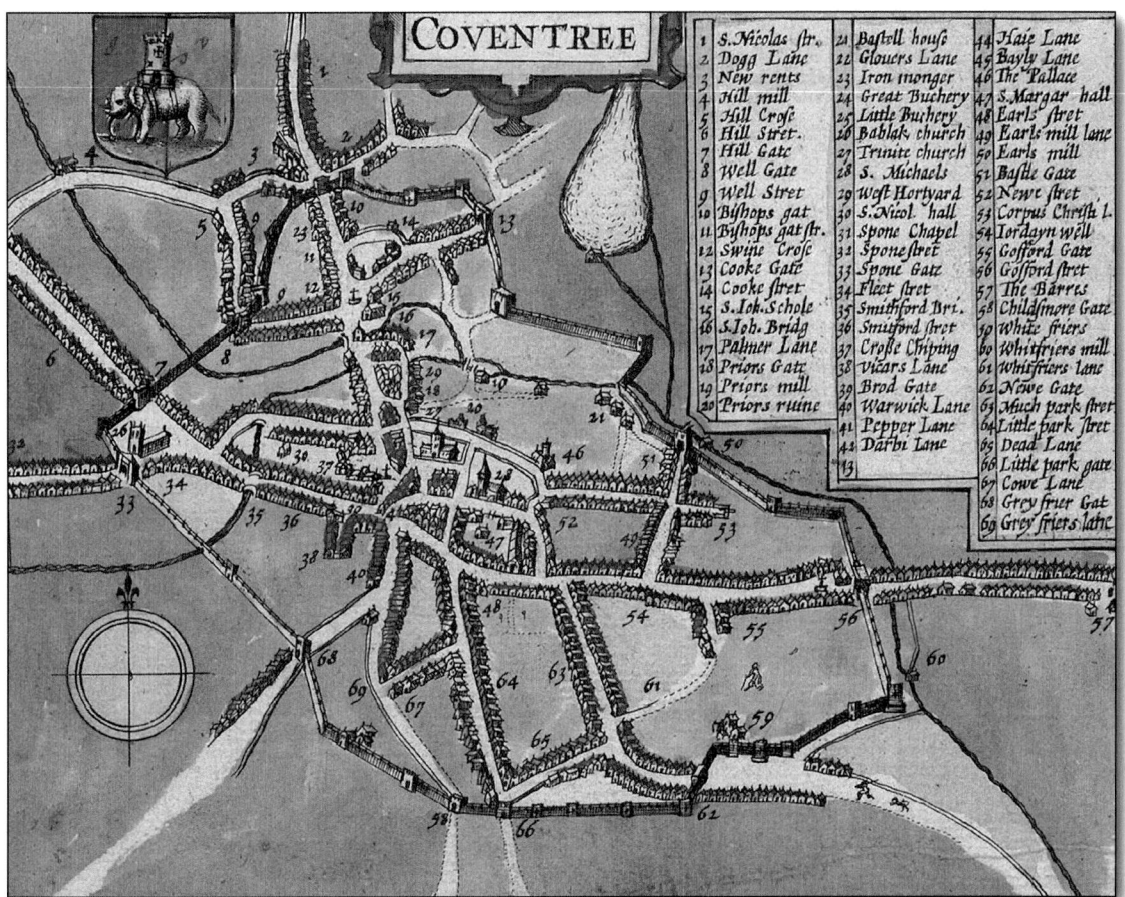

Map of Coventry by John Speed (1611).

regiment. The troop was listed on 24 January 1644 as containing a captain lieutenant, one cornet, one quartermaster, three corporals, two trumpeters, and 56 troopers, whilst payment was made to six officers and 50 troopers between 1 November 1644 and 31 October 1645.[13] The troopers, however, received only a third of their pay between April and August 1643, before they benefited from local assignations or taxes. Things improved somewhat between November 1644 and October 1645, when they got 90 percent of the money owed to them.[14] Flower's personal accounts show that he served as captain lieutenant to the troop from 1 November 1644 until 19 April 1645, 'before I received commission to be captain was 24 weeks, at which time I was allowed £3 10s. per week for my pay'.[15]

Like other Warwickshire Parliamentarian forces, Barker's troop was supplied from different sources. Under the Proposition scheme in 1643, John Featherston contributed to Colonel Barker:

---

13   WA, CR2017/C9, fol. 39v.
14   TNA, SP28/11/46, unf.
15   TNA, SP28/136/29, f. 2r.

to the use of the State the sum of £20 besides horse and arms voluntarily contributed by the said John Featherston in satisfaction of his fifth and 20th part according to the Ordinance of Parliament, the said John Featherston did contribute 1 horse with a saddle, bridle, and dragoon, worth £6 10s. at the least. And 1 complete armour for a horseman, and 1 pair of petronels, and 2 little pistols, and 1 other headpiece, in all worth £11 to the use of the State. The horse was sent to the late Lord Brooke deceased, and the petronels and arms before mentioned were delivered to Benjamin Lovell, clerk, then Captain of a troop of horse. So contributed in horse and arms by the said John Featherston to the use of the State to the value of £17 10s.[16]

Table 15 Purchases Made by Colonel John Barker for the Equipping of His Troop, March–May 1643 (TNA, SP28/136/19, ff. 3v.–23r.)

	£	s.	d.
Paid for the cornet, trumpet banner and staff	9	10	0
Paid for another cornet staff	1	15	0
Paid for carrying it to Coventry		1	0
Paid for a trumpet	2	10	0
Paid £1 5s. for a scarf and 9s. for a flask for Captain-Lieutenant Flower	1	14	0
Paid for 10½ yards of scarlet to make coats and suits for the trumpeters	4	3	0
Paid 9s. 10d. for 2 trumpets, £5 for banners and £4 10s. for strings.	9	19	10
Paid for 2 hats and feathers for the trumpeters		10	0
Paid for making their suits and cloaks	1	0	0
Paid for 20 bridle bits and 19 pairs of stirrups	5	5	0
Paid for 50 firestones for pistols and carbines		4	0
Paid to Robert Porter for 137 ammunition swords and belts, petronels and carbines	45	0	0
Paid for 2 carbines and 2 great saddles for the troop	2	0	0
Paid for a cornet staff		3	6
Paid for muskets and carbines	6	10	0
Paid for 3 saddles and bridles for the troop	1	14	0
Paid for 3 carbines and 4 petronels	2	0	0
Paid for mending 2 carbines, and for keys and stones		2	0
Paid for 2 saddles for the troop		9	0
Paid for a carbine box, belt and swivel		16	6
Paid to Robert Turner for carrying 4cwt of great saddles for the troop from London		18	0
Paid to John Baldwin in part for 30 pairs of petronel cases	5	10	0
Paid for 12 carbine belts		13	6
Paid for linings for 2 pairs of breeches for the troopers		3	0
Paid for making a pair of breeches, coats and linings		6	0
Paid for making 5 pairs of boots and 3 pairs of breeches		7	0
Paid for linings for 3 suits, and making a coat and breeches		6	6
Paid for cloth to make shirts	3	19	4
Paid for cloth to make troopers' clothes	18	9	0
Paid for making 2 coats, buttons and thread		2	6
Paid 1s. 6d. for a pair of shoes made from old boots, 3s. 8d. for making 2 pairs of breeches		5	2

---

16 TNA, SP28/184/4, ff. 1r.–v.

Colonel John Barker's Regiment of Foot

Colonel John Barker was commissioned to raise a Coventry-based regiment of foot on 27 June 1642. He recruited 1,150 men besides officers and raised a troop of horse in March 1643. In June 1645, Barker resigned under the terms of the Self-Denying Ordinance.

Table 16 List of Colonel Barker's Foot Regiment, Taken 24 January 1644

Colonel Barker, his company [see under his company below]	
Lieutenant-Colonel Phipps' company	
Captain Lieutenant	Lieutenant
Ensign	Ensign
4 sergeants	3 sergeants
4 corporals	3 corporals
1 drum major	
2 other drummers	2 drummers
105 common soldiers	85 soldiers, 8 are strangers
Sergeant Major Peter Burgoyne's company	Captain William Colmore's company
Lieutenant	Lieutenant
Ensign	Ensign
3 sergeants	2 sergeants
3 corporals	2 corporals
2 drums	1 drummer
70 soldiers, 20 are strangers	62 soldiers
Captain Willoughby's company	Captain William Purefoy's company
Lieutenant	Lieutenant
Ensign	Ensign
2 sergeants	2 sergeants
2 corporals	2 corporals
1 drum	2 drummers
70 soldiers	63 soldiers
Captain Samuel Ward's company	Captain Matthew Randell's company
Lieutenant	Lieutenant
Ensign	Ensign
2 sergeants	2 sergeants
3 corporals	2 corporals
2 drummers	2 drummers
60 soldiers	63 soldiers
Captain Robert Colmore's company	Captain Waldive Willington's company
Lieutenant	Lieutenant
Ensign	Ensign
2 sergeants	2 sergeants
2 corporals	2 corporals
1 drum	1 drum
62 soldiers	60 soldiers
Captain Willington's company is at Tamworth and Captain Robert Colmore's at Astley Castle. The regiment of foot being about half countrymen besides Captain Willington, his company.	

The total strength of the regiment was given as 30 commissioned officers, 62 non-commissioned officers, and 700 common soldiers.[17]

---

17 WA, CR2017/9, ff. 39r.–v.

Colonel John Barker's Company (Colonel John Barker's Regiment)

Originally part of Lord Brooke's Warwickshire regiment, in October 1642, the unit remained in the county and thus missed Edgehill. When the regiment was disbanded after Brooke's death, the colonel's company remained in the garrison of Coventry. Colonel Barker's own company was led by Captain Lieutenant John Brownell from June 1644 to June 1645, when he became captain of the company in his own right. This officer was a Coventry man and had previously served as lieutenant to Captain Samuel Ward.[18] The accounts of Nathaniel Hewitt, clerk to Barker's company, between 22 October 1643 and 12 January 1644 include the following muster list:

> Captain-Lieutenant John Brownell
> Ensign Richard Phillips
> Sergeant Phillips
> Sergeant Miller
> Sergeant Herbert
> Sergeant Todd
> Corporal John Wilkinson
> Corporal Joseph Carver
> Corporal Joseph Olde
> Corporal [unnamed]
> Drum-major [unnamed]
> Drummer Richard Barratt
> Drummer John Edwards
> 99 private sentinels.[19]

Moreover, 'the accounts of John Brownell, late lieutenant to Captain Samuel Ward for money by him received towards the payment of the said captain's company, 2 February 1644 to 18 May 1644', list the following commissioned officers, non-commissioned officers, and soldiers in the company, based upon disbursements made on 10 February 1644:

> Lieutenant Brownell
> Ensign Ash
> Sergeant Cooke
> Sergeant Perkins
> Corporal Thomas Southern
> Corporal Ayres
> Drummer Slade
> Drummer Kemp
> Lancepasando Thomas Ward
> 52 common soldiers.

---

18   TNA, SP28/145, f. 432r.; SP28/147/1, ff. 2v.–10r.
19   TNA, SP28/136/20, ff. 14r.–16r.

Cook Street Gate in Coventry's town walls. (Photo by author)

Similarly, those belonging to Sergeants John Teddsoe and Henry Buller record that, during this period, there were received 'for arming of divers soldiers of Colonel Barker's company in December 1644 38 swords, 3 pikes, 14 muskets, 24 pairs of bandoliers'; whilst, in February 1645, 22 swords, 12 pikes, 8 muskets, 24 belts, and 12 pairs of bandoliers came in, 'all of which were delivered to the corporals for those that wanted arms in their several squadrons'. In addition to the evidence drawn from the muster lists already given, Colonel Barker's company mustered three commissioned officers, nine non-commissioned officers, and 172 common soldiers from 1 October to 12 November 1643; the same officers with 134 soldiers from 12 November 1643 to 20 January 1644; the same officers and 130 soldiers from 20 January to 11 June 1644; the same officers plus 105 soldiers from 11 June to 6 August 1644; the same numbers on 28 January 1645; and between 66 and 71 private sentinels were mustered between July 1645 and January 1646.[20]

Colonel Thomas Willoughby's Regiment of Foot for the City of Coventry

Willoughby was of Sutton Coldfield and served as a member of the Warwickshire Committee before succeeding Barker as colonel of the Coventry-based regiment when the latter resigned in June 1645 under the terms of the Self-Denying Ordinance. Willoughby continued to command the regiment until its disbandment in March 1647.

Table 17 Colonel Willoughby's Company, Mustered 30 October 1645 (TNA, SP28/136/53A, ff. 79r.–80v.)

Captain-Lieutenant Robert Peake		
Ensign William Colman		
Sergeant Thomas Gunn		
Sergeant Thomas Humphrey		
Sergeant John Curtis		
Sergeant John Gunn		
Corporal John Peacocke		
Corporal Joseph Brooks		
Corporal Thomas Mousley		
Drum-Major John Edwards		
Drummer Arthur Harding		
Drummer James Spikes		
Samuel Baker – servant to the colonel		
Mostyn Launde – servant to the colonel		
Corporal Jeacocke's Squadron:		
Edward Withers	John Rodes	Thomas Packman
Richard Fox	Thomas Dolittle	William Welch
John Kendall	Thomas Bray	John Fox
Anthony Whatley	John Games	Henry Grimley
Thomas Read junior	William Cross	Thomas Boulte

---

20   TNA, SP28/136/20, ff. 17r.–19v., 22r., 71r.

THE PARLIAMENTARIAN GARRISONS OF COVENTRY AND KENILWORTH

Thomas Warren	John Berry	Joseph Moss
Thomas Grimes	John Wilson	
Josiah Allen	Thomas Randall	
Corporal Brooks' Squadron:		
Richard Stanton	John Rattly	George Hawkins
Thomas Stanton	Raphe Heath	John Roper
Isaac Stanton	Robert Rycraft	William Flint
George Wilson	Thomas Robson	Thomas Boult
John Dooley	John Gwilliams	Richard Baddley
John Marsh	Richard Lowe	Henry Hobly
Richard Smith	John Coleman	John James
Henry Manifold	Edward Barber	
Corporal Mousley's Squadron:		
Richard Brockhouse	John Board	Thomas Hands
Richard Cambridge	Raphael Smith	Thomas Cox
John Norton	Nathaniel Topley	John Harwood
Thomas Norton	Thomas Norris	Francis Stretton
Richard Parkes	John Ostler	George Shoreman
Thomas Hopton	George Bentley	Benjamin Smallbrook
Thomas Newton	Nicholas Clark	69 private sentinels
William James	John Sounden	
James Williams	Henry Bolte	

Table 18 Lieutenant Colonel Robert Phipps' Company, Mustered 30 October 1645 (TNA, SP28/136/53A, ff. 81r.–82r., 105r.–106v.)

Lieutenant Colonel Robert Phipps		
Lieutenant Thomas Hobson		
Ensign Thomas Priest		
Sergeant Thomas Hobson		
Sergeant Joseph Essex		
Sergeant Richard Brunt		
Corporal John Sesorson		
Corporal Samuel Bayes		
Drummer Frank Herbert		
Drummer John Croxon		
Frank Blakley	Edward Newman	Samuel Spencer
Henry Pugson	Thomas Mann	Richard Knight
Roger Frampton	Samuel Phipps	Richard Smith
Henry Clarke	William Herbert	John Stife
Thomas Berman	William Standen	William Deacon
Thomas West	Henry Gambole	William Lucas
John Nash	Hugh Auden	Ralph Ashe
Samuel Heap	Nicholas Powell	Richard Wright
John Gee	Thomas Avery	Nicholas Gibbs
Samuel Whitcroft	Richard Wale	Robert Courtney
Robert Waterhouse	Stephen Smith	Francis Beasley
Nicholas Baxter	Joseph Cathern	Edward Savin
Peter Lennon	John Francome	Bartholomew Sherwood
Peter Basnett	William Smith	46 private sentinels
William Bettridge	Arthur Jones	
Thomas Langson	Elias Churchman	

Lieutenant Colonel Robert Phipps was a physician in Coventry before hostilities and, sometime before December 1642, became lieutenant colonel of Colonel John Barker's regiment, holding that position throughout the First Civil War. Phipps was also on the county committee but seems to have fallen out with other members in mid-1643. Lieutenant Colonel Robert Phipps' company was particularly provided for by contributions from the inhabitants of Coventry. For instance, the constables of Bailey Lane Ward recorded payments 'for maintenance of soldiers', from 1 May 1643 to 13 November 1644 at 2s. 4d. per week; from 15 November 1644 to 12 June 1646 at 2s 6d. per week; and from 12 June to 22 August 1646 at 1s. 3d. per week. Abraham Watts paid 'Lieutenant Colonel Phipps his company per weekly tax for 3 years and 6 weeks ending 12 June last 1646 at 2s. per week'. Similarly, Francis Kerling provided the company from 27 April 1643 for 104 weeks at 18d. per week, the same for 40 weeks at 2s. per week, with a further 10 weeks' contribution at 9d. a week. Equally, in Bishop Street Ward, at an unknown date, William Stretton paid 10 weeks' assessment to Lieutenant Colonel Phipps' company, amounting to 10s.; the clothier Henry Wilkinson paid 5s. 4d. for the soldiers; whereas Ralph Phillips claimed 'for losses, taxes and free quarter since 10 May 1643, paid to Lieutenant Colonel Phipps' officers 13 March 1643 for 1 month 3s. 4d. for 3 months 10s. [and] paid his company £1 14s. from thence to 21 August 1646, being 10 weeks at 12d. 10s.'[21]

Sergeant Major Gamaliel Purefoy's Company (Colonel Thomas Willoughby's Regiment)

From Wolvershill, Warwickshire, Gamaliel was the father of Sergeant Major George Purefoy, Captain Michael Purefoy, Lieutenant William Purefoy, and Ensign Peter Purefoy and a relative of Colonel William Purefoy. As a member of the Warwickshire Committee, he served as captain in Colonel John Barker's regiment of the Coventry garrison, whilst, on 30 August 1645, he received a commission as sergeant major in the same regiment, then under the command of Colonel Thomas Willoughby.[22] According to his own financial accounts, Gamaliel's pay arrears amounted to the following:

> Due to me as captain from 14 June 1642, on which day I mustered my company in full, until 30 July 1643, being 58 weeks in sum of £304 10s., whereof I received at the same time £42; due to me also which I am out of purse for the raising of my company £43; to myself for pay from 30 July 1643 until 16 November 1644, being £219 15s.: to me from 15 November [1644] to 30 August 1645, being 41 weeks at £2 12s. 6d. per week, amounting to £107 12s. 6d.; to me as Sergeant Major from 30 August 1645 till 22 August 1646, being 51 weeks at £4 8s. per week, which comes to £260 8s.[23]

---

21 TNA, SP28/185/1, ff. 2r.–5v.; SP28/182/1, ff. 2r.–4v.
22 TNA, SP28/136/36, ff. 1r., 18r.; *CJ*, IV, p. 633.
23 TNA, SP28/136/36, f. 18r.

Table 19 Sergeant Major Gamaliel Purefoy's Company, 15 September 1645 (TNA, SP28/136/53A, ff. 83r.–84v., 107r.–110v.)

Sergeant Major Gamaliel Purefoy		
Lieutenant John Smalley		
Ensign Samuel Turner		
Sergeant Raphe Phillips		
Sergeant Richard Jellbrowne		
Sergeant Humphrey Baker		
Corporal Thomas Hanson		
Corporal Robert Godbey		
Corporal Humphrey Haynes		
Drummer William Cobley		
Drummer Job Howard		
Corporal Hanson's Squadron:		
Thomas Shepard	John Ward senior	Francis James
John Crowe	William Payne	Robert Wise
William Strickland	Richard Madelin	Thomas Wolfe
John Phillips	Robert Ashmore	Hugh Miller
Oliver Wolfe	Francis Madelin	John Tozier
John Frost	William Fletcher	Thomas Nicks
Thomas Perkins	Thomas Orton	Humphrey Miller
John Wooten	John Ward junior	
Corporal Godbey's Squadron:		
Samuel Harper	Edmund Lane	Edward Bartholomew
John Middleton	Richard Warren	Adam Harrison
Job Gibbs	Humphrey Parker	Richard Jackson
Gabriel Barr	William Warren	John Bristow
John Bunce	Maximillion Compton	Robert Oldbury
Richard Pearson	Rowland Elkins	John Bailey
William Farmer	Timothy Jenkins	Thomas Partridge
John Edwards	Humphrey Crewe	Thomas Goode
Corporal Haynes' Squadron:		
Samuel Legge	John Hall	Thomas Oldbury
Edward Dyke	Richard Crumper	Richard Arthur
Thomas Ripley	William Scott	Mark Gilfore
John Thread	Richard Abington	John Poynton
John Turvey	Thomas Hill	John Jakely
Robert Turvey	John Wittern	George Smallwood
James Cushing	John New	Samuel Jayne
William Crewe	Richard Saunders	
Hugh Atherton	Thomas Jeffcoate	

Between September 1645 and May 1646, the strength of Sergeant Major Purefoy's company remained constant, with a lieutenant, an ensign, 3 sergeants, 3 corporals, 2 drummers, and between 73 and 75 soldiers in receipt of pay; however, on 29 August 1646, a lieutenant, an ensign, 2 sergeants, 2 corporals, 1 drummer, and 50 men obtained a week's pay at the rate of £2 12s. 6d. for the sergeant major, £1 8s. for the lieutenant, £1 1s. for the ensign, 10s. 6d. for each sergeant, and 7s. for the corporals and drummer, being an overall sum of £18 7s. 2d. On 1 September 1646, the same number of commissioned and non-commissioned officers, plus 51 private sentinels, benefitted from a week's pay amounting to £19 1s. 10d.; on 10 October, the same, but 50 soldiers, were in receipt 'full pay for a week', totalling £18 7s. 2d.; whereas the same numbers were paid £229 2s. for a period of 12 weeks. Although pay rates for the common soldiers are excluded from these figures, it is possible to compute their daily pay as 5½d. (presumably the amount left after deductions for victuals, clothing, and quarter), an amount equating to the 3s. a week disbursed to those of Colonel John Barker's own company of foot in 1643.[24]

Captain Samuel Ward's Company (Willoughby's Regiment)

Of Coventry, Ward was captain of a company of foot in Colonel Barker's regiment by summer 1642 and still there in May 1646. His own accounts indicate the presence of 116 soldiers from August 1642 to February 1643; on 4 January 1643, 9 officers and 60 soldiers were mustered, whereas, between July 1645 and May 1646, there were 10 officers and between 58 and 70 men in pay. On 15 September 1645, Captain Ward's company mustered the following:

> Captain Samuel Ward
> Lieutenant Peter Herbert
> Ensign Robert Cooke
> Sergeant Thomas Perkins
> Sergeant John Joyner
> Corporal and clerk Thomas Botherne
> Corporal Edward Quale
> Corporal William Atherall
> Drummer John Flood
> Drummer John Kempe
> William Perkin, gentleman of the pike.[25]

Kenilworth

Although the armies of Charles I and Parliament passed though Kenilworth during their march to Edgehill in October 1642, and some Royalist troops under the Earl of Northampton were briefly located there later in the year, the medieval castle and town were properly garrisoned for Parliament by its governor, Captain Hastings Ingram, in January 1643. However, he was implicated in a plot to betray Warwick to the Royalists under armed guard in early April.[26] Imprisoned by the county committee, Ingram thereafter became

---

24 TNA, SP28/144/10; SP28/136/36, ff. 7v.–8r.; SP28/136/20, f. 23r.
25 TNA, SP28/136/53A, ff. 86r.–89r.
26 TNA, SP28/37, ff. 126r.–v.; SP28/139/3, f. 10r.; *The Last Weeks Proceedings of the Lord Brooke* (London: R. O. and G. D., 1643). TT, E91[19].

a supporter of the Earl of Denbigh in the Midlands.[27] In April 1643, the governorship of Kenilworth passed to Colonel John Needham, who acted in that capacity until 12 July 1645. His three sets of accounts show that Needham served as captain of a company of foot from 19 May to 25 July 1643 at 15s. per day, amounting to £602 5s., the half received coming to £301 2s. 6d.; moreover, he was governor of Kenilworth Castle from 19 May 1643 to 25 July 1645 at £2 per day, amounting to £1,606, the half owing £803.[28] A highly conscientious military officer and committeeman, Needham had previously been a captain in Brooke's association army and, upon his appointment as governor of Kenilworth, had taken his newly independent company with him to form the garrison. However, Needham was appointed governor of Leicester, and, on 28 July 1645, he was replaced at Kenilworth by Sergeant Major Peter Burgoyne, previously a trained bands officer and captain of an infantry company in the garrison of Coventry. Needham's commission as captain of a foot company expired on 25 July, and muster lists imply that Burgoyne commanded an entirely different unit, the former's command having been disbanded.

The financial accounts of John Mascall, treasurer of Kenilworth Castle, between 12 August 1644 and 4 February 1646 offer an insight into various payments to the garrison.

Table 20 Accounts of John Mascall, Treasurer of Kenilworth Castle, 12 September–28 November 1644 (TNA, SP28/136/6, ff. 264v.–270v.)

	£	s.	d.
12 September to 11 October 1644:			
Paid to 67 soldiers for a fortnight at 4s. 8d. per week	31	5	4
Given to the lieutenant to pay our soldiers which were at Abingdon in Sir William Waller's Army	16	0	0
Given to the lieutenant to pay our soldiers which were at Banbury in Sir William Waller's Army	15	8	2
Sent to Banbury to pay the soldiers for a fortnight's pay	33	0	0
Paid to 3 sergeants for a fortnight	3	3	0
Paid a corporal the same		15	0
Paid for a drummer and a porter the same	1	18	0
Paid 79 soldiers the same who were at Kenilworth Castle at 4s. 8d. per week	36	17	4
Paid the soldiers which came from Banbury, the soldiers being Corporal Hale, Drummer John Worsley, Francis Bowker, John James, Thomas Brimley, John Schofield, John Parker, and Edward Collet	21	18	1
14 November to 28 November 1644:			
Paid 2 weeks' pay to the governor, 1 lieutenant, 1 ensign, 3 sergeants, 5 corporals, 2 drummers, and 111 soldiers	[…]		
Paid Mr Sharrard the minister	12	6	0
Paid Mr Lee the surgeon for dressing the wounded soldiers for five weeks at 11s. per week	2	16	0
29 November to 12 December 1644 Paid 2 weeks' pay to the governor, 1 lieutenant, 1 ensign, 3 sergeants, 5 corporals, 2 drummers, and 110 soldiers	[…]		

---

27 TNA, SP28/37/126, unf.
28 TNA, SP28/136/3, f, 275r.

	£	s.	d.
4 January and 17 January 1645 Paid 2 weeks' pay to the governor, 1 lieutenant, 1 ensign, 3 sergeants, 5 corporals, 2 drummers, and 103 soldiers	[...]		
18 to 31 January 1645 Paid 2 weeks' pay to the governor, 1 lieutenant, 1 ensign, 3 sergeants, 5 corporals, 2 drummers, 93 soldiers.	[...]		

Between 30 October 1642 and 13 June 1643, Captain (then Colonel) Needham received various payments, such as £96 'from Colonel John Bridges towards the paying of my own foot company'; the sum of £9 14s. 11d. from Thomas Hynde by the hands of Corporal Williamson for his own pay and the pay of 25 soldiers, being one week and four days; and £30 from Sergeant Major Joseph Hawkesworth 'by the hands of Thomas Worthington, then my sergeant, towards the payment of my company'. Besides, a muster list of 11 January 1643 includes the following:

Lieutenant William Herring
Ensign Thomas Worthington
Sergeant Lawrence Wilkinson
Sergeant William England
Sergeant John England
Corporal William Shephard
Corporal George Jacye
Corporal Simon Bristol
Corporal William Baines
Corporal John Holding
Drummer John Worsley
Drummer John Travel
67 soldiers.[29]

Colonel Needham's third set of accounts record his receipts and disbursements from 13 April 1643 to 5 February 1646, a selection of which is provided below:

Table 21 Colonel John Needham's 'Account of what arms I received from the State since I received my commissions' (TNA, SP28/136/4, f. 282r.)

From Captain Bradshaw, one belonging to the magazine for arms at London, and delivered by virtue of a warrant from the Close Committee at Westminster – 72 firelocks
From Coventry by order there of the Committee – 30 muskets These muskets and firelocks are now in the garrison, and some that were broken by overcharging, and some others were left at Sir Thomas Holt's house, Beely House, Compton House and Banbury Castle being stormed, which the use of these arms being (as were as I can guess) – 20 lost
For swords I never received any from the State, but furnished my soldiers at my own charge – £40

---

29 TNA, SP28/136/2, ff. 211r.–213v.; SP28/136/3, f. 275r.–289v.

Table 22 'An account of what horses have been in the castle of Kenilworth and how disposed of them from 12 May 1643 to 5 April 1644' (TNA, SP28/136/4, ff. 281r.–v.)

Taken from Mr Gardner 8 horses, mares and colts; 1 mule is dead; 2 of then sold, the captain accounting for 1
A horse given to Dunn of Kenilworth that had his horse killed in the service, commanded 40 by the Earl of Denbigh; 1 of them is dead, 2 of them are now in the garrison, 1 of them given to Obadiah Brooksby for 1 that he lost in the service, he himself now being in the garrison
Given 1 more of them to Mr Brooks of Stonly that had his killed in the service, commanded out by the Earl of Denbigh
Taken from Mr Woolston 3 mares and 2 colts, 1 of which is dead, the other stolen, 1 other was given to Dunn of Kenilworth, the first that was given being dead
The 2 colts sold by Mr Ingram, overseer of the stables, for which he had given account to the treasurer, they were sold for £4 6s. 8d.
1 grey nagg which was taken from a malignant person, which Mr Ingram has sold, his price being 12s.
Taken from Mr Gardner 1 of the same 2 mares, 1 of them was sold to William Floyd, groom to the stables, for £2 which he had abated from his pay, that was behind; the other was lost
Taken from Mr Langham of Poulton 1 horse, which is now in the garrison

Such lists of mounts indicate that the garrison of Kenilworth did not only consist of infantry units. Hence, albeit briefly, a dragoon company, commanded by Captain Samuel Hill, was also present. In January 1646, he wrote to the Committee of Accounts:

> I am very ready to render an account of my employment [in Warwickshire], particularly at Kenilworth, though it more properly belongs to Captain Ingram, who was governor of the Castle, and from whom I received orders and did nothing otherwise. It is true that, being commanded by him, I fetched in divers malignants with whom he compounded and received their money, and what I had to pay my dragoons I had from him, which when I can call to mind I will inform you. I never received any myself from any of them, but left it wholly to him, who commanded in chief. If any horses were taken from any upon groundless information of their malignancy, they must not blame the messengers, but him who sent them.[30]

As was the case with other civil war garrisons, the one at Kenilworth received both financial and material support from local civilian communities. Although a substantial number of officers and soldiers were quartered by householders, quantities of bedding and other items were supplied. From the parish of Honiley, John Knight claimed that he 'had taken from him by the soldiers under the command of Mr Ingram, governor of Kenilworth Castle 1 old flock bed, 1 pair of sheets, 1 blanket, and 1 bolster worth £7', whereas John Tibbets provided a wool bed and blanket 'by the command of Captain Needham into Kenilworth Castle'. Another parishioner maintained that he had contributed 'bedding, 3 strikes of oats, 1 loaf of bread, 2 cheeses, 2 muskets, 1 set of bandoleers, which were taken from me by some of Mr Ingram's soldiers, and for working at the bulwarks, and for the carriage of 1 load of hay to Kenilworth Castle in Captain Needham's time [worth] £12 2s.' Similarly, William Matthew of Kenilworth Duchy in Kenilworth Parish

---

30   *CSPD 1645–1647*, p. 310.

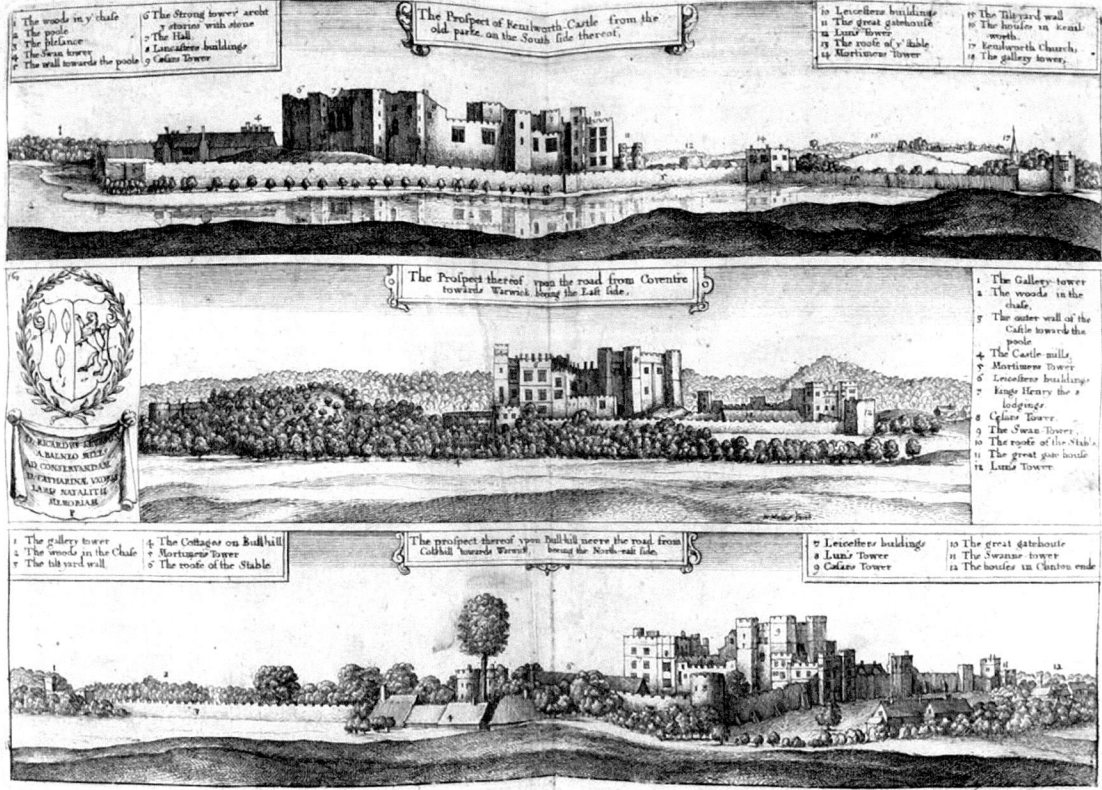

Prospect of Kenilworth Castle, from William Dugdale, *Antiquities of Warwickshire* (1653).

noted his delivery to Governor Needham and his soldiers of a flock bed, one pair of sheets, two blankets, and one pillow.[31]

The garrison was also furnished with large quantities of timber for building and firewood. Hence, it was claimed that, in April 1643, 28 trees were felled in the King's Wood at Kenilworth 'by Captain Needham's appointment'. Among these, eight were taken from Paryer's Coppice by Sergeant England, William Peawood, John Clements, and Thomas Aldridge; six 'good oaks' were felled for firewood in Harper's Coppice, and a further eight from Whorstone Coppice. Moreover, the same persons gathered two loads of underwood in Strabery Coppice and the same quantity in Buttons Coppice during Whitsun week 1644. It was also reported that:

> about Midsummer a little before Nasby fight, were felled in the chase by Sergeant England and others by the appointment of Captain Needham to make a mill for the castle, 2 oaks; the number of these oaks be esteemed worth at least £49, likewise the loads of underwood worth £38s. The wood and trees for firewood felled and cleft upon the chase and park, which was by the appointment of Captain Needham for his own use and others in the castle from the beginning of his time of coming to July 1645 worth at least £300.

---

31 TNA, SP28/183/21, ff. 4r.–5v.; SP28/185, ff. 4r.–9r.

Additionally, a document entitled 'The accounts for the garrison of Kenilworth Castle for such monies as were received for the bark, lops, and tops of such trees as have been felled in the years 1643, 1644, and 1645, which was in the time that Colonel John Needham was governor of that garrison' contains the following entry from John England:

> Paid to myself at several times by the allowance and appointment of Captain John Needham, governor, being head workman for felling the timber, contriving the form of the works both for earth and timber; and for my constant labour in the 3 years beforementioned. And also for the making of the outward gates, the drawbridge, and the bulwark of timber in the head of the pool without the wall. Total received by me £11 14s. 10d.[32]

Amongst the loss accounts for Kenilworth Duchy are 'What losses payments and hindrances Gilbert Howe, gentleman and housekeeper of Kenilworth Castle has made since the first putting in of a garrison into the castle of Kenilworth which was done on 12 September 1642 by Mr Stoughton and Mr Fish of Warwick'. These include claims for the following quantities and values of grass and animals taken for the garrison, presumably upon the authority of warrants from the governor:

> I have also lost 3 years' benefit of the grass within and without the castle walls, and all the profit of the orchards and gardens to the value of for 4 years unto us 20 nobles a year, in all £26 6s. I have likewise for 3 years been trespassed in my grounds and grass in the park by falling firewood trees, and cleaving of them for the use of the garrison, and the daily carriage of it into the castle and town with carts and wains, and by cutting of turf for bulwarks, and the daily high way made through my grounds whereby I have been damnified £20.
>
> 1643 Captain Needham, being then governor of the castle had also going in my grounds 800-odd sheep, cows, and mares and colts in the summer, and 50 ewes and lambs, and 10 mares and Colts in the winter besides other cattle valued at £12.
>
> 1644 Captain Needham told me that he was allowed by the Committee of Coventry for the garrison horses the harbaging of the park grounds, which he had fully to himself and took monies for the joisting of 30 cattle which went in it from which my tax being deducted there remains £40.
>
> 1645 in the beginning of these times I had about 100 sheep 40 head of cattle of all which I have now left but 10 by reason my grass was eaten up by the garrison horses and other cattle of theirs so that I was forced to put off my stock to pay my rent I have also lost these years past in the sale of young cattle and wool of lambs above £30, so in all £80.[33]

Moreover, from Kenilworth Augmentation in Kenilworth Parish, some items were supplied to the Parliamentarian garrison during the time of its occupation, including 'bedding and beer to the Castle' by John Lane costing

---

32 TNA, SP28/136/3, f. 1r.
33 TNA, SP28/185, ff. 8r.–9r.

£2 8s.; 13 heifers taken and killed at the castle by Captain Harvey's command to the value of £7 10s.; a hogshead of beer and 200 of coals 'in Captain Ingram's time taken to the castle'; and the services of Henry Power, who provided a team of draught horses for eight days when Captain Needham was governor of Kenilworth Castle.[34]

---

[34] TNA, SP28/182/1, ff. 2r.–4r.

Bibliography

Manuscript Sources

Aberystwyth, National Library of Wales
Chirk Castle Mss B35A/16; B16C/41; B86/95
Clenennau Letters and Papers 539

Aston, Cheshire
Unlisted warrants, 1643–1645

Aylesbury, Buckinghamshire Archives
D159/35

Brighton, East Sussex Record Office
DAN4/1/38; DAN4/1/42; DAN4/1/50

Chester, Cheshire Archives
CR63/1
DCH/X/15/14
DDX/428
QJF 78/4; QJF 79/1; QJF 82/4

Chippenham, Wiltshire and Swindon Archives
A1/110A
X3/119

Coventry, Coventry Archives
BA/H/11

Exeter, Devon Record Office
1392M/L 1644/22

Kew, The National Archives
C66/780 Chancery and Supreme Court of Judicature
E101 Exchequer accounts: Royal Household and Wardrobe
E121 Trustees for the Sale of Crown Lands: Interregnum Certificates
HL/PO/JO/10/1/224 Articles of the surrender of Halton Castle, 20 July 1643
PROB 11/220/237 Will of Katherine Brooke, 21 April 1651
SP16 State Papers Domestic, Charles I
SP19 Petitions to Parliament, 1644–1648
SP21 Committee of Both Kingdoms: Books
SP23 Committee for Compounding with Delinquents: Books and Papers
SP28 Commonwealth Exchequer Papers
SP29/196 Secretaries of State: State Papers Domestic, Charles II: Letters and Papers, 1667
SP44 State Papers: Entry Books

WO47/1 Ordnance Office minute book, 1644–1645
WO49/55 Ordnance Office Debenture book, 1625
WO49/82 Ordnance Office Debentures Book, 1644–1650
WO55/423 Ordnance Office warrants, 1642–1644
WO55/457 Ordnance Office warrants, 1642–1643
WO55/459 Ordnance Office warrants, 1643–1644
WO55/460 Ordnance Office Book of Warrants for Deliveries, 1643–1645
WO55/1646 Ordnance Office Book of Deliveries with Corresponding Warrants, 1644–1646
WO55/1647 Ordnance Office Book of Deliveries, June–October 1645
WO55/1660 Ordnance Office Stores and arms received (Oxford), 1642–1643
WO55/1661 Ordnance Office Stores and arms received (Oxford), 1624–1646
WO55/1662 Ordnance Office Receipts Book, 1644–1645

London, British Library
Mss Add. 986; 11331–11333; 18980; 18982
Mss Harley 1943; 1970; 1999; 2018; 2119; 2126; 2128; 2137; 2166; 6802; 6804; 6833; 6851; 6852

London, London Museum
Tangye Collection Manuscripts 46-78/708

Oxford, Bodleian Library
Ms Ashmole 830
Ms Carte 103
Ms Clarendon 28
Mss Eng. hist. C14; C244
Ms Fairfax 36
Mss Firth C6–7
Ms Rawlinson D395
Mss Tanner 58; 60; 62

Reading, Berkshire Record Office
R/Z3; R/Z6; R/Z7; R/Z10
D/EZ179/1
W1/FA 1/2

Stafford, William Salt Library
Mss Salt 463; 477; 482; 564

Warwick, Warwickshire Archives
CR2017/C9–10

Windsor, Windsor Castle
RCIN 404917

Worcester, Worcestershire Archives
BA1714/899

Printed Primary Sources

Contemporary Newsbooks

A continuation of certaine speciall and remarkable passages from both houses of Parliament, 23–30 August 1642. TT, E114[36]
A Perfect diurnall of the passages in Parliament, 7–14 November 1642. TT, E240[14]; 26 December 1642–2 January 1643. TT, E239[9]; 2–9 January 1643. TT, E240[14]; 9–15 January 1643. TT, E240[14]; 16–23 January 1643. TT, E240[21]; 13–19 February 1643. TT, E240[19]; 22–26 March 1643. TT, E239[14]; 27 March–3 April 1643. TT, E247[9]; 3–9 April 1643. TT, E202[29]; 3–10 June 1643. TT, E239[18]

Mercurius Aulicus, 22–28 January 1643. TT, E244[20]; 1–7 March 1643. TT, E244[16]; 9–15 April 1643. TT, E246[10]; 16–22 April 1643. TT, E246[16]; 23–28 April 1643. TT, E246[19]; 20 May 1643. TT, E246[26]; 8 June 1644. TT, E244[30]; 25 June 1643. TT, E246[9]; 9 September 1643. TT, E245[36]; 20 September 1643. TT, E264[16]; 27 April 1644. TT, E246[16]; 23 November 1644. TT, E246[26]
Mercurius Britannicus, 21–28 October 1644. TT, E68[5]
Perfect Occurrences, 20–27 December 1644. TT, E49[18]
Speciall Passages and Certaine Informations, 18–25 April 1643. TT, E116[41]; 21–27 June 1643. TT, E89[14]; 11–18 September 1643. TT, E117[41]
The Kingdomes Weekly Intelligencer, 21–28 February 1643. TT, E85[15]; 7–14 March 1643. TT, E93[6]; 25–27 May 1643. TT, E75[17]; 1–7 April 1645. TT, E276[22]; 13–20 May 1645. TT, E284[23]; 28 July–4 August 1646. TT, E306[22]
The Moderate Intelligencer, 23–29 April 1645. TT, E337[20]
The Weekly Account, 13–20 November 1644. TT, E81[2]; 20 December 1643. TT, E250[13]

Contemporary Tracts and Pamphlets

A Briefe and exact relation of the most material remarkable passages that hapned in the late well formed (and as valiantly defended) Siege laid before the City of Glocester (London: Thomas Vnderhill, 1643). TT, E67[31]

A famous victory obtained by the citisens of Coventry, and the Parliaments forces, under the command of the Lord Brooks, and colonell Hambden, against the Kings army, August 22 (London: R. Wood, 1642). Dr Williams' Library, F390A

A Fuller Relation of the Victory obtained at Alsford, 28 March, by the Parliaments forces (London: Laurence Blaiklock, 1644). TT, E40[1]

A Glorious and Happy Victory obtained by the Volunters of Buckingham, Bedford, Hariford, Cambridge, Huntingdon and Northamptonshire against Lord Wentworth nere Alesbury and Wickham (London: I. H. and J. Wright, 1642). TT, E129[17]

A letter from Collonell Bridges goverer of Warwick Castle to a freind of his in London, dated the 20 of April 1645. Wherein is sett forth a great victory obtained by the said collonell against Prince Maurice his armie on the 17 of this instant Aprill (London: R. B., 1645). TT, E278[27]

A most famous victory obtained by that vallant religious gentleman, Collonell Venne, against Prince Robert, who came against Windsor on Munday the 7th of November, promising Collonell Vann great preferment if that he would deliver up the said castle to his Majesites use, also Collonell Vens answer to Prince Roberts propositions likewise declaring how the said towne is beat downe, and men, women, and children, forced to fly into the woods to save themselves from the cruelty of the cavaliers (London: J. Rich, 1642). TT, E126[42]

A True and exact relation of the manner of His Maiesties setting up of his standard at Nottingham on Munday the 22 of August 1642 (London: F. Coles, 1642). TT, E115[4]

A true and perfect relation of the first and victorious skirmish between the army under the conduct of the Right Honourable the Lord Brooks, the Lord Grey, Collonel Hampden, Collonel Hollis, Collonel Chomley, and others members of the honorable Houses of Parliament (London: Matthew Walbanck, 1642). TT, E114[25]

A True Relation of a Great Fight Between the Kings Forces and the Parliaments, at Chinner neer Tame on Saturday last (London: B. A., 1643). TT, E55[11]

A True Relation of a Great Victory obtained by the Parliament Forces in Cheshire, under Sir William Brereton, against the King's Forces, under the command of Sir William Vaughan, near Denbigh (London: Edward Husband, 1645). TT, E308[14]

A True Relation of the late proceedings of the London Dragoneers, sent down to Oxford, consisting of foure Companies under the command of Sir John Seaton (London: Henry Overton, 1642). TT, E118[39]

A True Relation of the Lord Brooke's Settling of the Militia in Warwickshire (London: R. O. and G. D., 1642). TT, E669[50]

A Worthy Speech Made by the Right Honourable the Lord Brooke, at the election of his Captaines and Commanders at Warwick Castle, as also at the delivery of their last commissions (London: John Underwood, 1643). TT, E90[27]

Abingtons and Alisburies Present Miseries etc. (London: Rich Herne, 1642). TT, E128[33]

Cheshire's Successe since their pious and truly valiant Colonel, Sir William Brereton, Baronet, came to their rescue, &c. (London: Thomas Vnderhill, 1643). TT, E94[6]

Exceeding true and happy newes from the Castle of Windsor. Declaring how severall troopes of dragooners have taken possession of the said castle, to keepe it for the use of the King ann Parliament (London: T. Franklin, 1642). TT, E123[20]

Good and Joyfull Newes Out of Buckinghamshire, being a True and Exact Relation etc. (London: Francis Wright, 1642). TT, E126[99]

Good and true newes from Redding, Being an exact relation of the proceedings of his Excellence the Earl of Essex, since he advanced from Windsore (London: J. G., 1643). TT, E99[2]

His Highnesse Prince Ruperts Late Beating up the Rebels Quarters At Post-comb and Chinner in Oxfordshire. And his Victory in Chalgrove Field, on Sunday morning June 18, 1643 (Oxford: Leonard Lichfield, 1643)

His Majesties Proclamation and Declaration Concerning a Clause in One of the Late Articles at Reading (Oxford: Leonard Lichfield, 1643). TT, E669[13]

Magnalia Dei. A Relation of some of the many Remarkable Passage in Cheshire before the Siege of Namptwich, during the continuance of it: and at the happy raising of it by the victorious gentlemen Sir Tho. Fairfax and Sir William Brereton (London: Robert Bostock, 1644). TT, E31[13]

Most Happy Newes from the Earle of Essex. Wherein is declared the relation of two famous Victories obtained by the Parliament Forces (London: T. Rider, 1643). TT, E85[30]

The English intelligencer, shewing the true and most remarkable passages that have hapned in this kingdome (London: Francis Wright, 1642). TT, E127[26]

The Kings letter intercepted coming from Oxford with a ioyful and true relation of th[e] great victory obtained by Sir Thomas Fairfax, Sir William Brereton, and Sir William Fairfax, against the Irish at the raising of the siege at Nantwich on Friday last January 26, 1643 (London: Andrew Coe, 1644)

The Last Joyful Intelligence from his Excellency his Quarters at Reading, since the surrendering of the town (London: Thomas Watson, 1643). TT, E100[5]

The Last Weeks Proceedings of the Lord Brooke (London: R. O. and G. D., 1643). TT, E91[19]

The Latest Intelligence of Prince Rupert's Proceedings in Northamptonshire and Also Colonel Goodwin's at Brill (London: Publisher unknown, 1643). TT, E88[3]

The Latest remarkable truths (not before printed) from Chester, Worcester, Devon, Somerset, Yorke and Lancaster counties (London: Thomas Vnderhill, 1642). TT, E240[23]

The manner and good successe of the Lord Brookes forces in pursuing the cavaliers from Coventry. In a letter to an honourable person in London, August 24. 1642 (London: Humphrey Blunden, 1642). BL, 669, ff. 6r.–v.

The Second intelligence from Reading. Dated from His Excellency his quarters before Reading, 24 April (London: Samuel Gellibrand, 1643). TT, E99[19]

The third Intelligence From Reading. Dated from His Excellency His Quarters Before Reading, April 26. at night (London: Samuel Gellibrand, 1643). TT, E99[29]

The True Proceeding of the Severall Counties of Yorke, Coventry, Portsmouth, Cornwall (London: Richard Best, 1642). TT, E114[6]

Two letters of great consequence to the House of Commons: the one from Alisbury in Buckinghamshire, dated March 22. 1642. and signed by Col: Arthur Goodwyn: Col: Bulstrode: Col: Hampden: Tho: Terrill: Esq; the other from Sir William Brereton to a member of the House of Commons (London: Edw. Husbands, 1642). TT, E94[2]

Vicars, John, *Magnalia Dei Anglicana. Or, England's Parliamentary Chronicle* (London: J. Rothwell, Tho. Vnderhill, 1646). TT, E247[32]

Victory Proclaymed, in an exact relation of the proceedings of the Parliament Forces in their Siege before Reading from April 15 to 27 (London: Benjamin Allen, 1643). TT, E100[4]

Reports of the Historical Manuscripts Commission

Eighth Report, App. I (London: HMSO, 1881)
Twelfth Report, App. IX (London: HMSO, 1891)
Thirteenth Report, App. I (London: HMSO, 1894)
Fourteenth Report, App. IV (London: HMSO, 1894)

Books and Edited Collections

Andrews, George (ed.), *Rural Economy in Yorkshire in 1641: Being the Farming and Account Books of Henry Best, of Elmswell, in the East Riding of the County of York* (Edinburgh: William Blackwood and Sons, 1857)

BIBLIOGRAPHY

Anon., *Journals of the House of Commons* (London: HMSO, 1802), vols II–VII
Anon., *Journals of the House of Lords* (London: HMSO, 1767–1830), vols III–X
Beale, Stewart, Hopper, Andrew, and Hughes, Ann (eds), *The Household Accounts of Robert and Katherine Greville, Lord and Lady Brooke, at Holborn and Warwick, 1640–1649*, Camden 5th Series, 68 (Cambridge: Cabridge University Press, 2024)
Boyle, Roger, Earl of Orrery, *A Treatise of the Art of War Dedicated to the King's Most Excellent Majesty* (Savoy: T. N., 1677)
Clark, Andrew (ed.), *The Life and Times of Anthony Wood, Antiquary, of Oxford, 1632–1695, Described by Himself* (Oxford: Clarendon Press, 1891–1892), vols I–II
Cruso, John, *Militarie Instructions for the Cavallrie* (Cambridge: Cambridge University, 1632)
Day, William A. (ed.), *The Pythouse Papers: Correspondence Concerning the Civil War* (London: Bickers and Sons, 1879)
Dore, R. N. (ed.), *The Letter Books of Sir William Brereton*, Record Society of Lancashire and Cheshire, 123, 128 (Liverpool: Record Society of Lancashire and Cheshire, 1984, 1990), vols I–II
Elton, Richard, *The Compleat Body of the Art Military* (London: Robert Leybourn, 1650)
Firth, C. H., and Rait, R. S. (eds), *Acts and Ordinances of the Interregnum, 1642–1660* (London: HMSO, 1911), vols I–III
Green, Mary A. E. (ed.), *Calendar of the Proceedings of the Committee for Advance of Money, 1642-1656* (London: HMSO, 1888), vols I–III
Guilding, J. M. (ed.), *Reading Records: Diary of the Corporation* (London: J. Parker, 1892–1896), vols I–IV
Hall, James (ed.), *Memorials of the Civil War in Cheshire and the Adjacent Counties by Thomas Malbon, of Nantwich, Gent., and Providence Improved by Edward Burghall*, Record Society of Lancashire and Cheshire, 19 (London: Record Society of Lancashire and Cheshire, 1889)
Hamilton, W. D., and Bruce, J. (eds), *Calendar of State Papers Domestic: Charles I, 1625-1649* (London: HMSO, 1858), vols I–XXIII
Helsby, Thomas (ed.), George Ormerod, *The History of the County Palatine and City of Chester* (Revised and enlarged edition, London: Routledge, 1882), vols I–III
HMC, *Calendar of the Manuscripts of the Marquess of Ormonde, K. P., Preserved at Kilkenny Castle* (London: HMSO, 1902–1920), vols II–VIII
Hobson, M. G., and Slater, H. E. (eds), *Oxford Council Acts 1626-1665* (Oxford: Clarendon Press, 1933)
Hogan, James (ed.), *Letters and Papers Relating to the Irish Rebellion between 1642–46* (Dublin: Stationery Office, 1936)
Hopper, Andrew (ed.), *The Papers of the Hothams, Governors of Hull during the Civil War*, Camden 5th Series, 39 (Cambridge: Cambridge University Press, 2011)
Lewis, John (ed.), *The Siege of Chester: Nathaniel Lancaster's Narrative* (Nottingham: Raider Books, 1987)
Long, Charles E. (ed.), *Diary of the Marches of the Royal Army during the Great Civil War; Kept by Richard Symonds*, Chetham Society, Old Series, 74 (Westminster: J. B. Nichols and Sons, 1859)
Macray, W. D. (ed.), *Beaumont Papers: Letters Relating to the Family of Beaumont of Whitley, Yorkshire* (London: Nichols and Sons, 1884)
Macray, W. D. (ed.), Edward Hyde, Earl of Clarendon, *The History of the Rebellion and Civil Wars in England* (Oxford: Clarendon Press, 1888), vols I–VIII
Markham, Francis, *Five Decades of Epistles of Warre* (London: Augustine Matthewes, 1622)
Ormerod, George (ed.), *Tracts Relating to Military Proceedings in Lancashire during the Great Civil War* (Manchester: Chetham Society, 1844)
Peachey, Stuart, *The Edgehill Campaign and the Letters of Nehemiah Wharton* (Leigh-on-Sea: Partizan Press, 1989)
Pennington, D. H., and Roots, I. A. (eds and intro.), *The Committee at Stafford, 1643-1645* (Manchester: Manchester University Press, 1957)
Roy, Ian (trans. and ed.), *The Royalist Ordnance Papers, 1642–1646* (Oxford: Oxfordshire Record Society, 1964, 1969), vols I–II
Rushworth, John, *Historical Collections of Private Passages of State* (London: D. Browne, 1721), vols I–VIII
Rye, Walter (ed.), *State Papers Relating to Musters, Beacons, Ship-money, &c. in Norfolk from 1626 Chiefly to the Beginning of the Civil War* (Norwich: Goose and Son, 1907)
Slingsby, Sir Henry, *The Diary of Sir Henry Slingsby* (London: Longman, Rees, Orme, Brown, Green, and Longman, 1836)

Sprigge, Joshua, *Anglia Rediviva or England's Recovery* (London: R. W., 1647)
Taylor, John, *A Catalogue of the Taverns in Ten Shires about London* (London: Henry Gosson, 1636)
Tibbutt, H. B. (ed.), *The Letter Books of Sir Samuel Luke, 1644-45* (London: HMSO, 1963)
Vernon, John, *The Young Horseman, or, the Honest Plain-Dealing Cavalier* (London: Andrew Coe, 1644)
Walker, Sir Edward, *Historical Discourses upon Several Occasions* (London: W. B., 1705)
Warburton, Eliot, *Memoirs of Prince Rupert, and the Cavaliers* (London: Richard Bentley, 1849), vol. II
Warwick, Sir Philip, *Memoirs of the Reign of King Charles I* (London: Ri. Chifwell, 1702)
Whitelocke, Bulstrode, *Memorials of the English Affairs* (London: Nathaniel Ponder, 1682)
Young, Peter, and Tucker, Norman (eds), *Military Memoirs of the Civil War: Richard Atkyns and John Gwyn* (London: Longmans, 1967)

Secondary Sources

Books and Reports

Abram, Andrew, *Dragoons and Dragoon Operations in the British Civil Wars, 1638-1653* (Solihull: Helion & Co., 2023)
Abram, Andrew, *More Like Lions than Men: Sir William Brereton and the Cheshire Army of Parliament, 1642-46* (Solihull: Helion & Co., 2020)
Abram, Andrew, *Supplying the New Model Army: Logistics, Arms, Ammunition, Clothing, Victuals and the Matériel of War, 1645-1646* (Solihull: Helion & Co., 2024)
Abram, Andrew, *The English Garrison of Tangier: Charles II's Colonial Venture in the Mediterranean, 1661-1684* (Solihull: Helion & Co., 2022)
Arni, Eric Gruber von, *Justice to the Maimed Soldier: Nursing, Medical Care and Welfare for Sick and Wounded Soldiers and Their Families during the English Civil Wars and Interregnum, 1642–1660* (Aldershot: Ashgate, 2001)
Atkin, Malcolm, *Worcestershire under Arms: An English County during the Civil Wars* (Barnsley: Pen & Sword, 2004)
Beamont, William, *A History of the Castle of Halton and the Priory or Abbey of Norton* (Warrington: Percival Pearse, 1873)
Brown, Fraser, and Howard-Davis, Christine, *Norton Priory: Monastery to Museum, Excavations 1970–87* (Lancaster: Oxford Archaeology, 2008)
Bull, Stephen, *The Furie of the Ordnance: Artillery in the English Civil Wars* (Woodbridge: Boydell, 2008)
Dugdale, Sir William, *The Antiquities of Warwickshire* (London: Thomas Warren, 1656)
Hughes, Ann, *Politics, Society and Civil War in Warwickshire, 1620-1660* (Revised edition, Cambridge: Cambridge University Press, 2002)
Israel, Richard, *Cannon Played from the Great Fort: Sieges in the Severn Valley during the English Civil War 1642-1646* (Solihull: Helion & Co., 2021)
Jennings, Stuart B., *Royalist Newark, 1642-1646: Sieges and Siege Works* (Solihull: Helion & Co., 2024)
Lawrence, David R., *The Complete Soldier: Military Books and Military Culture in Early Stuart England, 1603–1645* (Brill: Leiden, 2008)
Memegalos, Florence S., *George Goring (1608-1657): Caroline Courtier and Royalist General* (London: Routledge, 2007)
Morrill, John S., *Cheshire 1630-1660: County Government and Society during the 'English Revolution'* (Oxford: Oxford University Press, 1974)
Nugent, George, *Some Memorials of John Hampden, His Party and His Times* (London: Chapman and Hall, 1854)
Scott, Christopher L., and Turton, Alan, *Hey for Old Robin! The Campaigns and Armies of The Earl of Essex during the First Civil War, 1642–44* (Solihull: Helion & Co., 2017)
Sherwood, Roy, *The Civil War in the Midlands, 1642-1651* (Stroud: Sutton, 1992)
South, Raymond, *Royal Castle, Rebel Town: Puritan Windsor in the Civil War and Commonwealth* (Buckingham: Barracuda, 1981)
Stoyle, Mark, *Soldier and Strangers: An Ethnic History of the English Civil War* (New Haven, CT: Yale University Press, 2005)

Tennant, Philip, *The Civil War in Stratford-upon-Avon: Conflict and Community in South Warwickshire, 1642-1646* (Stroud: Sutton, 1996)
Wanklyn, Malcolm, *Decisive Battles of the English Civil War* (Barnsley: Pen & Sword, 2006)

Articles and Chapters

Abram, Andrew, '"Sufficiently Different' to the Rest of the Army": The Cheshire Parliamentarian Dragoons in the First Civil War', *JSAHR*, 98 (2020), pp. 220–38

Atherton, Ian, 'Royalist Finances in the English Civil War: The Case of the Lichfield Garrison, 1643-5', *Midland History*, 33 (2008), pp. 43–67

Atherton, Ian, 'The Accounts of the Royalist Garrison of Lichfield Close, 1643-5', *Staffordshire Studies*, 18 (2007), pp. 63–96

Dyson, Tony, 'Colonel Moore's Offensive against Wirral, November 1643', *THSLC*, 162 (2013), pp. 29–48

Dyson, Tony, 'The Oaths at Woodchurch, 1643-1644: Tensions in Civil-War Wirral and Its Aftermath', *THSLC*, 164 (2015), pp. 1–20

Edwards, Peter, 'The Supply of Horses to the Parliamentarian and Royalist Armies in the English Civil War', *HR*, 68 (1995), pp. 49–66

Edwards, Peter, 'Turning Ploughshares into Swords: The Arms and Military Equipment Industries in Staffordshire in the First Civil War, 1642-1646', *Midland History*, 27 (2002), pp. 52–79

Gilboy, Roger, 'Crisis Mortality in Civil War Oxford, 1642-1646', *Oxoniensia*, 82 (2017), pp. 83–104

Gratton, Malcolm, 'Liverpool under Parliament: The Anatomy of a Civil War Garrison, May 1643 to June 1644', *THSLC*, 156 (2007), pp. 51–74

Hardacre, P. H., 'Colonel John Bridges: A Cromwellian in Ireland', *JSAHR* (1983), 61, pp. 3–9

Hopper, Andrew, '"Tinker" Fox and the Politics of Garrison Warfare in the West Midlands, 1643-50', *Midland History*, 24 (1999), pp. 98–113

Hughes, Ann, 'Warwickshire on the Eve of the Civil War: A "County Community"?', *Midland History*, 7 (1982), pp. 42–72

Lee, F. G., 'A Letter of Sir John Culpeper to Prince Rupert, Informing Him of the State of the Aylesbury Garrison 1643', *Records of Buckinghamshire*, 3:3 (1864), pp. 99–101

Lowe, John, 'The Campaign of the Irish Royalist Army in Cheshire, November 1643-January 1644', *THSLC*, 3 (1959), pp. 47–76

Marsh, Simon, 'The Arming of the London Auxiliary Regiments to the Trained Bands during the Civil War', *Arquebusier*, 34:6 (2016), pp. 1–19

Worton, Jonathan, '"Coursing the Tinkerley Fox": Tactics of Garrison Warfare in the West Midlands during 1643 and 1644', *Midland History*, 47 (2022), pp. 38–56

Unpublished Theses

Nagel, Lawson C., 'The Militia of London 1641-1649', PhD thesis (University of London, 1982)

Robinson, Gavin, 'Horse Supply in the English Civil War 1642–1646', PhD thesis (University of Reading, 2001)

About the Author

Dr Andrew Abram served in the British Army between 1978 and 1991. In 2007, he gained a doctorate in History at the University of Wales, Lampeter. Andrew was a lecturer at Lampeter until 2015, followed by a spell as associate lecturer at Manchester Metropolitan University. Dr Abram's interest in the British Civil Wars, and seventeenth-century conflicts more generally, has led to the publication of five monographs by Helion & Co., in addition to various journal articles and chapters in edited collections. Andrew is currently secretary of the Battle of Winwick Society and lives with his family in the Peak District.

About the Artist

Seán Ó'Brógáin is based in Donegal, Ireland. He studied Scientific and Natural History illustration from Lancaster University and works for a wide range of international clients. His previous artwork for Helion has included *St Ruth's Fatal Gamble: The Battle of Aughrim 1691 and the fall of Jacobite Ireland*, *Raw Generals and Green Soldiers: Catholic Armies in Ireland 1641-43*, *The King's Irish: The Royalist Anglo-Irish Foot Of The English Civil War*, and *Of Kerns and Gallowglasses: Irish Armies of the 16th Century 1487*.

Other titles in the Century of the Soldier series

No 39 *In The Emperor's Service: Wallenstein's Army, 1625-1634*

No 40 *Charles XI's War: The Scanian War Between Sweden and Denmark, 1675-1679*

No 41 *The Armies and Wars of The Sun King 1643-1715: Volume 1: The Guard of Louis XIV*

No 42 *The Armies Of Philip IV Of Spain 1621-1665: The Fight For European Supremacy*

No 43 *Marlborough's Other Army: The British Army and the Campaigns of the First Peninsular War, 1702-1712*

No 44 *The Last Spanish Armada: Britain And The War Of The Quadruple Alliance, 1718-1720*

No 45 *Essential Agony: The Battle of Dunbar 1650*

No 46 *The Campaigns of Sir William Waller*

No 47 *Wars and Soldiers in the Early Reign of Louis XIV: Volume 2 - The Imperial Army, 1660-1689*

No 48 *The Saxon Mars and His Force: The Saxon Army During The Reign Of John George III 1680-1691*

No 49 *The King's Irish: The Royalist Anglo-Irish Foot of the English Civil War*

No 50 *The Armies and Wars of the Sun King 1643-1715: Volume 2: The Infantry of Louis XIV*

No 51 *More Like Lions Than Men: Sir William Brereton and the Cheshire Army of Parliament, 1642-46*

No 52 *I Am Minded to Rise: The Clothing, Weapons and Accoutrements of the Jacobites from 1689 to 1719*

No 53 *The Perfection of Military Discipline: The Plug Bayonet and the English Army 1660-1705*

No 54 *The Lion From the North: The Swedish Army During the Thirty Years War: Volume 1, 1618-1632*

No 55 *Wars and Soldiers in the Early Reign of Louis XIV: Volume 3 - The Armies of the Ottoman Empire 1645-1718*

No 56 *St. Ruth's Fatal Gamble: The Battle of Aughrim 1691 and the Fall Of Jacobite Ireland*

No 57 *Fighting for Liberty: Argyll & Monmouth's Military Campaigns against the Government of King James, 1685*

No 58 *The Armies and Wars of the Sun King 1643-1715: Volume 3: The Cavalry of Louis XIV*

No 59 *The Lion From the North: The Swedish Army During the Thirty Years War: Volume 2, 1632-1648*

No 60 *By Defeating My Enemies: Charles XII of Sweden and the Great Northern War 1682-1721*

No 61 *Despite Destruction, Misery and Privations..: The Polish Army in Prussia during the war against Sweden 1626-1629*

No 62 *The Armies of Sir Ralph Hopton: The Royalist Armies of the West 1642-46*

No 63 *Italy, Piedmont, and the War of the Spanish Succession 1701-1712*

No 64 *'Cannon played from the great fort': Sieges in the Severn Valley during the English Civil War 1642-1646*

No 65 *Carl Gustav Armfelt and the Struggle for Finland During the Great Northern War*

No 66 *In the Midst of the Kingdom: The Royalist War Effort in the North Midlands 1642-1646*

No 67 *The Anglo-Spanish War 1655-1660: Volume 1: The War in the West Indies*

No 68 *For a Parliament Freely Chosen: The Rebellion of Sir George Booth, 1659*

No 69 *The Bavarian Army During the Thirty Years War 1618-1648: The Backbone of the Catholic League (revised second edition)*

No 70 *The Armies and Wars of the Sun King 1643-1715: Volume 4: The War of the Spanish Succession, Artillery, Engineers and Militias*

No 71 *No Armour But Courage: Colonel Sir George Lisle, 1615-1648* (Paperback reprint)

No 72 *The New Knights: The Development of Cavalry in Western Europe, 1562-1700*

No 73 *Cavalier Capital: Oxford in the English Civil War 1642-1646* (Paperback reprint)

No 74 *The Anglo-Spanish War 1655-1660: Volume 2: War in Jamaica*

No 75 *The Perfect Militia: The Stuart Trained Bands of England and Wales 1603-1642*

No 76 *Wars and Soldiers in the Early Reign of Louis XIV: Volume 4 - The Armies of Spain 1659-1688*

No 77 *The Battle of Nördlingen 1634: The Bloody Fight Between Tercios and Brigades*

No 78 *Wars and Soldiers in the Early Reign of Louis XIV: Volume 5 - The Portuguese Army 1659-1690*

No 79 *We Came, We Saw, God Conquered: The Polish-Lithuanian Commonwealth's military effort in the relief of Vienna, 1683*

No 80 *Charles X's Wars: Volume 1 - Armies of the Swedish Deluge, 1655-1660*

No 81 *Cromwell's Buffoon: The Life and Career of the Regicide, Thomas Pride* (Paperback reprint)

No 82 *The Colonial Ironsides: English Expeditions under the Commonwealth and Protectorate, 1650-1660*

No 83 *The English Garrison of Tangier: Charles II's Colonial Venture in the Mediterranean, 1661-1684*

No 84 *The Second Battle of Preston, 1715: The Last Battle on English Soil*

No 85 *To Settle the Crown: Waging Civil War in Shropshire, 1642-1648* (Paperback reprint)

No 86 *A Very Gallant Gentleman: Colonel Francis Thornhagh (1617-1648) and the Nottinghamshire Horse*

No 87 *Charles X's Wars: Volume 2 - The Wars in the East, 1655-1657*

No 88 *The Shōgun's Soldiers: The Daily Life of Samurai and Soldiers in Edo Period Japan, 1603-1721 Volume 1*

No 89 *Campaigns of the Eastern Association: The Rise of Oliver Cromwell, 1642-1645*

No 90 *The Army of Occupation in Ireland 1603-42: Defending the Protestant Hegemony*

No 91 *The Armies and Wars of the Sun King 1643-1715: Volume 5: Buccaneers and Soldiers in the Americas*

No 92 *New Worlds, Old Wars: The Anglo-American Indian Wars 1607-1678*

No 93 *Against the Deluge: Polish and Lithuanian Armies During the War Against Sweden 1655-1660*

No 94 *The Battle of Rocroi: The Battle, the Myth and the Success of Propaganda*

No 95 *The Shōgun's Soldiers: The Daily Life of Samurai and Soldiers in Edo Period Japan, 1603-1721 Volume 2*

No 96 *Science of Arms: the Art of War in the Century of the Soldier 1672-1699: Volume 1: Preparation for War and the Infantry*

No 97 *Charles X's Wars: Volume 3 - The Danish Wars 1657-1660*

No 98 *Wars and Soldiers in the Early Reign of Louis XIV: Volume 6 - Armies of the Italian States 1660-1690 Part 1*

No 99 *Dragoons and Dragoon Operations in the British Civil Wars, 1638-1653*

No 100 *Wars and Soldiers in the Early Reign of Louis XIV: Volume 6 - Armies of the Italian States 1660-1690 Part 2*

No 101 *1648 and All That: The Scottish Invasions of England, 1648 and 1651: Proceedings of the 2022 Helion and Company 'Century of the Soldier' Conference*

No 102 *John Hampden and the Battle of Chalgrove: The Political and Military Life of Hampden and his Legacy*

No 103 *The City Horse: London's militia cavalry during the English Civil War, 1642-1660*

No 104 *The Battle of Lützen 1632: A Reassessment*

No 105 *Monmouth's First Rebellion: The Later Covenanter Risings, 1660-1685*

No 106 *Raw Generals and Green Soldiers: Catholic Armies in Ireland 1641-1643*

No 107 *Polish, Lithuanian and Cossack armies versus the might of the Ottoman Empire*

No 108 *Soldiers and Civilians, Transport and Provisions: Early Modern Military Logistics and Supply Systems During The British Civil Wars, 1638-1653*

No 109 *Batter their walls, gates and Forts: The Proceedings of the 2022 English Civil War Fortress Symposium*

No 110 *The Town Well Fortified: The Fortresses of the Civil Wars in Britain, 1639-1660*

No 111 *Crucible of the Jacobite '15: The Battle of Sheriffmuir 1715*

No 112 *Charles XII's Karoliners Volume 2 - The Swedish Cavalry of the Great Northern War 1700-1721*

No 113 *Wars and Soldiers in the Early Reign of Louis XIV: Volume 7 - Armies of the German States 1655–1690 Part 1*

No 114 *The First British Army 1624–1628: The Army of the Duke of Buckingham (Revised Edition)*

No 115 *The Army of Transylvania (1613–1690): War and military organization from the 'golden age' of the Principality to the Habsburg conquest*

No 116 *The Army of the Manchu Empire: The Conquest Army and the Imperial Army of Qing China, 1600–1727*

No 117 *French Armies of The Thirty Years' War 1618–48*

No 118 *Soldiers' Clothing of the Early 17th Century: Britain and Western Europe 1618–1660*

No 119 *Novelty and Change: Proceedings of the 2023 Helion and ompany 'Century of the Soldier' Conference*

No 120 *Peter The Great's Disastrous Defeat: The Swedish Victory at Narva, 1700*

No 121 *Royalist Newark, 1642–1646: Sieges and Siege Works*

No 122 *The Battle of Fribourg 1644: Eughien and Turenne at War*

No 123 *Science of Arms: the Art of War in the Century of the Soldier 1672–1699: Volume 2: Cavalry, Artillery & the Conduct of War*

No 124 *Supplying The New Model Army: Logistics, arms, ammunition, clothing, victuals and the matériel of war, 1645-1646*

No 125 *Wars and Soldiers in the Early Reign of Louis XIV: Volume 7 - Armies of the German States 1655–1690 Part 2*

No 126 *War and Soldiers in the Early Reign of Louis XIV: Volume 7- Armies of the German States 1655-1690 Part 3*

No 127 *Confrontation of Kings, 1656: The Three-Day Battle of Warsaw in the Swedish Deluge, 1655-1660*

No 128 *The Battle of Lens 1648: Conde beats the Spanish*

No 129 *Ukrainian Cossacks from the late 16th century to the early 18th century: Organisation, clothing, equipment, armament*

No 130 *War and Soldiers in the Early Reign of Louis XIV: Volume 8: The Armies of Denmark, Courland and Danzig, 1655-1690*

No131 *No More Time To Lose : The Battle of Kahlenberg and the Relief of Vienna, 12 September 1683*

No 132 *Garrisons and Garrison Warfare in the British Civil Wars, 1638-1653*

SERIES SPECIALS:

No 1 *Charles XII's Karoliners: Volume 1: The Swedish Infantry & Artillery of the Great Northern* War *1700–1721*